From F to Phi Beta Kappa

Lance Ong has written a well-thought out, comprehensive, and highly readable guide to becoming a superior student. That alone would make this a valuable book. I am particularly impressed, however, by how much more he achieves. In a lively, personal voice, he talks to students as one who has been where they are, who recognizes their self-doubt and uncertainty about how to approach the complex process of learning, and who offers them unflagging encouragement and common-sense strategies on which they can rely. Best of all, in my view, he speaks joyously of the love of learning for its own sake and the rich opportunities the university years offer for self-development, reminding his readers that "college is not ultimately about your grades, it's about you."

—Robert A. Corrigan, Ph.D.
President, San Francisco State University

This is a well-organized and good book with excellent advice. If I were a college student again I would appreciate your book.

—Eugenie Clark, Ph.D.
Professor Emerita, University of Maryland
appearing in *Who's Who* and Encyclopedia Britannica
Honorary Doctorates from University of Massachusetts, Dartmouth,
University of Guelph, Ontario, and Long Island University

As one who has taught for many years in the university, I see it as a book that would be most welcomed by a substantial number of first- and second-year students. In my experience, fear and confusion is common among such young people who, irrespective of their abilities, are confused and intimidated in that new world; I believe they would see this book as much-needed aid for doing their studies properly and well.

—Douglas Dowd, Ph.D.
Has taught economics at Cornell University, Johns Hopkins University, University of California (Berkeley), State University of California (San Jose and San Francisco), and, presently, University of Modena

...The blend of motivation materials in Part I and the very specific, practical, and detailed study techniques presented in Part II provide a healthy and desirable approach to the book....Specifically, we believe that the materials on note-taking, speeches and class presentations, writing papers, and exam preparation speak directly to areas in which many college (and high school) students fall apart....The book addresses areas of great importance to the academic success of college students.

—William H. Thomas
Educational Consultant for assessment of student performance and teacher licensure, former Program Director for Educational Testing Service

—Margaret M. Thomas
Educational Consultant for teacher licensure,
Former Assistant to the Dean of Faculty, Mills College

As a college teacher for over 30 years, I welcome Mr. Lance Ong's new book focusing on academic success. Shedding new light on age-old terrain, it's a much-needed guidebook, really, for students grappling with the often perplexing demands and rigors of college life.

In reviewing Mr. Ong's typescript, my students at City College and I find that the author imparts valuable, tried-and-true wisdom on each page. As one might suspect, rarely does one achieve greatness without the requisite painstaking hard work which brings it to life. As a former struggling college and university student himself, Mr. Ong has tasted his share of trials and tribulations on the road to scholastic distinction. The fact that Mr. Ong is no stranger to the sting of failure and the ecstasy of success, from a student standpoint, makes his work all the more credible and accessible.

There is much to gain from Mr. Ong's helpful and earnest approach, and we commend his innovative "Guide to Student Success" wholeheartedly.

—Victor Turks
English teacher, City College of San Francisco

Universal tips that every student can practice with good results.

—Victoria R. M. Scott
Freelance editor for Harvard and Stanford University Presses

Student Praise

This reading gave me a new energy and motivation to study and achieve my goals.

The author's experience in college was very similar to mine, so I felt very intimate....Very interesting to read. Familiar situation got me into these words.

It is so amazing that if somebody wants to be a good student, there is a formula.

[What] I liked about this reading was the author's great encouragement to college students.

This reading can help thousands of students who are "lost."...he gives you his techniques...and I love it.
—**Students**
City College of San Francisco,
an institution with California's largest undergraduate enrollment

FROM F TO PHI BETA KAPPA

Supercharge Your Study Skills

Lance O. Ong

Chromisphere Press
San Francisco

Copy Editing	Victoria R. M. Scott, Michael McGee
Design and Production	Side By Side Studios
Indexing	Thérèse Shere
Proofreading	Elisabeth Beller
Cover Photos	Graduation © Myron Jay Dorf/CORBIS
	Study group © Tom & Dee Ann McCarthy/CORBIS
Back Cover Photos	Graduation companions © Ariel Skelley/CORBIS
	Author photo by Kingmond Young Photography

GMAT is a registered trademark of the Graduate Management Admission Council.
Phi Beta Kappa is a registered trademark of the Phi Beta Kappa Society.
Post-it is a registered trademark of 3M.
Scantron is a registered trademark of Scantron Corporation.

Attention universities, junior colleges, libraries, and high schools: discounts are available for quantity purchases. Please contact Chromisphere Press for ordering details at P.O. Box 470743, San Francisco, CA 94147.

Printed in the United States of America
International Standard Book Number: 0-9744274-0-3
Library of Congress Control Number: 2003099752

Although exhaustive efforts have been made to ensure the accuracy of information contained herein, neither Chromisphere Press nor the author shall be held liable for any errors, omissions, inconsistencies, or inaccuracies. This book is read with the understanding and agreement that the publisher and author are providing information and not professional services. The publisher and author disclaim liability for any and all damages incurred directly or indirectly from the use of information in this book.

This book is printed on acid-free paper

To those who believed in me

Brief Contents

Contents

III KEEPING A BALANCED PERSPECTIVE   193

List of Illustrations

List of Tables

Acknowledgments

I wish to thank the following people for their support for writing this book: Angie Annotti, Eugenie Clark, Ph.D.; Douglas Dowd, Ph.D.; Jade Snow Wong, L.H.D.; Donald Asher; Alice Filmer, Ph.D. Student; Janice Newfield, Education Consultant; Victoria R. M. Scott; and Victor Turks.

A special thanks is given to Robert A. Corrigan, Ph.D., President, San Francisco State University, and Ms. Sheila A. McClear, Director of Special Projects, for their gracious input and encouragement. San Francisco State University has contributed most significantly to my education.

Finally, a special thanks goes to the warm-hearted people, here and abroad, all of whom are too modest to have their names mentioned, who unselfishly gave their advice at timely points along my journey. Their kindness has helped me more than they may know.

About the Book

This book details the strategies that lifted a three-time F student to Phi Beta Kappa membership and five other academic honors. I was that student. Failing in school is a demeaning experience—but I am living proof that a good study strategy can turn all that around. After graduating, I felt a strong desire to help other students, whose grades range from B to F, by sharing my tips. I tried to write this book in a succinct, straightforward, and readily usable form that won't take too much time away from your homework. These are the methods that yielded tangible results for me.

Please note that although some quotations selected for this book refer only to men, I include women in the text on an equal footing, as I recognize and salute their contributions to our world. Throughout the book, I use "semester" to represent an academic term, quarter, or semester.

Founded in 1776, Phi Beta Kappa is America's oldest and most prestigious academic honor society. Its distinguishing principles are friendship, morality, and learning. Phi Beta Kappa is an honor conferred upon senior undergraduates by the Society's chapters at four-year colleges and universities.

This book is for students of all majors, declared or undeclared.

COLLEGE AND YOU

1

The Journey from F to Phi Beta Kappa

Draw from others the lesson that may profit yourself.
—Terence [Publius Terentius Afer], ca. 190–159 B.C.E.[1]

In my senior year of high school, I relied on cramming. I'd stay out until 2:30 a.m. on school nights playing arcade games, wake up at 6:00 a.m. to read text assignments, fall asleep during class, go home in the afternoon to collapse on the couch, and wake up in the evening ready to go out again after dinner. My worst final course grade was a C. I thought I could do more of the same in college. Big mistake. As a college freshman, I failed for the first time in my life—not once but three times.

The first year of college was stressful for me: living away from home for the first time; not knowing anyone or having friends there; living with a roommate for the first time; not knowing how to study well when other students appeared to be totally composed and keeping up with their studies; and being unsure of my capabilities. Amidst these problems was a heavy, unrelenting homework load, with set deadlines and unforgiving consequences.

It is only the ignorant who despise education.
—Publilius Syrus, fl. first century B.C.E.[2]

Adjusting to a new environment was difficult for me, but it was my reaction to these new challenges that really sabotaged my learning and my grades. Depressed and disenchanted, I cut classes, skimmed but didn't absorb text readings, ignored lectures, doodled in my notebook, used recreation to forget about study problems, stayed up late to play video games, didn't get enough sleep, dozed off in class, didn't attend teacher-assistant study sessions, fell behind in assignments, crammed for exams the night before, and waited until the last week of class to visit professors during their office hours. In one course, I handed in three overdue papers (written in one sitting the night before) to the teacher's mailbox instead of attending the last class. I blamed external circumstances for my own mistakes, laziness, and failure to concentrate.

It is worse still to be ignorant of your ignorance.
—St. Jerome, ca. 342–420[3]

I applied minimal effort just to get things done, being a great proponent of the philosophy, "Out of sight, out of mind." This was a disservice to my parents, who had worked hard to pay for my tuition, and it also crippled my own growth in the process. Thousands of dollars were wasted discovering my own ignorance. Yet I had no idea how to improve myself. A scowl began to appear on my face each day.

Years later, when I resumed college, I still had a weak academic record and no plan for performing well, though I did want to prove to myself that I wasn't a failure. I wanted to succeed by my own wits and ability. The lazy approach had proved too degrading to repeat. I had to consider putting in some hard work. The idea was noble, but I mostly wanted to see results. I didn't want to labor over a mountain and receive a pebble as a reward. I independently conceived a strategy to become a better student, using every idea I could come up with to progress. My strategies were tested in school over a period of four years.

My reentry into college began with an intensive Mandarin language program in Singapore. In clean, air-conditioned, well-lit rooms with large windows looking out on lush tropical landscapes, I competed with students who in many cases spoke little or no English. Chinese classmates already spoke the language and were simply learning to read and write. Japanese classmates were familiar with Chinese characters and their meanings. Several students spoke more than three languages, and one was fluent in five. My main goal was not to go home in disgrace. I kept telling myself, "Whatever happens, I can't afford to fail."

Lectures were in Mandarin, not English. Developing an ear for the language, doing daily homework, being quizzed on ninety-eight new characters per week, and answering on-the-spot questions in class required my constant attention. There was no room for ignoring lectures or for doodling this time around.

On the morning of the final exam, my head was filled to the brim with memorized information. As I walked to class, all I could see were my notes flashing through my mind. But a surprise awaited me. Upon arrival, I was directed to a medium-sized room I hadn't seen before. There the exam was administered by teachers I had never met. Seats were assigned by a teacher escort. When the test began, you could have heard a pin drop.

Midway through, I was interrupted for the oral portion of our exam. After turning over my answer sheet on my desk, a teacher walked me down the hallway to another room I hadn't before seen. The small room was sparsely furnished, its shades drawn to block out the bright morning sun. Two teachers whom I knew were seated at a desk facing an empty chair, where I was to be tested. They asked me hypothetical questions to measure my diction, range of vocabulary, command of idioms, and general fluency. The topics ranged from social etiquette to the causes of a four-car accident and how to speak to a Chinese doctor when sick. Then it was back to the first room to complete the written exam. I was one of the last two students to finish the test.

Afterward, there was an enormous feeling of relief. The pressure was off, and though I was unsure of how I had done, I had to wait for the scores to be announced the following week. I walked downstairs to browse in the campus bookstore, where I heard the lyrics "Through the Fire" sung by Chaka Khan on the shop music system. My newly created strategies had undergone their first major test during those three hours that day. A week later, I was informed that I had placed second in my class overall.

After returning to America, I decided that I needed my bachelor's degree. Although my overseas experience showed that I could excel when I applied myself, the stakes were different this time. This was mainstream American academia, where I had failed before. I didn't know whether the strategies that had worked so well in Southeast Asia would work in America too. The program abroad had required rote learning, a focus on diction, and completely different writing and grammatical skills than classes at an American university, which would demand independent critical thinking, logical reasoning, and endurance for three years. I felt that if I made every effort to do well, I stood my best chance of succeeding. I first resumed my bachelor's program at the University of Hawai'i at Manoa. A tuition increase took me back to California, where I completed my degree at San Francisco State University. To set a realistic goal, I merely sought to pass my classes, learn well, and obtain my diploma to acquire a good job. I kept the techniques from Singapore that I thought would work and also added some new strategies.

Creating and applying my own strategies was both scary and thrilling. It was scary because my grades were on the line, and the only way to test the strategies' worth was to use them under real conditions. The thrill lay in seeing my test scores, grades, and cumulative grade-point average climb into the stratosphere. I worked primarily to better myself. I had no notion of earning formal honors. As long as I received passing grades, I felt, the diploma would take care of itself. My strategies continued to work, and I placed first in seven of twenty-one consecutive classes. (In one of these courses, I tied for first with two other students.) Then, toward graduation, a few surprises occurred. I received six forms of recognition:

- Phi Beta Kappa: I was one of 19 students so honored out of a graduating class of 5,101; only 1% of U.S. college seniors receive this;
- Magna cum laude (a rule change effective the semester of my transfer disqualified me from summa cum laude);
- Golden Key National Honor Society, a recognition awarded to the top 15% of U.S. undergraduates (in one of the more than 150 schools with chapters at the time) for maintaining a 3.5 grade-point average into their junior or senior year;
- All-University Honors, awarded to the top 10% of San Francisco State's graduating class;
- Departmental Honoree, elected by eight academic advisors for high achievement; and
- The Dean's List for six consecutive semesters.

These rewards were unanticipated but brought closure to my three Fs.

During my miserable freshman year, I knew that I was acting irresponsibly, but I wasn't aware of the serious ramifications of doing so. I wanted someone to talk to me in nonderogatory terms and tone of voice, someone to sit down and tell me, "Lance, what you're doing is counterproductive because…," and then name all the reasons. I wanted someone to provide me with the direction and techniques that would help me recover my grades. Such advice was not forthcoming.

In other words, I remember wanting to correct myself but not knowing how. But there's no reason for you to repeat the same miserable experience if you get such advice now. *This book contains everything I wanted to know as a struggling student but had to figure out on my own.* Whether you're an F, D, C, or B student, here are the same strategies and philosophies that took me from three Fs to six academic honors, a two-year 3.92 grade-point average, and a bachelor's degree. I share my formula in detail. I don't claim that these methods will transform you into an A student overnight because that depends on your abilities and how well you adapt this book's information to your circumstances. But unless you're trying to overcome more than three F course grades, I can't see where these tips can take you except up. My experience points to a conclusion about succeeding in college: you can succeed with a simple strategy but it has to be very well planned, organized, and thorough. Your strategy ought to be simple; the complex information will be your course material.

Basically, a full-time student's life is centered on attending class, completing homework assignments, and preparing for tests. These challenges caused me the most stress in my early college years. Being overstressed is not necessary if you know how to surmount your obstacles. You'll see the problems coming at you, but you'll know what needs to be done and how to do it well. Using my techniques, a large portion of stress can be reduced for you. With less stress, you will be able to *see and feel* your college experiences with greater appreciation and fulfillment. Going to college is all about becoming the best you can be in life. By doing your best and using the tips in this book, you will be a giant step closer to achieving that goal.

My views are based on my experiences as a full-time student taking twelve units per semester. My assertions are based on the belief that rare exceptions don't negate general truths. My central message is to strive to achieve your best because your total development in the grand scope of life is more important than what's printed on paper. Recognition (inevitable if your grade-point average is high) and grades, though very important, are incidental results rather than primary ends in themselves.

2

Your Duty to Yourself

Duty is the sublimest word in our language. Do your duty in all things.
You cannot do more. You should never wish to do less.
—Robert Edward Lee, 1807–1870[4]

The duty to:

- develop to *your* intellectual potential;
- be as perceptive as *you* can be; and
- get the most out of your education.

What's good about going to college?

Your key to a fulfilled life is your ability to learn, acquire information, and use it wisely. College is not ultimately about your grades; it's about you. It's about maximizing your lifelong productivity by training you to become as resourceful as you can be. College develops critical thinking that can be used in and out of the classroom, a strong memory, and skills in organization, time management, and problem-solving. You learn to formulate intelligent strategies with proven results and to ask good questions to understand situations more precisely. College helps you hone your verbal, written, and interpersonal communication skills. It instills awareness of the world around you and an acquired intelligence that no one can take away from you. The knowledge you gain from college allows you to make more reasoned choices in life. In the process you develop the self-confidence, maturity, and self-discipline to pursue and achieve your goals. A college degree also results in higher job qualifications, increased earning potential, and upward social mobility.

For many professions, a college degree is mandatory. Other employers view your degree as a sign of success, that you've proven your competence in a long-term regimen, and that you'll be a productive employee. Your education opens doors to career prospects, whether or not your job is directly related to your major field. You learn research skills that you can use in your personal life to answer your own questions.

Seldom do people remark that they regretted having gone to college.

The difficulty in life is the choice.
—George Moore, 1852–1933[5]

You shape yourself by your thoughts and actions, whether in reaction to something or by exercising free will. The more knowledgeable you are, the more reasoned your decisions, the greater your chances of satisfaction and success. You're at an advantage when you're empowered by choice. Without acquired intelligence, you will perceive less, which will confine the breadth of your decisions and limit your progress in life.

Undergraduate study is a once-in-a-lifetime experience that shapes the course of your life. Four to five years seems like a long time but is, in fact, only 1/14 of an average human life span of seventy years. Within the next ten to fifteen years, you may come to realize that life is actually short. This doesn't mean that you have to agonize over the brevity of life, but simply that it makes sense to appreciate the time and opportunities you have now. All study strategies, course selections, extra-curricular activities, and your major revolve around you and how you wish to sculpt yourself. Take the time to sculpt well.

Seeking Your Potential

No one knows what he can do till he tries.
—Publilius Syrus, fl. first century B.C.E.[6]

Innate talents and strengths are your potential. Everyone has an intellectual potential. It is up to you to find, develop, and reach yours to become the best that *you* can be.

You need to determine your full capabilities. Throughout your college years, you will be defining these abilities. How far you develop your intellectual skills in relation to your full capability is something that you determine and control: you decide how to apply yourself.

I've seen some students achieve 4.0 cumulative grade-point averages. Some even triple-majored or earned their degrees in less than four years while graduating in the top percentage of their class. Their accomplishments were superb.

But what about people like you and me? To fulfill your particular potential doesn't mean you need to become the next Nobel Prize winner or Olympic gold medalist, though if this is within your capability, I fully endorse your pursuing it. Some students may not obtain silver or gold but emerald or jade instead. As long as you are truly doing your best to learn and to apply what you learn, you'll get the most you can out of your education.

Being entirely honest with oneself is a good exercise.
—Sigmund Freud, 1856–1939[7]

Up until college, parents and family members may have been supportive of your efforts to learn. You may have griped at times, but they stood behind you daily, reassuring you that you were doing what everyone needs to do. Now that you're in college, such constant reassurance may not be there; you are left to guide and develop yourself alone.

Doing your best requires self-honesty and believing in yourself. You need to believe that you can go the distance, that you are fully capable of achieving your learning goals if you try. Being self-driven to do your best is hard. It requires more than doing "whatever, whenever," however much or little that may be. You won't come close to becoming your best unless you're honest about (a) what you're capable of achieving, (b) how hard you're capable of working, and (c) whether you're being too easy or too hard on yourself. Listen to your inner voice (not the one that rationalizes) when asking if you're doing the best you can.

Being honest about yourself also means not denying mistakes. Ignoring deficiencies that can be changed or making excuses to evade responsibility will actually curtail your long-term progress. Monitoring yourself isn't easy or pleasant, but neither does it require being a perfect person. It merely means that to become your best, you cannot put blinders on yourself. There is more beyond that. Once you perceive something, it is up to you to act—to achieve, amend, or correct. *Awareness, self-honesty, astute tactics, a balanced philosophy, continuous learning, and discipline are the main elements that will carry you through.* There will always be those who won't try and won't make the most of themselves, but you don't have to be one of them.

The desire to define, develop, and know my potential was one reason I didn't choose classes based on their quizzes, cumulative exams, or grading scales. I believe you develop greater versatility at problem-solving by being tested under a variety of conditions and levels of difficulty. Such training also dispels any fear of facing academic challenges. As long as a teacher was good, I accepted the tasks that came with his or her course. I also didn't depend on caffeine or sleeping pills, opting instead to be more self-reliant via time management, regular sleep, diet and exercise, planning, and a positive attitude. I'm not suggesting that every reader must do the same. An F or D student obviously needs to improve his or her grade-point average through strategic enrollment, whereas a B student can fully challenge him- or herself. Judge what's proper for you.

Do You Doubt Yourself?

If you doubt your abilities to succeed in college, be reassured. You're already capable of passing your courses. If the admissions board didn't see your potential based on your prior academic record, you wouldn't have been admitted to your college in the first place. Having resolved this, the rest is a matter of perseverance and working effectively. From this point on, it's not a matter of *whether* you'll graduate but *how well* you'll graduate. Your path to graduation may not be straight or fast, but that doesn't matter. Given determination, brains, and hard work, college is a level playing field where you're judged primarily on how you apply yourself.

Is It Too Late If I've Already Failed a Class?

> Diligence is the mother of good fortune.
> —Miguel de Cervantes, 1547–1616[8]

No, it's not too late to change and clean up your study habits and skills. You can still dig yourself out and raise your grades—as long as you apply yourself diligently. Here are seven points to consider about Fs (as one who's been there):

- You weren't admitted to college by being F caliber.
- Fs erode your grade-point average, making it difficult for you to restore good academic standing.
- You may have to repeat a course that's unpleasant (due to content or teacher), not offered every semester, or both.
- Fs adversely affect self-esteem.
- You spend more time and money to graduate. Calculate the tuition for a course, and I'm sure it's an amount you wouldn't want to throw away.
- Fs jeopardize your qualifications for scholarships and graduate school.
- What's constructive about an F? At most, you discover that time and money are wasted while putting yourself at severe academic disadvantage, sabotaging your learning, and halting your progress.

Unless there is some profound reason that it can't be avoided, I don't recommend failing a course.

We endowed you with the brains—use them!
—A friend's mom

I believe that Fs often result from not trying rather than from a low IQ. (An exception is when one encounters a professor who flunks 30–50% of the class every term; but this is very rare.) In one of my largest classes, with 138 students, 6 students failed because they didn't hand in homework, missed one or more exams, attended few sessions, or didn't officially drop the course after ceasing to attend. Two of them scored a 76 on one midterm. Another scored 89 on the group project but missed one midterm and a homework assignment. Given the percentage weights for grading at the time, even a D on both missed assignments would have allowed that person to pass the course. These students had it in them to succeed. It's as if these people wouldn't even try.

If you're not going to stay in a particular course, be sure that you drop it before the official deadline and that your school's enrollment confirmation reflects this. Such an administrative error on a student's part is a costly mistake. (If you're receiving financial aid, ensure that dropping a course doesn't disqualify you or carry any penalty.)

In one of my most intense classes, we had five midterm exams. Lectures were loaded, penalties for late or missed homework were severe, limited time was allotted for essay tests, assignments were frequent, the comprehensive final exam was 40% of our grade, grade scales were raised (95 for an A and 85 for a B), and ten of the thirty-three enrolled students had mid-semester cumulative scores at 90 or above. I was surprised to see one student with an F cumulative grade eight weeks into the course. On the first exam, I had outscored that person 95 to 82, but she clobbered me on the second and third exams (103 and 94, versus my 102 and 86, respectively) by earning bonus points on essay answers. With such a strong mind for nailing the tests, what caused her grade to plunge? She simply didn't hand in homework. Exams occurred biweekly. During a six-week period, this student failed to hand in weekly written assignments. For reasons unknown, she missed our fourth exam. Whether or not she was able to recover her grade via the fifth test and comprehensive final exam is unknown. What is apparent, however, is that being absent for an exam and missing deadlines not only ruined an otherwise splendid track record, it also destroyed her grade.

If you've failed a class, test, homework assignment, or have a failing grade at midsemester, do your best to understand why this happened and seek not to repeat the same pattern of conduct. Once you see your grades waning, regardless of your level, pay immediate attention and take serious steps to correct the problem. Analyze what's causing the deficiency—whether missed or late assignments, inadequate note-taking, lack of concentration, insufficient test preparation, or any of the other mistakes I made as a freshman. Maintaining or elevating your grade-point average on a long-term, sustained basis is the goal: letting it regress is not.

College is the time of shouldering responsibility. How far would I have gotten had I kept my freshman attitude? Even when there are some legitimate reasons beyond your control, accepting partial responsibility is only realistic. Some people deny mistakes and leave problems uncorrected. I don't think this is prudent. It's okay to admit to yourself that you made a mistake. Nobody needs to know unless you want to share it with them. If you know how to correct your F habits, you can resolve the conflict privately. If you need help, seek advice and feedback from your teachers, friends, or a counselor. In any event, your priority should be regaining your equilibrium. Put yourself back together, address the issue, learn from it, and correct the problem. Being self-reliant includes not flaking out on yourself when your personal growth is on the line. Remember that you're shaping your life as you go along. *One of the surest ways to avoid Fs is to attend every class, keep up with your studies, hand in all assignments on time, and always be present for your tests.*

Don't Take Undergraduate Learning for Granted

The fact is that a college education feeds an adolescent in one end and gets a young adult out the other.
—Dr. Leroy S. Rouner, Boston University[9]

You entered college as a teenager. You leave as an adult. The years you spend in college have far-reaching effects, both personally and careerwise. How well you apply yourself as a teen has a significant effect on your progress in adulthood.

Lacking a college education is very limiting. You only need look at the majority of those who don't have a college education to see their limitations in critical reasoning, articulating their thoughts, solving problems in constructive and intelligent ways, or writing English. Government statistics reveal that those without a post-secondary degree have considerably lower annual incomes. You have before you the opportunity to go further. You have dozens of teachers and professors, expert in their fields, willing to impart their knowledge to you. You have full access to school facilities to help you grow. Seize this opportunity. The tools and the help are around you; it's just a matter of finding and applying them, whether they be your instructors, resources available on campus or in your community, or the tips given in this book.

I Just Want the Piece of Paper

Conduct is three-fourths of our life and its largest concern.
—Matthew Arnold, 1822–1888[10]

Deliberate mediocrity is not being mediocre compared to others; it's choosing to achieve less than you actually can. Some of my classmates complained about classes and homework more than they cared about doing a good job on their studies. To me, this is missing the big picture. Some students focus mainly on acquiring a certificate or diploma. They "just want to get by" and don't bother applying what they learn to life outside of class. Some students enroll in courses offered by teachers reputed to be easy graders. Such grades strengthen your grade-point average but don't prepare you to handle tough classes, nor do they help you reach your full intellectual potential. There is also a personal cost.

Nothing is stronger than habit.
—Ovid [Publius Ovidius Naso] 43 B.C.E.–ca. 18 C.E.[11]

Long-term behaviors are habit-forming—their cumulative effects need to be watched. But being aware of what becomes second nature is tough. Attitudes and their associated practices carry over to your life beyond college. With an "I'll just get by" attitude, where will you be five or ten years from now? Answer: probably not anywhere near where your potential could have taken you. The longer you repeat a counterproductive habit, the more difficult it is to change. Furthermore, long-term practices tend to catch up with you in life, sometimes sooner, sometimes later. This is not meant to paralyze you with fear about leading a full life, but simply as a word of caution about continued indiscreet behavior.

A good mind possesses a kingdom.
—Lucius Annaeus Seneca, 8 B.C.E.–65 C.E.[12]

Some people maintain that their college learning was meaningless because they don't use their specific academic knowledge for their jobs. I disagree. What matters is what college does for you as a total person, which depends on how well you apply yourself and what you learn. True, I did not use my figure drawing when I worked as a logistics coordinator. True, I did not use Venn diagrams when I was a purchasing supervisor for an international deluxe hotel. But this is only looking at things superficially. I've used knowledge gained from studies in critical thinking, management theory, international business, law, and transportation management on the job. Studies in speech communication improved my interviews, interpersonal skills within organizations, customer service, and nonbusiness communications. I've applied studies in art to scrutinizing proofs and making printing decisions about corporate graphics. Writing skills were used for cover letters, résumés, documenting incidents for insurance purposes, business reports, memorandums, and correspondence with customers, vendors, and suppliers. Studies in human biology gave insights into how the body functions, how it's adversely affected down to cellular levels by poor health practices or exposure to toxic agents, and how to maintain good health. Studies in ethics expanded my awareness of a variety of issues that allow for more comprehensive decisions. Moreover, in college you develop self-assurance from passing the challenges in dozens of courses. True, course materials change from class to class, but this only makes you more adaptable, skillful, and experienced at situational problem-solving.

Although it may not be apparent when you're struggling to find your rhythm, you are laying the foundation of your fundamental pattern of self-discipline in life. *Choosing the academic path of least resistance or minimal effort will not fully develop you.* For example, some students seek courses that are graded on a curve, without cumulative final exams, essay tests, quizzes, and mandatory attendance—without making quality of learning a prime consideration. (Further discussion appears in Chapter 5 in the section "Substance First, Tactics Second.")

For the same time and money spent on school, you will learn less. In effect, you limit your knowledge by choice. Is such conduct really doing the best for yourself? College is not the time to be satisfied with being mediocre but the time to encourage yourself to bloom. You can make it happen if you try.

Discipline is required for any form of success. The idea of discipline isn't inviting at face value, but it doesn't mean a lot of hard work without reward of any kind. When you use effective strategies, you see results—and these results reinforce your motivation and belief in yourself. Can you think of any actor, musician, artist, Olympic athlete, professor, engineer, scientist, entrepreneur, trade expert, or body-sculpted model who didn't use discipline to achieve his or her success? Even the talented must develop their skills through practice and training. They may enjoy what they do, which makes it easier, but they still use discipline. And if you look carefully you'll see that successful people don't simply work hard in a haphazard way—they have definite goals and definite strategies. These people seek to develop their talents in the most efficient manner. They persevere both because they believe in themselves and because they get results. You can do the same. It seems hard because you are just starting to develop your strength of mind. But the basic discipline you practice now will serve you for years beyond college. It is a gift no one else can give you.

Even though your future employers may not scrutinize your grades, if you're an A- or B-caliber student setting your sights on B or C grades, you're harming yourself. Focus on doing your best in your studies. Your diploma and résumé will fall into place as a result. Even if you've already decided on your career and its requisite major, do step A well (studies) before worrying about steps B (diploma), C (résumé), and D (the job after graduation). Each one is predicated on its predecessor.

Finding Your Major

Be a first-rate version of yourself, not a second-rate version of someone else.
—Judy Garland, to her daughter, Liza Minelli[13]

There's nothing wrong with not declaring a major in your early college years. It may be fashionable to appear decisive and ambitious, but as a freshman, you need not feel pressured—there's already enough on your plate. Most colleges have general education requirements for all majors. You can spend your first year or two taking these courses needed for graduation. Meanwhile, take the time to make a sound decision about your major.

When searching for an appropriate major, I was faced with a choice: do I major in something enjoyable or something that will make money after graduation? I remember people asking me, "What are you majoring in?" and "What sort of job will that get you?" At times, I found these questions intrusive. These people wouldn't be shouldering my schoolwork for four years, nor would they shoulder any unhappiness if I majored in something I didn't like, so why need I answer to them?

It's my belief that a college major shouldn't be viewed as vocational preparation alone. Money and happiness are not mutually exclusive, but they are not always synonymous, either. Of course, it would be good to find a major that you like *and* that lands you a good job. But if you're faced with an either-or situation, the question you need to ask is, "What suits me best?" The answer depends on your values, priorities, and aspirations. For some, majoring in a field that will equip them to earn a high salary is a necessity, perhaps even a tolerable sacrifice for being happy. I cannot say which avenue is right for you—my best advice is to be true to yourself and your values. I myself would major in whatever I was most enthusiastic about, whether in the liberal arts or in a technical or scientific field. Whatever you select, you don't want to be ambivalent about your major.

When I asked my most trusted friends about this, they endorsed choosing a major that I liked. Their consensus was that making a lot of money isn't very meaningful if you're unhappy with what you do. Dr. Leroy S. Rouner cited a poster at the Boston University School for the Arts that reads, "Learn what you love." He also noted that "You can't predict what is going to be useful even if you know what you want to do in the future"[14] and added that:

> Love as a criterion guarantees that you will work to your highest potential, because you are self-motivated: you love it. Finally, it provides the surest basis for life-long learning—which we all extol, but which often doesn't happen—because it is part of who you are, and not just something you think, often wrongly, that you can use.[15]

Some people believe your major sets the course for your career immediately after college. Vocational or technical majors aside, this is not always so. Some firms hire primarily on the basis of intelligence, interpersonal skills, and problem-solving ability. One controller of a major international hotel chain told me that he hired people for their positive attitudes—the skills needed could be acquired subsequently through training. (In the years beyond college, it's common for people to change occupations several times before they retire; your major doesn't determine the course for the rest of your life). Your major may not ultimately be what your job entails, but that's okay: you learned what you loved, you developed your discipline and potential, you became able to write well, and you had a good college experience. If you've seasoned yourself in school, complete with internship and studying abroad in your junior or senior year (see Chapter 16), you'll stand out from other recent graduates when you apply for work.

In some cases, your internship employer may welcome your return but with compensation.

The best decisions are made with complete information. Considering you'll be studying a major for several years or more, it's worth making a full investigation of the subject, its industry personality, and how it suits you, your personality, and your values. Take aptitude tests. Visit teachers or contact trade professionals for informational interviews. Enroll in or audit some of the courses in question. It's good to know what a field is like from a participant's point of view—what you'll be swimming in every day, for weeks on end, for several years.

My approach was to go to the campus bookstore and browse through all the shelves of textbooks from A to Z. As I flipped through the books, I usually had one of four reactions:

1. "This subject is definitely not me" (i.e., so incompatible that I wouldn't survive the major).
2. "Too dull."
3. "Okay but not of great interest" (I could do it if I had to, but I wouldn't be enthusiastic).
4. "Hey, I can do this! And I can do this well!" (the topic had instant appeal). The subjects that gave me this reaction were those I explored for possible majors.

This method helps reveal the subjects for which you have a natural affinity. If you come across a subject that really grabs you, you won't say with a scowl, "Ugh; I have to do this for the next four years?" You'll be more enthusiastic about seeing whether there's an existing major for the subject and forecasting your academic schedule up to graduation.

You can also use this method to select the required liberal arts courses that are of most interest to you. You could also compare textbooks of different sections of a specific course as a partial basis for determining in which to enroll.

In my case, I didn't find a ready-made major that fully appealed to me. Several subjects interested me: international business, business law, and ethics. After reading through my college catalog, I came across an individually designed major. This allows a student to design his or her own major curriculum, subject to quite a few requirements. I had to fulfill more than fifteen criteria, such as (1) writing a proposal to explain my objectives and the connection between my chosen courses and theme of study; (2) designing a curriculum substantially different from those of existing majors, spanning three departments in at least two colleges, and comparable in quality to the curricula of other majors offered through the school; (3) ensuring that four-fifths of total major units were upper division and that only six units were used to fulfill requirements outside the major; (4) maintaining a minimum cumulative grade-point average of 3.0, or B level; (5) course selection that could not breach individual department regulations; (6) chronological order of courses planned to avoid missing classes required for graduation; (7) written authorization from my academic advisor, department chairs, and the dean of undergraduate studies; (8) completing at least two-thirds of the total major units after formal permission was granted; and (9) not being able to change the curriculum without approval from my academic advisor. The learning experience, however, was very beneficial for me. One classmate designed her major to include international relations, economics, and international business. Another incorporated conflict resolution. Wow! These students could definitely think big.

If your interests are multifaceted, I suggest that you look into the possibility of such a major. If offered at your school and appropriate for you, be sure to find out all rules and restrictions. Your self-designed major may need to include extra courses in case some of your original selections aren't available during subsequent semesters. Professors may be on sabbatical, and some courses may be discontinued, offered biannually, or not offered every semester.

To determine what class to take when, I saved all my course schedules from previous semesters. While still fulfilling my general college requirements, I looked in the course schedules to see the semesters, days of the week, and times of day my contemplated classes were offered. At times, I even telephoned or visited the department secretary six to twelve months in advance to see when a course would be offered. This helped me project my semester schedules for spring and fall of each year up to graduation. By knowing which courses were only offered once a year, I knew whether I needed to take them in the spring or fall semester. Prerequisites determined which courses I had to take first. Other courses were scheduled around these. Beyond that, I chose order of course enrollment to create a more interesting blend of subjects within a semester. This not only stretches your mind more for learning, it's also less boring than taking similar courses during the same semester. Diverse topics make it easier to separate, discern, and retain subject information for learning and exams. Choosing your electives can be lots of fun, too.

The quality and scale of difficulty of your chosen courses will shape a big chunk of your intellectual growth and college experience. The curriculum, especially if it's to prepare you for a particular sector of the job market, will shape a large part of your qualifications. Such a curriculum, of course, can be noted during your job interviews or on your cover letters and résumé. If you design your own major, you may have to maintain a higher grade-point average than other students. Your designated name for your major may appear on your diploma and résumé. You will need to explain your major at interviews and social events to those unfamiliar with custom-designed majors.

If you're learning what you love, none of this will intimidate you because you'll be driven by your personal interests. If you design your major, your academic advisor may become a key person guiding you through your college's administrative procedures, from your planning stages to verifying your fulfillment of all criteria and processing your final paperwork needed for graduation.

I used a highlighter in my college catalog, and also bookmarked it with Post-it notes, to mark the courses that sounded interesting to me. I'd then write a list of courses to explore through informational interviews or browsing at the bookstore. Your college catalog will also indicate specific course prerequisites and enrollment restrictions.

Whatever you choose, your best major lies wherever your passion, interests, and skills are greatest. With such a major, you'll have a sense of meaning, direction, and fulfillment each day, and will be happier with yourself. You won't mind putting in the work to learn. You'll also retain the information better because of your natural inclination for the subject.

Value Your Liberal Arts Courses

Most undergraduate programs include general liberal arts requirements, even for technical majors. Although some of my classmates griped about this, it is these courses that underlie your overall development. I attribute the core of my intellectual growth to my liberal arts courses. I remember sitting in a Critical Thinking class one day and saying to myself, "These liberal arts courses give more understanding to life at large than my technical major courses." Other such classes are Speech Communication, English Composition, and Human Biology.

This is not to devalue technical courses, for they give you the specific knowledge to succeed in your trade of choice. But the liberal arts educate you to be a literate, cultured human being. It is fine to pursue a technical major and career, but you owe it to yourself to develop your personal culture through liberal arts while fulfilling your graduation requirements.

Many of my classmates merely wanted to pass liberal arts courses to fulfill their requirements. Some resented taking these classes because they lowered their grade-point average. Others asserted that general education courses were useless since they weren't directly related to their projected job. They took notes, memorized information, passed exams, dismissed practically everything, and walked away with little more than the grade. "I'm a business major, so why must I study biological science?" These people were good at their trades but they weren't in tune with the qualitative aspects of health, human relations, warmth, arts and culture. "You're taking the classes anyway, so why not extract what's valuable and apply it to your life?" I used to think to myself. It's very easy to overlook the value of liberal arts, especially with the trend of seeking instant money and ambitious career results upon graduation. Your career growth is important, but so is your personal development. More than pure academic learning can occur in liberal arts classes. How a subject is presented and how it can be adapted outside of class are two different things. Using your own introspection and creativity, you can apply what you learn in both personal and professional contexts. Doing this expands your vision, deepens your thinking, broadens your decision-making capacity, and increases your human capital. Research the course offerings to find those of greatest interest. Appreciate the value of your liberal arts courses. Examples are given in Part III.

3

Work Hard **and** Wisely

I keep six honest serving men
(They taught me all I knew);
Their names are What and Why and When
And How and Where and Who.
—Rudyard Kipling, 1865–1936[16]

College-level homework is challenging. It's supposed to be. When you reflect on your previous years of school, you can see you had to put in work to acquire your present knowledge. No one would develop intellectually if he or she stayed at the same course level year after year, studying the same material over and over again. Just as the body needs a variety of exercise, so the mind needs new information and new challenges to grow.

You cannot fly like an eagle with the wings of a wren.
—William Henry Hudson, 1841–1922[17]

People have said that some students have more raw intelligence than others. Beyond innate talents and acquired IQ, a lot comes down to how well you apply yourself. Inborn intelligence is no guarantee of high exam scores or a stellar grade-point average. Exams test you on what you've learned. A naturally intelligent student who doesn't study won't score well. A student of less so-called intelligence can achieve higher test scores. What makes the difference? The capacity to acquire knowledge, using an efficient strategy, discipline, and perseverance are the compensating factors. I didn't consider myself to be particularly smart: I simply worked at it.

Throughout college, your native intelligence will be combined with new information to shape your unique fund of knowledge. This fund will be expanding exponentially. To reach your potential you need to plan and work well, to give yourself the focus and means to attain your goals.

Nobody graduates without putting in work. But working hard doesn't mean expending lots of time and energy for tiny returns. Laboring without an organized plan can make you feel like a fly trying to find a way through a windowpane. However, if you work hard *and* efficiently simultaneously, you will make your greatest gains.

In the course of working hard and efficiently, some people develop into a state of intelligence without conscience. So there's no misunderstanding: you'll be a finer person when you maintain your conscience throughout your stages of development rather than casting it aside as many seem to do to "get ahead." Remember who you are. As you evolve, don't let a quest for efficiency cause you to deny your ethics.

I don't believe in taking longer than necessary to do something, but I believe in doing things very well. If something required a month to complete, I would take a month. But I wouldn't labor over something for three hours when two would do.

In his *Encyclopedia of Modern Bodybuilding*,[18] Arnold Schwarzenegger spoke of ways to increase athletic training intensity: "by doing the same amount of work in less time" and "by doing an increased amount of work in the same time." You can apply these principles to your study strategy. They point you to the idea of working efficiently. Accordingly, your study strategy must be as streamlined as you can make it (without compromising quality). Efficiency requires organization. To be organized requires planning. And planning requires time and attention. But all this allows your talents and energies to produce your best within a given period.

The right strategy allows you to accomplish your work faster, finish more work in the same time, *or complete your finest work on time*. Give yourself the wings worthy of an eagle by supplying yourself with an astutely planned strategy, being mindful about yourself, and following through with practice.

Persevering

The secret of success is constancy to purpose.
—Benjamin Disraeli, Earl of Beaconsfield, 1804–1881[19]

Our most successful people did not get to where they are overnight. They worked hard and wisely, and they persevered. You've developed perseverance in school up to college. College is harder, but you're also more learned now and have more tools available to help you succeed.

The beginning is always the most difficult. This can discourage novices very quickly. But things get easier. By working hard *and* efficiently, you develop discipline. As time goes by, it's easier to motivate yourself, focus, and perform; and you'll be inspired by greater results (especially if you're studying what you enjoy). You'll build and reinforce your discipline, confidence, and motivational strength on each accomplishment, one by one, stage by stage. Once you become accustomed to keeping up with your studies, you'll hit your stride. It is a good feeling. You will also discover what you can do and what you're made of. You'll gain more from your courses, your grades will improve, and your self-discipline will stay with you beyond college, setting you apart from others in the workplace.

What about those who need to overcome deficiencies before they can find their rhythm in their studies? Deficiencies can be compensated for if you give this priority, use the right plan, and then follow up with practice. In the long run, a less-gifted person working hard and efficiently will progress farther than a naturally gifted person who doesn't apply him- or herself. If you have deficiencies to overcome, don't be discouraged. The recovery may not be immediate, but your productivity and long-term gains are what counts. Going from three Fs to six honors wasn't about luck: it was about carrying out these principles on a daily basis.

There is no substitute for hard work.
—Thomas Alva Edison, 1847–1931[20]

At times, you may be neck and neck with other students. Surprising as it may sound, the difference can come down to who works harder. I wasn't the brightest person in my classes—I simply worked at things more, and out-persevered classmates who gave up after a certain point. In one of my most competitive classes, ten other students had test scores comparable or superior to mine. I ultimately outranked them because they didn't keep up with their deadlines: they failed to turn in two to three weekly written assignments. You may also find that other students know what's required to do well, yet they simply don't follow up with practice.

Pace Yourself

The bow too tensely strung is easily broken. *and*
It takes a long time to bring excellence to maturity.
—Publilius Syrus, fl. first century B.C.E.[21]

Considering the time, money, and work you'll invest, it's sensible to make your college experience as beneficial as possible. You'll be in school for two to five years, but you only need to advance one step, day, and semester at a time. You can take breaks along the way to refuel yourself and get a second wind. If you're after top scores and seeking to develop your potential, each stage will be hard enough. As long as you're maximizing each step, week, and semester without setting yourself back from overwork, you'll get the most out of your education. This isn't a race against time. You will finish eventually. The key is to have learned the most according to your abilities in the process. Don't burn yourself out.

Overstudying is analogous to sprinting from the start of a stage race: you'll exhaust yourself before the finish line. But unlike a race, you'll also be penalized with lower grades for poor performance. Burnout can lead to decreased motivation, concentration, learning, memory, and quality of work. You won't absorb as much information, and your test scores will be affected. Your grades may drop and you may become discouraged or disgruntled as a result. This is not a productive path toward graduation.

During study sessions away from class, monitor yourself. When your learning curve begins tapering off due to exhaustion, take a break in some form or another. Visit friends, take a walk, exercise, telephone a classmate—whatever refreshes your state of mind without setting back your time schedule. If you get into a rut, pull yourself out. If tired, take a nap. Studying hard is an admirable aspiration, but there's nothing smart about burning yourself out. In fact, taking a day off can provide mental relief that allows you to return to your work in a fresh state of mind, thus maintaining or increasing your productivity.

I made it a general policy to take one day off on weekends, to maintain my sanity. My fall and spring semesters were so intense that I didn't bother with summer school. I knew that if I didn't take summer vacation, I would soon become sick of studying, in which case my education would go down the tubes. I've heard of people preferring summer school because classes are smaller, easier to enroll in, and have fewer competitive students in them. Although I never attended summer courses or winter session, these are worth considering if this kind of strategy works for you.

To pace myself at one point near midterm exams, I went with a roommate to see a horror film. The movie provided a ninety-minute diversion. My roommate's editorial after the show was: "You were sick of studying and wanted a no-brainer." I agreed with a smile. I had absorbed so much academic information that I didn't want to see any movie requiring me to analyze its deeper meaning. The break got me out of the dorm, out of a study rut, and gave me some relief. At other times, I simply exercised at the gym, took a bicycle ride, or had dinner with friends.

Ideally, choose the maximum study pace at which your performance peaks, but not ebbs. Your peak capacity will change as you become more seasoned, so your limits will be redefined over several years. Also, your endurance and intensity spans will vary depending on your courses' contents, which will be changing every semester. Through experience, you'll learn to feel when you can take on more or when you've reached saturation point.

Pacing yourself also means not taking on more units than you can handle. One elder student criticized me for not taking sixteen semester units, and thus for "wasting my time." Come on, now! That student had skipped her third and seventh grades due to intellectual merit, entered junior college at age sixteen, became salutatorian, and graduated with her bachelor degree at twenty. She took sixteen and a half units every semester for four years straight, double majored in economics and sociology, and graduated Phi Beta Kappa with a 4.0 grade-point average! Okay, I had to respect that achievement. After rebutting that she didn't have a life outside of studying, I had to pause and think for a minute. Scrutinizing myself confirmed that I had already chosen my proper path. I knew my limits and that I was doing everything I could to do well. There is a point up to which your maximum efforts yield maximum results. This is also the point beyond which you become strained so that your performance begins to decline from overwork and excessively divided efforts. Taking more semester units for lesser results would have caused my morale to suffer, my learning to be compromised, and money to be wasted—all because someone else felt I should rush my way through college. I wanted a balanced life outside the classroom, so that

I could exercise regularly and occasionally have some social activity. (There was less time for play since I was digging myself out of the Fs.)

One classmate completed her bachelor program in less than three years. She took twenty-one units per semester and trained herself to live on five hours sleep each night! I don't know how many units may have been fulfilled by transfer or challenge by examination, but her g.p.a. was at least 3.6 to make Phi Beta Kappa and she finished well within the top 10% of my graduating class! Two of my colleagues, both Phi Betes, remarked that taking such an intensive load could be a recipe for a nervous breakdown. Perhaps, in fact, that was that student's maximum pace; she obviously had superior intelligence. Though unusual, there are students who can handle heavy unit loads. It is important, however, to maintain perspective on what's appropriate for *you*. Some people naturally need less sleep than others. Some students can surmount sixteen or more units; some cannot. Some take the heavy load, pass the courses, but experience burnout nonetheless.

Whether your load is twelve, sixteen, or twenty units, be true to yourself. Choose a load and pace where your performance is at or near its peak while you're neither over nor under challenged. Also get the sleep *you* need.

Give Yourself Enough Lead Time to Do Assignments Well

Nothing can be done at once hastily and prudently.
—Publilius Syrus, fl. first century B.C.E.[22]

Know the right timing.
—The Seven Sages, ca. 650–ca. 600 B.C.E.[23]

Procrastination is easy, especially when an assignment turns you off. It is also easy to be turned off when you don't have a clear idea of how to attack your homework. One aim of this book is to reduce such uncertainty of method.

I wouldn't make it a general policy to think "the greatest labor-saving device ever invented is 'tomorrow.'" Procrastination causes more work to accumulate. You rush to meet immediate deadlines. This reduces reading comprehension, leads to cramming for tests, and causes nervousness which detracts from clear thinking. Cramming for tests doesn't allow you to score your best. Assignments completed in haste don't represent your best work. Accordingly, you receive grades that don't reflect your true abilities because teachers can only judge you by what you hand in. Also, because your long-term practice is based on a string of work that's below your full capabilities, you only develop a fraction of your potential.

If you give yourself generous head-start times and work consistently up to your deadline, you'll be less rushed while achieving better results. Allowing yourself enough time to review for exams is another blessing. Using your course syllabi, begin from your due dates and work backward, stage by stage, to calculate the overall time you need to complete your work. Then apply this timeline in forward sequence, starting on the day you've determined (for details, see Chapters 5 and 6).

Know When to Put Fun on Hold

Enjoy when you can, and endure when you must.
—Johann Wolfgang von Goethe, 1749–1832[24]

Finding time for leisure activity isn't a problem for most students. Managing time for their studies is. You can still enjoy leisure activity, you just need to know when it's okay and when you need to stay put and study. Managing time includes calculating how much you can allocate away from your studies and—equally important—when it's time to leave an activity and return to studying. *Don't wait until tomorrow to do what needs to be done today.* It's important to keep a disciplined policy and not let leisure activity preempt your studies. It's very easy to lose track of time when you're having fun. Hours go by, and then you may be too tired to study afterward. Even if you plan to work in entertainment, consumer recreation, or video electronics, you'll still need to study well and pass your courses if you care about your duty to yourself. You'll be competing with others in the work world. Your degree of self-discipline and intellectual development will be apparent after college, indicating who you are and what you did with yourself there. Applying yourself well in college gives you the work habits that will help you stand out from the crowd.

I remember playing a computer video game, for a time, that was a gift from a classmate. Bombing the computer's enemy base camp left me with mixed feelings: I got my mindless relief from studying, delight from defeating the program on its hardest setting, and a minor sense of completeness over a frivolous computer game. I also felt strangely hypocritical because I was enrolled in an international Peace Law and Human Rights course. But I always knew that 15 to 35 minutes was long enough to play before returning to other obligations or homework, so I made it a point to beat the game's artificial intelligence as fast as I could.

To ensure that he didn't lose track of time, a friend used a kitchen timer for video-gaming during college. Once the timer went off, he disciplined himself to leave the game and return to his homework. I endorse having brainless relief when you need it. But don't forget that you're engineering your learning habits and intellectual makeup as you go along. Have your fun when it's needed, but remember that studies are your priority.

Goal-Setting

First say to yourself what you would be; and then do what you have to do.
—Epictetus, ca. 50–120 C.E.[25]

Wanting to do well is your catalyst for achievement. You then need to see many study-related issues to have clear goals. These issues are described in detail throughout this book. Clearly defined goals help you craft your strategies with greater precision.

John Naber, a 1976 Olympic gold medalist in the men's backstroke, is a good goal-setting model. Four years before his Olympic competition in the 100-meter event, Naber projected his then-closest competitor's progress. "I didn't predict he'd *swim* that fast, I predicted he would be *capable* of that. Therefore, for me to win, I had to swim a time faster than what I thought he was capable of doing."[26] Naber projected his opponent's winning time, in four years, to be 55.5 seconds. Naber's fastest time was 59.5 seconds. Accordingly, Naber sought to reduce his overall time by 4 seconds.

Naber didn't try to accomplish his task with one great attempt or by blindly swimming as fast as he could during training. "I did not stand on the blocks and say, 'I'm going to break a world record, everybody watch me now.'"[27] Naber divided his goal into stages. He aimed to reduce his finish time by 1 second each year, 1/12 of a second each month, leading up to the Olympic competition. This goal-setting strategy allowed Naber to set a new world record at 55.49 seconds.[28]

Certain goals or challenges may appear overwhelming if you try to attain them in one effort. But if you divide your goal into incremental stages, it will be more manageable for you to achieve. By planning each stage, your progress is more efficient, with more certain results. This can be applied to reading chapters of a textbook, to the number of days over which to divide your exam reviews, and to the stages devoted to long-term writing projects.

I once applied this goal-setting model to drawing a still life with black and white charcoal for art class. I had three subjects arranged on a table: a black leather glove, a Bartlett pear, and a silver goblet. Each day I drew at the same time for several hours, since the natural lighting and shadows from my windows remained consistent. What I didn't plan on was a sudden rise in our autumn weather temperatures. Each day I was bewildered why the fruit didn't match its position on my drawing; the pear was ripening and leaning to the side more each day. I sped up the drawing by lengthening each stage and having fewer sessions; an overripe pear would stain the glove. Moral of the story: if perishables are involved, check the weather forecast, your room temperature, and your subject's degree of perishability when planning your approach!

Make a Master Checklist of All Criteria Needed for Graduation

Make yourself a list of all the courses and requirements for graduation. Group courses alphabetically by category. The purpose of this list is twofold:

■ It gives you an instant readout of which requirements you've fulfilled and what's pending; and

■ It's an instant readout of your track record. Think of this as an academic balance sheet and progress record. Your morale will be boosted as you see your list of accomplishments growing.

Here's a hypothetical example:

Table 1 Master checklist of criteria for graduation

Courses	Units	Your Final Course Grade
General requirements for all students	*(15 units)*	
Course 1	3	A
Course 2	3	B
Course 3	3	C
Course 4	3	A
Course 5	3	B
Area Requirements		
English-Language Proficiency Test		Passed
Math Proficiency Test		Passed
Arts and Humanities	*(9 units)*	
Course 1	3	A
Course 2	3	B
Course 3	3	C
Language and Literature	*(9 units)*	
Course 1	3	A
Course 2	3	B
Course 3	3	C
Sciences	*(9 units)*	
Course 1	3	A
Course 2	3	B
Course 3	3	C
Social Sciences	*(9 units)*	
Course 1	3	A
Course 2	3	B
Course 3	3	C

Major Courses	Units	
List of lower-division classes		
Course 1	3	A
Course 2	3	B
Course 3	3	C
And so on…		
List of upper-division classes		
Course 1	3	A
Course 2	3	B
Course 3	3	C
And so on…		

Electives		
Course 1	3	A
Course 2	3	B

Unit total required for graduation:	120	g.p.a.	3.105 (based on above hypotheticals)

All other criteria needed for graduation

1. Minimum cumulative grade-point average
2. Deadline to apply for graduation
3. Library books to be returned before applying for graduation
4. Administrative requirements
5. Successfully complete all courses during final semester

Note: Plotting your major curriculum helps you avoid schedule conflicts or missing a course essential for graduation. Some classes may not be offered every semester or not offered until after you wish to graduate. Save all your course schedules to track their availability. When in doubt, call the department secretary. This will help you plan future semesters' course combinations.

Your checklist may change after you choose or change your major, when certain courses are discontinued, or when new courses are added.

Given a Choice, Schedule Strategically

When living on or near campus, class schedules are easily managed. Having to commute long distances is more involved. I preferred consolidating classes into two or three days a week—whenever possible, back to back on Tuesdays and Thursdays. Some foreign language classes meet daily, however, which is, of course, practical because the frequency of exposure and practice enhances your learning.

Some of my required upper-division courses met only once a week, usually at night. In these cases, there was no alternative. Though convenient, once-a-week lecture courses ran for three hours, were very intensive, required great endurance in attention and concentration. Your mind gets saturated, and it's harder to remain sharp and focused than in shorter classes.

I always enrolled in twelve semester units. When I could consolidate my schedule, I had four-day weekends every week, during which I could concentrate on readings, exam preparation, writing stronger term papers, and getting regular exercise. The extra time wasn't for partying. Living an hour away from school with a Monday through Friday schedule would mean ten hours each week—nearly a full day—lost to commuting alone. Contrast this with a Tuesday and Thursday schedule with only four hours a week in transit. Six extra hours per week is considerable. Assuming sixteen weeks per semester, a Monday through Friday schedule would require 160 hours in transit versus 64 hours with a Tuesday and Thursday schedule. By consolidating classes, 96 hours were saved over the course of the semester—a very significant amount when it comes to homework, deadlines, and more sleep each night. If my required courses met on Monday, Wednesday, and Friday, I'd try to consolidate all my other classes into these three days instead. I'm not suggesting that you choose convenience of schedule over quality of education. But all other things being equal, the greater the consolidation, the better the use of your time. An added perk of a Tuesday and Thursday schedule is that your spring breaks will be longer: Friday to Monday instead of Saturday through Sunday.

At large colleges, registering for courses can be more involved because of limited space per course. Students are assigned enrollment priorities based on year (senior, junior, sophomore, freshman), major, military status, and other criteria. The dates on which you are permitted to register for courses reflect your priority status. Register for your courses the minute your priority allows. As a freshman and sophomore, it is common to find courses already full when you attempt to register.

Speed is a factor because a multitude of students will be snatching slots in the same courses. If you discover that a course is full, choose another section of the same course or an entirely different required course as quickly as possible because you won't know how many remaining slots are open. The sooner you act, the greater your chances of getting into your alternative course or courses.

To minimize lag time in selecting classes, have at least four to six different semester schedules already planned. Label these plan A, B, C, D, and so on. Order these plans from the most to least preferred schedule. When registering, I had my schedules written out. If one didn't work, I'd try the next. I seldom had to rely on Plan D.

When you must enroll in courses you find dull and hard, it helps to distribute them one per semester over numerous semesters rather than consolidating them back to back in succession.

TECHNIQUES
THAT WORK

4

Core Study Principles and Policies

You know you're successful when you remember to do everything.
—Anonymous

For me, in addition to points already covered, doing well in school came down to these main elements:

- Cultivating good critical-thinking skills;
- Analyzing course syllabi carefully;
- Mapping out your entire semester calendar within the first week of class;
- Planning time effectively;
- Reading chapters before the scheduled lectures;
- Being punctual for all classes and meetings;
- Having good note-taking skills;
- Getting enough sleep each night, especially before exam day;
- Concentrating during every phase of study;
- Having effective methods for absorbing new material;
- Retaining new material effectively;
- Taking breaks as needed to alleviate mental exhaustion or stagnation;
- Preparing thoroughly for exams;
- Maintaining good recall and thinking clearly during tests; and
- Not getting lazy until the last graded assignment is turned in.

There are only so many hours and only so much energy you can expend in a day in relation to other demands. Every time-saving measure that aids learning should be used within ethical boundaries. Given demanding classes and the need for regular exercise, I used these core principles and methods:

■ If you can make learning one of your lifelong values, your college task will be a lot easier and more meaningful.

■ College is the time to put yourself to the test. You can't know your strengths until you're tested. Also, view exams as ways to prove, better, and learn more about yourself.

■ Time is one of your most valuable assets; plan it well. Many students are overly optimistic about time and don't react until a deadline is right around the corner. *Make lack-of-planning desperation a thing of the past.*

■ College is not forgiving of ignorance. Grades are not forgiving of mistakes. As a fundamental philosophy, I adopted two principles of Total Quality Management:[29]
(1) Aim to do things right the first time, and
(2) "Make continuous improvement a way of life."[30]

As an ongoing practice, keep what works, throw out what doesn't, and create your own improvements as you advance through the semester. As you become a more seasoned student, your strategies will become more polished.

Note: *Doing things right the first time* refers to applying foresight and planning before you take action. Incorporating upstream preventative measures in your strategy works better than relying on downstream corrections. It takes more time and work to put things right than to do things right the first time. This principle does not apply literally to writing or creative work because these need refinement. However, by proper planning and having clear direction and goals, your first draft or form will be off to its best start.

■ Take the time to do your assignments right. "Right" means your best work. Take as long as you need to do a very good job, but don't take longer than necessary to get the job done well.

■ There are three general elements to studying: *time*, *work*, and *quality*. Quality should be your number-one objective, with work and time centered on that goal. It's up to you to find the most efficient ways of producing your best work.

■ There are four steps to studying well:
(1) Defining your course criteria,
(2) Setting clear goals,

(3) Planning your strategy, and

(4) Following through.

Keeping your focus throughout every stage is paramount.

■ In a strategy, everything counts. Every tactic you employ, whether adopted or self-created, should be honest and designed to move you forward efficiently in both the short and long term. Strategies should be planned to minimize time and energy wasted. Seek to have no superfluous steps in your procedures. The fewer uncertainties you give yourself, the better you can concentrate and work. Also, the more organized your time, the clearer it will be how much time you can devote to fun or extracurricular activities.

■ Plan to have your knowledge and memory of a subject peak on the date and at the time of an exam.

■ If you're after top scores, you must take every assignment in every course seriously. By top scores, I mean the highest within your individual capabilities. Every point *within your reach* matters.

■ This is your time to shine—and you will—but *you* have to make it happen. Facing your challenges strengthens your will to deal with and surmount problems. This may be hard to do in the beginning, especially if certain courses appear intimidating. However, the more you practice such courage and determination over time, the easier it becomes to summon your strength of will *at will*. Monitor the changes within yourself over the next two to four years. *If you practice the strategies suggested in this book, you will see noticeable results.*

■ Assignments and tests with the most percentage weight determine the bulk of your course grade: give them special attention and perform them well. High scores on these help buffer your grade if you've scored below par on other assignments. (This is discussed more in Chapters 5 and 13.)

■ Aim to score well on all assignments, quizzes, and tests leading up to the final exam. This has three benefits:

(1) The stronger your semester grade going into the final exam, the easier it is to keep it, which is always preferable to trying to overcome a deficit.

(2) Less pressure to score high on a final exam means that you have more time and energy to devote to other course finals.

(3) A teacher may even exempt you from a final exam if your semester grade is good. With fewer divided efforts, you have a greater chance of performing well on your remaining exams and, thereby, raising your grade-point average.

One of my professors exempted students from the final if our semester grade was B or higher. The final exam was not only cumulative but also constituted 40% of our total grade. For me, being exempted was a big load off of my shoulders. Coincidentally, a second class that same semester exempted me from its final. This led to my attaining As in all courses that term; in one class, I had the highest score among 138 students.

■ *Concentration is everything.* Your study environment and seating should allow your mind to concentrate 100%, free from interference and distractions. It should be quiet: no radio, music, television, noise, or other people talking. Seating should be comfortable for prolonged studying. During exam reviews, your focus should be reduced to only two things: *you and your notes.*

Note: Choose your study environments where interruptions are nonexistent, or seek to prevent interruptions. Regaining your train of thought and rhythm after an interruption can take up to twenty minutes or more; if this happens three or four times a day, you'll lose more than an hour from interruptions alone. During critical study sessions at home, I would shut off the telephone ringer and let the answering machine take incoming calls. If you're interrupted, mark your spot in any way you can to give yourself a guidepost for resuming.

■ Your aim to maximize your grade starts *before* the first day of class. After registering for your courses, buy your textbooks. If you're uncertain whether a given course section is right for you, interview your teacher before you enroll in his or her section and/or go to the bookstore before your registration day to scan your choice of textbooks. In class, listen carefully to your teachers' expectations to give you direction and aim. Working with incomplete information can cause misunderstandings, incorrect or excess work, false starts, lower grades, and frustration.

■ Understand everything covered in class to be in control of all your assignments and test preparations, and to minimize stress due to uncertainty.

- Keep up with *all* assignments. Don't hand them in late. Performing well on regular assignments is the best way to keep your grades strong. Don't put yourself at a disadvantage by falling behind.
- Extra-credit assignments are opportunities to boost or buttress your course grade. They should not be viewed as substitutes for completing regular homework (except in an emergency, where they may help recover your grade if you've missed an assignment). If extra-credit tasks would jeopardize your ability to handle current work loads, however, don't pile more on your plate. Moreover, not all instructors will give extra-credit assignments. You can always ask; the worst they can say is "no." Generally, keeping up with and scoring well on your regular assignments is preferable because you'll have less work overall and can concentrate on doing fewer assignments better.
- At times, learning requires a student to make order out of chaos. To understand new material being taught, I determined things in this order:
  (1) The What (what's the name, description, category, or definition of the subject?)
  (2) The Why (why is the subject important—its purpose, significance, benefit, or consequence?)
  (3) The How (how does it work or occur—its procedure, process, or formula?)

Note: Some teachers, student speakers, and trainers tend to jump right into How or Why first, which can confuse a first-time learner. In addition, some inadvertently omit one or more parts to a sequence, which can cause misunderstanding on the part of the learner. Asking good questions comes into play here.

- When learning a procedure, seek to learn it in sequential order. First grasp the full process before digesting its parts. This will be useful not only in school but during on-the-job training as well.
- Be able to succinctly define and articulate a problem.
- Take breaks between reading sessions to give your eyes, mind, and body a break.
- Read your college catalog to determine your school's expectations for academic and personal conduct.
- Attend every class.

- ■ Ask questions about what you don't understand.
- ■ Take solid notes.
- ■ Eat a balanced, nutritious diet everyday.
- ■ Always get enough sleep to be fully alert the next day. Don't form a pattern of sleep deprivation. Be careful that playing long and hard doesn't cause you to defer and extend your sleep hours when homework is waiting to be done the same or next day.
- ■ If you get tired during hours of study outside class, take a nap, but be careful not to upset your regular sleep cycle.
- ■ If a class meeting or exam is rescheduled, ensure that you have no other appointment conflict.
- ■ If you suffer from allergies, take the appropriate prescription medications so that your symptoms don't distract you from your lectures or tests. One of my classmates sniffled throughout a lecture that ran nearly an hour and a half. Also, find out whether your medication causes drowsiness that will interfere with concentration during note-taking or exams.
- ■ Although it's tempting toward the end of a semester, don't get lax until after you've handed in your last assignment to be graded. You may want to get things over with, but hang in there and wait until it's really over to have fun!

This last perspective also applies when you have only one class during your last semester before graduating. With the finish line in sight, I've known some classmates to disregard performance as long as they pass the course. They just wanted to get out of school. This made things hard for their teammates in group projects, where each member received the same grade regardless of each person's work.

I had only one course during my last term before graduation. The previous semester had been my most difficult. I could easily have rationalized putting in minimal effort to pass. I'm glad I didn't because I learned valuable skills in that course that I still use today. The course was Speech Communication, which enhanced my communication skills used at school, work, and during social activities. Furthermore, two other classmates depended on me for their group project and shared grades. Knowing how frustrating it is to be disadvantaged by an undependable team member, I sought not to repeat the same inconsideration.

5

Analyze Your Course Criteria

Well begun is half done.
—Aristotle, 384–322 B.C.E.[31]

You cannot put the same shoe on every foot.
—Publilius Syrus, fl. first century B.C.E.[32]

Logical consequences are the scarecrows of fools and the beacons of wise men.
—Thomas Henry Huxley, 1825–1895[33]

The beginning of wisdom is the definition of terms.
—Socrates, 469–399 B.C.E.[34]

All teachers have their criteria for assigning grades, whether or not they are disclosed verbally or in writing. It is up to you to ascertain what these criteria are. Knowing this helps you plan your strategies and work in the most efficient way. While no two teachers' grading criteria are identical in every way, they will most likely include some or all of the following:

- attendance;
- text readings;
- deadlines for homework assignments;
- quizzes;
- midterm and final exams;
- the quality of your questions or remarks during class participation or discussions;
- technical specifications for assignments (such as font sizes, margins, formatting, folders, presentation, etc);
- penalties for late work, absences, or missed exams;

- the percentage of your course grade that each assignment constitutes;
- calculating course grades by curve or using a 100-point scale (this is revisited later in the chapter);
- the point scale used for assigning grades on each assignment, quiz or test;
- type of final exam (essay, multiple choice, true or false, fill in the blanks; open or closed book; or take-home);
- the cut-off points for letter grades used by your teacher;
- group projects;
- speech presentations;
- extra credit assignments; and
- make-up work.

Determine these criteria within your first two class meetings, particularly the percentage weight that each assignment contributes toward your course grade.

If your teacher does not disclose his or her grading stipulations in syllabus form, your option is either to find out by asking him or her directly, querying students who have already taken his or her course, or simply doing your best on every assignment since you won't know what percentage each assignment counts toward your overall course grade. It is very likely, however, that midterm and final exams or major projects will be weighed more heavily than, say, a quiz or extra credit assignment.

However, it is common for teachers to distribute syllabi that detail the criteria for their courses. Your course syllabus is the best basis for formulating your strategy in each class. Syllabi set your entire semester calendar. Classes vary in terms of assignments and policies but your strategies need to suit the particulars of a course. *Write any amendments or clarifications your teacher makes in class on your syllabus.* This may include changes to assignments, deadlines, or test content. Also use a highlighter to mark important areas on your syllabi. Analyze your syllabi thoroughly both in class and again at home. Overlooking details can lead you to perform your work incorrectly, put your grade at risk, and prevent you from receiving the grades commensurate with your hard work. Also, if you're after maximum points, it's essential to notice certain things that may not be immediately obvious.

The following examples are provided to show how different criteria set the stage for different approaches. No two classes are exactly alike, but these examples will give you insight for analyzing details to succeed in your courses. You will then be in a position to see nuances or similarities by which to fine-tune your own strategies.

Class A had a grade percentage breakdown: class participation 10%, written analyses 15%, first midterm exam 15%, second midterm exam 20%, term paper 30%, and final exam 10%. There were three significant indications. First, the term paper weighed the most of all assignments. Although not due until later in the semester, it had to be well written; hence, it was important to start early to allow enough time for study, research, composition, and revisions. Second, the final exam was only 10%, which meant that (a) it had less effect on your semester grade than four other assignments; and (b) scoring well on the midterms, analyses, and term paper was critical because they shaped the bulk (80%) of the course grade. The third factor, class participation, was less obvious because it constituted only 10% of our grade. But class was held in an auditorium-sized room with more than 100 enrolled students. To fulfill your 10% for participation required asserting yourself amongst a sea of students. I contributed on a regular basis, and ensured that the professor verbally acknowledged my name and marked his book at the same time. (The professor's policy was to flag a student's name for participation. If you're a shy student in a sizeable classroom, gather the gumption to say your name or approach the teacher after class while both your memories are fresh, and verify that he or she has recorded your name. Some teachers may recognize you by sight when you participate and will automatically credit your name without prompting). Sitting at the front of the class was essential in order to be easily seen by the professor when I raised my hand. Arriving late could thus cost me points because all seats in front were usually taken.

The parameters were very different in Class B, in which one midterm and final exam each comprised 50% of my grade. Here the strategy was straightforward: attend lectures, take thorough notes, and ensure that you prepared for and did well on both exams. On the one hand, there were fewer assignments. On the other hand, each test was more intensive. Periodic quizzes counted as extra credit, but they couldn't offset a poor performance on either exam. But for those with strong exam scores, the quizzes would push their overall points above the competition.

Class C had a seven-page syllabus. This was a writing-intensive course in which 45% of our grade hinged on writing quality and another 45% depended on two tests. The complete breakdown was as follows: class participation 3%, classroom writing 5%, other writing assignments 5%, quizzes 5%, class presentation 2%, written case analyses 20%, term paper 15%, midterm exam 15%, and final exam 30%. In-class writing and class participation meant that attendance was important. 8% of your course grade could mean the difference of a full letter grade. It was mandatory that photocopies of all references be attached to our homework papers. Late assignments were not accepted. Time management, research, and revisions of papers were even more important.

This class was hard on students who found writing difficult. English-as-a-second-language students dreaded this course. Here a writing enthusiast could thrive. If others wrote equally well, the difference came down to planning, organization, depth of content, creativity, and quality of revisions. Deadlines were fast and frequent. Endurance and constant discipline were required to produce consistently good work on time, especially with other courses' assignments pending. Rather than cringe at the idea, I saw this as an opportunity to improve my writing. Of course, it involved a lot of work, but constant practice is what most improves your skills. And there were two comforts for the apprehensive student: (1) rough drafts could be submitted in advance for review, thereby allowing a student to hand in a better paper on the due date, and (2) revisions to graded papers were allowed to improve your score. (If writing is difficult for you, you can ask your teachers if they will grant you either or both of these options—the worst they can do is say "no.")

Class D differed in three significant ways. First, at the beginning of the semester, students were given two weeks to choose a subject for their term project. They were then given another two weeks' grace period to change their subject if necessary. Second, the term project constituted 30% of the overall grade. Of this 30%, 70% (0.3×0.7, or 21% of one's total grade) was weighted toward the written report and 30% (0.3×0.3, or 9% of one's total grade) was for the oral presentation. Third, 5% extra credit for the whole semester could be earned by giving the oral presentation on one of five days during the second-to-last month of class. This had instant appeal because it merely entailed early performance, not additional work. A sign-up sheet was left at the first aisle of the classroom for us to view during our break time. Later, out of curiosity, I walked over from the far side of the room. I immediately noticed that, during these five days, there were far fewer slots in relation to the number of students enrolled. Hence, making a lightning-fast decision was essential before every slot was filled. Slow reaction or hesitation worked against a student here.

Presentation dates couldn't be changed once you signed your name. I first searched for the last available extra-credit day. If that day was full, I looked for the next to last day available, and so on. The logic was that (a) by signing up within that period, you were guaranteed a 5% boost to your course grade; (b) choosing the last day available during the period gave the most time to prepare your presentation; and (c) as classmates gave their presentations during the first four days, your could gauge your own, gain new ideas on how to improve it, and avoid committing the errors that detracted from their presentations, especially if the teacher commented on something. The backbone of my presentation was written well in advance and was subject to the same stringent revisions as all my written papers and speeches. Modifications to my presentation during the four-day observation period were not extensive but did give it more polish.

Class H's most notable criteria related to class attendance and participation: 10% was deducted from a student's total grade upon a third absence, 20% upon the fourth, and the fifth resulted in an F for the course. Merely attending class did not suffice. At the semester's end, your cumulative score (from all homework, quizzes, and tests) was multiplied by a number between 0.9 and 1.1, predicated on the quality of your class participation. Thus no participation considerably reduced your cumulative point total, whereas good participation had the opposite effect. This was significant for students whose grades were borderline before the 0.9–1.1 multiplication as it was for students seeking to maximize their scores.

In various courses, missed deadlines or incomplete work incurred penalties, some of which were severe. Class C gave zero credit for late assignments. Class D didn't accept late papers caused by computer file corruption, accidental erasure, or any other technical fault. Class J had weekly assignments, each of which lost 50% credit during the first delinquent week, 75% the second, and 100% thereafter. In Class O, homework that was less than 50% complete received zero credit, plus a whopping 50-point deduction from one's semester total! Sock it to me, why don't you! If you're putting in the work, you deserve every point you can get. *It's a shame to lose points due to a missed deadline, so plan your work well.*

In Class K, a group project shaped a major portion of your course grade. The class had three exams weighted at 15% each, a group project at 35%, 10% for a paper, and 10% for attendance. Its multiple-choice tests were straightforward, so I focused on the group project. The term project required forming our own groups and would yield a shared grade. Group projects involve mutual dependence. Each member needed to be reliable, aiming for the same grade, prompt for meetings, motivated, good at reasoning, and dedicated to finishing his or her work on time. In effect, having the right people in your group affected a large portion of your grade. (See Chapter 8 for more on group projects.)

Class L didn't allot weights to assignments and tests; your course grade was calculated by a straight average of all your scores. This class's biggest challenge was its mixed-configuration exams. Four midterms meant that fewer chapters were covered per test. However, our study guide handouts for each of the four contained 99 to 132 topics. Besides the sheer volume of detailed information you needed to learn and memorize, there were some tough fill-in questions on the exams, with up to six blanks per question or lengthy sentence completions. No word list was provided on the test, so we couldn't use the process of elimination. What appeared to be correct by common reasoning wasn't necessarily correct, so these tests were much harder than multiple-choice exams.

Because the fill-in questions required very specific answers, test reviews involved an enormous amount of preparation. Memorization couldn't be by rote because certain topics dovetailed with those for essay questions that were worth up to 25 points each. The way to prepare for the exams was to use class handouts as a basis for writing your own study notes. The handouts were reasonably specific. For example, some indicated whether a topic involved a specific number of steps to a process. But each topic was quite detailed and extensive. One set of my study notes spanned thirteen pages but resulted in a score of 98 on the exam.

Another very important criterion concerns make-up exams. Not all instructors give make-up tests. Some teachers may grant make-up exams only when they receive a written medical notice, on letterhead, stating the nature of the emergency that caused your absence. One of my science courses had midterms weighted at 30% of our total grade so that missing a test without mitigating circumstances was certain disaster. In another course, failure to notify the instructor of your absence beforehand resulted in an automatic F for the test (which was also weighted at 30%). In Class O, missing an exam without the professor's written consent incurred an F for the course regardless of your other assignments or tests completed!

Never miss an exam. If you must miss one, ensure that you have a very legitimate reason *and* get the form of proof stipulated on your syllabus to justify a make-up test. If you anticipate an absence, meet with your teacher at the earliest opportunity before the exam to discuss the best way to handle the situation.

Attendance and note-taking were the two most critical parts of Class M. There was a 25% midterm and a 50% final exam. Attendance and participation were worth 25%—as much as the midterm. Students in this class needed to attend every session anyway: tests were based solely on lectures that did not mirror text readings, though this wasn't apparent until three weeks into the semester. Absences were costly. Moreover, although half the semester's material was condensed into its midterm, there was no study guide handout, nor were we told what topics would be on the test. The midterm had four essay questions worth 25 points each. This was a three-hour lecture class but we were limited to an hour for the test. Three minutes were taken for the teacher to distribute the exam and go over instructions. If you opted to factor in 4 minutes for proofreading answers, your total test time was 53 minutes. This was an open-note test, but 13.25–14.25 minutes still isn't a long time in which to frame a comprehensive, concise, well-organized answer and write it out neatly. Such an exam became a race against time. Under such pressure, answers may not necessarily reflect one's best quality of expression. The best insurance was to study very carefully, be clear on all information, and apply it quickly and comprehensively when answering hypothetical questions.

The higher the percentage weight of an assignment or test, the more important it is to score well on it. Since these shape a greater part of your overall grade, they provide buffers against mistakes made on a final exam. In other cases, they can position you to jump to the next higher letter grade if you do well on your last test.

Assessing grade scales is another important criterion. Compare these two courses:

Table 2 Comparison of point cut-offs for assigning letter grades

	Class 1	Class 2	Grade
Points	92–100	95–100	A
	89–91	92–94	A–
	86–88	89–91	B+
	83–85	85–88	B
	80–82	82–84	B–
	78–79	80–81	C+
	72–77	75–79	C
	70–71	70–74	C–
		68–69	D+
	60–69	65–67	D
	0–59	0–64	F

Compound these grade scales with exam types, percentage weights, and total points per test. If Class 1 administered a fifty-question multiple-choice exam while Class 2 gave essay tests worth 28 to 36 points, Class 2 would clearly give less margin for error on exams. (This is revisited later in this chapter.) In Class 2, mistakes, laziness, forgetfulness, or being casual about test reviews had a more dramatic effect on your grade.

This is a good time to caution the C-aspiring D student: *Select your classes carefully according to your temporary limitations.* In other words, it's okay to avoid an overwhelming challenge *temporarily* for the sake of your long-term progress. A student just climbing out of an F or a D will be better off in Class 1 than Class 2, given a choice between the two. While you are trying to develop into your best, you don't want to take on something that may intimidate and dishearten you. But once a former F or D student has a few Cs under his or her belt, he or she should shed this conservative approach and ascend into the next realm of challenge.

Some teachers assign course grades based on class curve. With curving, you're graded in relation to your classmates as opposed to a fixed 100-point scale. There are numerous ways to curve. Some instructors may assign As to the top 10% of your class, Fs to the bottom 10%, Bs to the second highest 15–20%, Ds to the second lowest 15–20%, and Cs to the rest. Some teachers use the highest exam score achieved in your class to base their standards. Scoring, 90–100% of this class-high score would merit you an A, 80–89% of it a B, and so on. This can help salvage your grade when you're in a super tough course or when a teacher writes a test that proves to be too long for its given exam period. Bear in mind that grade cut-offs after curving may be adjusted differently. Some instructors will peg the class median at 75% and use this for determining grades. Others may mark grade cut-offs in between distinct clusters of students' test scores. Additional policies may apply—for example, students whose scores after curving fall below 70% may receive failing grades. These, and other factors, depend on your school's grading policies and your instructors' practices. You could ask your teachers what curving method they use if it's not stated on your syllabi. Whether it's best to pose this question in class or privately in their office is something you must determine. (Grade calculations are further explored in Chapter 13.)

Although the aforementioned courses had very different grading criteria, one central principle applied to all of them (and will apply to your classes now): *Not paying full attention to the syllabus, overlooking details, and neglecting to fit these criteria to your circumstances could cost you valuable points.* A sure way to keep your grades up is not to incur penalties. You needn't become nervous about this: simply being mindful of applicable restrictions, going about your work, and finishing on time will suffice. Although scrutinizing these criteria and going to great measures to fulfill them may appear extreme to average students, the concern here is to develop and perform to the best of your abilities rather than deliberately remaining mediocre. This doesn't make penalty avoidance the primary basis for your actions—it's ensuring that you don't lose points unnecessarily. Your learning and development are primary; it's only your strategies that are centered on your syllabi criteria.

I'm not suggesting that you cultivate a defensive attitude about syllabi, nor that my teachers were trying to thrash students. They weren't. These were their rules, just as your teachers will have theirs. Some students might gripe about stringent syllabi criteria, *but exacting syllabi are actually preferable for students seeking to do well.* Specific criteria and restrictions allow you to set clearer goals and formulate your strategies with greater precision. This gives you the best chance of succeeding in a particular course.

All classmates have access to the same syllabus, but whether they read it thoroughly and assess it accurately is another matter. You may also notice that students' intentions may be good and their theories sound in the planning stages, but not everyone follows through with appropriate actions. Seeing is one thing; following up is another. You can't act effectively before seeing. By the same token, seeing what needs to be done won't result in strong scores if you don't follow through. Seeing *and* doing are what's needed. Carefully tailoring your approaches to the syllabus criteria will give you an advantage over those who don't pay full attention. If other classmates do perceive all the restrictions, then quality of work will be a larger determining factor.

Ambiguous syllabi make it harder for you to know what a teacher expects and what criteria you must meet. Yes, you are there to learn, but your teacher has his or her requirements. If you don't fulfill these while you learn, you'll receive a lower grade. Why not get a good grade while you learn? Vague criteria mean that a student can't precisely plan how to perform assignments well. What should be a matter of learning the course subject can become one of learning how to work for a teacher who doesn't communicate specifically what he or she wants. In such cases, self-motivation is key. Unless you ask questions to clarify such ambiguities, you run the risk of wasting time and energy on the wrong kind of work, which may result in a mediocre grade. When in doubt, don't assume—always ask.

Substance First, Tactics Second

Some students don't go to college for an education; they go for a degree.
—Charles Haase, Ph.D., Economics

Learning well on your own merit is the first priority. To optimize your college experience, I would spare nothing within the bounds of honesty to give yourself every advantage to learn well. Tacticians typically seek paths of least resistance with quality of learning being secondary. You've probably heard students with the attitude, "Just tell me what's on the test so I can get my ticket punched." You may hear others saying that grades don't matter because your employer won't ask about your grade-point average. True, most probably won't ask. However, if you've lazed your way through school, your intellectual depth will show it, as will the quality of your decisions and work on the job. Conversely, suppose your résumé states: cum laude, award for academic excellence, graduated in top 10% of class, or other distinctions based on your grade-point average? This will give added weight to your qualifications. It is true that there are other factors to career success, such as networking, good conversational skills, knowing how the system works, having key contacts, interview skills, résumé writing, grooming, and timing. These are important, and you should know their finer points and not live in an ivory tower. But job-hunting strategies should be distinguished from, and not be acquired at the expense of, your personal intellectual development.

Two professors, one of economics for fifty years, now teaching at University of Modena, another of music for forty years, now at The Juilliard School of music, agree that students often memorize material without understanding the messages contained therein. I remember that, as a student, grades were very important. You needn't retain everything covered in every course; such would be impossible. In addition, there may be isolated cases when you're sweating through a course and rote memorization may be your only way to survive, keep pace, or maintain your momentum.

Within academia, the tactics you apply will be tools for learning well—not a substitute for doing so. No student can achieve four years of As on tactics alone. Some of my tactician classmates said, "You can't get good grades without learning." This is true to an extent. But, here we must discern between a college-long strategy based primarily on "parrot and forget" versus one that includes assimilating information to deepen your free thinking outside school.

Your learning comes first; your grades are incidental. But while you are pushing yourself, you deserve the best grades you can get. This is proper recognition. Aim for the grades that are commensurate with your caliber. Unless you're in a class where reciting a teacher's views verbatim is the only way, good grades show that you've learned the material and applied your strategies well. A higher grade-point average shows you are self-motivated, organized, an effective time manager, able to follow directions and complete multiple tasks under pressure, and have good communication skills—things employers value. On a personal level, your grade-point average shows that you cared enough to push yourself to reach your potential. It also proves your self-discipline and versatility at problem-solving because your teachers will throw a barrage of homework at you.

Good grades also reinforce your motivation and morale to continue. You see real results from your planning, creation of strategies, and work. Your self-confidence and self-esteem increase. Your diploma, scholarships, academic honors, and future graduate school are affected by cumulative scores. Grades do matter. Learning well and using efficient, honest tactics is the prudent way to go.

Determine What You Need for Good Grades in a Course

To dial in your strategy, determine all the following for each of your courses within the first week of your semester:

- Grade scale
- Grading method (absolute scale versus curving)
- Dates of all your final exams (The more days in between each exam, the more time you have to prepare. The less time between exams, the more intensive your study load, the more divided your efforts, and the more important it is to score higher early in the semester to alleviate pressure at the term's end.)
- Percentage weight itemization for all assignments
- Percentage weight of your final exam
- How to position yourself so that strong scores on assignments and tests bearing greatest percentage weight will clinch your target course grade

Once you set your strategy into place, it's important not to let hard calculation ruin the joy and quality of learning. I didn't remind myself repeatedly about specific grade percentages—I simply did my best on every assignment. With the constant reassurance that I was doing my utmost, I could accept the results, high or not.

Enjoy your learning as it occurs. Agonizing over numbers, grades, and tactics will divert you from focusing primarily on learning. Learning shouldn't be reduced to a cut-and-dried cost-benefit analysis. Your education isn't a mere scorecard. We're talking about your personal development and quality of life, not about training to become a machine. Your college experience enriches you and should not be viewed as mere data on paper.

Assess Your Exams for Content, Format, Total Points, and Grade Weight

I typically examined the content of a course's first test, which told me whether a teacher based the exam solely on lecture notes or on a combination of text readings, lectures, and handouts. This determined my review strategy for all subsequent tests in that course.

Not knowing the nature of a first midterm, and to be fully prepared, I would review both my notes and text for the class. Generally, if I saw that the first test only included information from lectures, that's all I would study for subsequent exams. This allowed me to invest greater effort in learning, absorbing, and applying the material because courses that only required studying notes typically gave me the hardest exams. If I saw that tests covered notes and readings, then all my subsequent test reviews for that course would include both.

Being complacent is not what I'm suggesting. Although the majority of my teachers didn't change their test patterns throughout the semester, several of them did—and when they did, our exams shifted significantly. These changes were unannounced beforehand. These changes in test patterns separated ordinary students from the sharp ones.

For example, in one course the first test was based on lecture notes, but the second also included detailed text information. Because the midterm constituted 30% of the course grade, under-preparation would be even more punishing on it. My only recourse was to study all notes, text readings, and handouts for subsequent tests. Being caught off guard was more than just a wake-up call. Points missed as a result could mean the difference between a C and a B, or a B and an A, on the test. Even if you changed your subsequent exam reviews, this surprise exam score could compromise your semester cumulative score—which could mean the difference between a B+ and an A- at the semester's end. Any student striving for his or her best knows that a final course grade of 3.7 (A-) is preferable to a 3.3 (B+), and that a 2.7 (B-) is preferable to a 2.3 (C+). This difference is significant for those aiming for scholarships or other personal targets predicated on points. The saving grace, of course, is if the class is graded on a curve. (Education can be a competition with yourself to do your best possible job; in courses graded on a curve, it can also be a competition against others.)

Although some students at the top of the class may be caught by surprise, the class average will suffer even more. If you find yourself in such a situation, it might seem comforting to be above the median. However, depending on your teacher's curving method, you must not lose sight of your closest competitors because they affect your class curve. You can identify your strongest competitors by looking at post-test results disclosed by your teacher. (This is described in Chapter 7, in the section "General Tips on Taking Notes.")

Such calculation of test patterns and preparation is something only you can make, based on your gut feelings about your teacher and your degree of risk—namely, the percentage weight of a test and how high you've set your sights in terms of scoring well.

You may notice other students' test scores improving after they see how a teacher structured the first test. Doing well on exams can be a matter of getting used to a teacher's test style. Monitor the content patterns of your tests. Alter your strategy immediately according to changes that occur. To be safe, it is important to prepare thoroughly to score as high as you can beginning with your first test. Even though the rest of the class may react and score better on subsequent exams, if you've scored high from the onset and then keep your scores strong throughout the term, you'll always be one step ahead of your competitors.

The preceding assumes that you cannot see samples of exams previously administered by your teacher. Viewing old tests can help you anticipate an exam's content, patterns, question style, and degree of difficulty. Knowing this, especially before a first test, can place you at an advantage since you can fine-tune your preparations more definitively. Not all teachers, department secretaries, or school libraries keep such copies for review by students, but some may. It doesn't hurt to ask them, your teacher assistant, or your school librarian.

In unusual circumstances, the option to view old tests may be a necessity. One friend was required to pass a comprehensive exam for her entire major curriculum before qualifying to graduate. For such an enormous challenge, she was able to obtain copies of previous tests from the department secretary. She structured her exam reviews based on these samples, while also using her notes and text readings. The actual exam questions were different from those on the samples, but her extensive preparations enabled her to answer them correctly (and pass with flying colors). She also noticed that the questions were so difficult that merely studying notes or text information wouldn't have been sufficient in and of itself.

Total Test Points Indicate Your Margin of Error

How many points your exam is worth affects your margin of error. For example, some of my courses included multiple-choice tests with fifty questions. All things being equal, on a 100-point scale without grading on a curve, each question was worth 2 points. You could ruin five questions and still squeeze out an A-, ten questions for a B-, and fifteen questions for a C- (or 10, 20, and 30 points, respectively). These tests were more forgiving of errors than tests with fewer points. For example, in Class 2 mentioned earlier, our exam had only 28 points, so each test point was worth 3.57 points on a 100-point scale. Combined with the Class 2 grade scale given earlier, errors were more costly.

Table 3 Total test points indicating margin for error

Test Score	100-Point Scale	Letter Grade	Margin of Error on Test (in points)	
28	100	A	0	
27	96.43	A	1	
26	92.86	A–	2	(grade cut-off)
25	89.29	B+	3	
24	85.71	B	4	
23	82.14	B–	5	(grade cut-off)
22	78.57	C	6	
21	75.00	C	7	
20	71.43	C–	8	(grade cut-off)
19	67.86	D+	9	(grade cut-off)
18	64.29	F	10	
17	60.71	F	11	
16	57.14	F	12	

You had to be very accurate on this type of test to earn the same grades as in the first example: to get an A required no more than 2 points deducted; a B, 5 points; a C, 8 points; and a D, 9.

The fewer the points in a test, the more each point is worth, the more damaging each point deduction is, the smaller your margin of error, the harder it is to score high, and the more you must prepare for the test. These two examples represent near extreme opposites; most tests will fall somewhere in between.

In addition, the less time allotted for your exam, especially if it is intensive or an essay, the faster and more accurately you must perform. *If you're after top scores, you must notice these nuances beforehand and prepare thoroughly for the test.*

There can be an exception, however, if grading is calculated as a percentage of the total test points or based on class curve. This, too, can be taken into account as you define your parameters.

Take Every Quiz Seriously

Seek to score 100% on your quizzes for the following reasons:

1. They involve smaller lots of information that are relatively easy to absorb, giving you better odds of getting a perfect score. A perfect quiz score shows you're learning well. It is also a psychological boost and prelude to your midterm exam score.
2. Keeping up with quizzes is one of the best ways of stay fit for midterms and finals because you'll have less come-from-behind learning to do.
3. If you're after top semester scores, acing each quiz positions you closer to that goal.
4. Mistakes on quizzes tell you where you need improvement before you face your exams.
5. If you are allowed to keep your quiz questions, they're very good study aids because similar or identical content may appear on your tests.

Some courses give many quizzes. Some instructors will omit your lowest quiz score when calculating your grade. If your teacher doesn't drop your lowest quiz score, you have a smaller margin for error. If he or she does drop your lowest quiz score, this saves your grade if you have an off day. But even with such a cushion, try not to have more than one weak quiz score. Even seasoned students can have a bad day. I remember scoring 100 on one macroeconomics quiz and 20 on the next. I wasn't upset, but I certainly made sure I understood how I'd erred to avoid a worse disaster on the midterm.

It's best not to bomb a quiz out of being lax and thinking you'll do well on others. You can't predict whether or not another quiz will catch you on an off day. Laziness or complacency are not only risky grade-wise, they're bad study practices and put unnecessary pressure on you.

Thus it's better to strive to do well on every quiz rather than take it for granted that one score will be deleted. Even if it's your last quiz in the class, you don't know whether or not you'll do better on it than on previous ones (unless all your quizzes have been, say, 96 to 100%). As a general policy, it's simpler to do well on every assignment to cushion a bad quiz day. Then if your lowest quiz score is dropped, your quiz average and cumulative scores are only strengthened.

In my most difficult general education course, quizzes were used in a novel way to enforce attendance. There were over eighty-five enrolled students, and the class average score going into the final was in the mid-sixties or a D. "Here comes a curve!" one of my graduate classmates said as a group of us discussed this over lunch in the cafeteria. The professor was tough as iron. In reflecting upon students' excuses and requests for leniency in grading and policy enforcement, he proclaimed to us, "I've heard everything!" Dr. Iron gave quizzes a slightly different twist. Weekly quizzes constituted 15% of our grade. In auditorium-sized lecture courses, when quizzes are given at the beginning of class, you commonly see students hand in their quizzes and walk out. Not so in this class. Quizzes were given at the end of our lectures, and an attendance sheet for student signatures was collected early in class. This was reasonable because students should attend in any case. But it made it harder to retain information for our quizzes since intensive lecture information was given in the interim.

6

Groundwork

[A student has] The Moral Obligation to Be Intelligent.
—John Erskine, 1879–1951[35]

Meet All Your Deadlines

Part of being in control of your studies is not falling behind in any assignment. Deadlines are disclosed either on your syllabus or verbally by your teacher. Be sure to finish every assignment on time to avoid penalties. Meeting your deadlines includes: keeping up with chapter readings; allowing enough time to write papers with at least several revisions; preparing thoroughly for exams and speeches; and practicing group presentations with your teammates beforehand. To determine the time needed to complete an assignment well, start from your deadline, work backward, and trace each step of your work process in reverse order. After that, apply your solution in forward order.

Calendar Your Deadlines

Within the first week of class, mark your deadlines on a calendar that's mounted in an area seen daily in your abode. Alternatively, you could use a datebook that you'll carry every day. The calendar or datebook should provide a month view and contain large boxes so your writing is clearly visible from a distance. *For all important dates for your entire semester:*

1. Highlight a bold box;
2. Write in *all deadlines* for *all courses*, giving the class name, a brief description of the assignment, and its percentage weight.
3. For quizzes, indicate chapter numbers. For final exams, note whether or not they are comprehensive.
4. Mark the dates:
   - when you must begin papers, reports, and test reviews;
   - for school holidays;
   - for group project meetings (indicating place and time);
   - on which a class is canceled (as stipulated by your teacher); and
   - to which exams are rescheduled.

If a class meeting or exam is rescheduled, ensure that you have no other appointment conflict.

When you're given a choice of due dates for an assignment, pick a day that's spaced as far from your other deadlines as possible. An exception is when a teacher grants you extra credit for early performance. At that point, you'll have to determine which option is best for you.

The following page provides an example of calendaring. Deadlines have been consolidated into the same month for purposes of illustration. Actual deadlines will vary depending on your course schedule.

Note: After calendaring your entire semester, you may notice that a considerable number of deadlines awaits you. Do not be intimidated. The visual display of tight deadlines not only reminds you of the need to keep pace but also your prompts enable you to manage your time more efficiently.

If you opt for a wall-mounted calendar, you can also mount next to it your syllabus schedules, if provided, to have a week-by-week reference for chapter readings and lecture subjects. If you don't wish to detach these schedules from your original syllabi, photocopies will suffice.

Calendar the Dates of Your Final Exams as Soon as Possible

Ideally, you'll have several days or more between each final exam. In actuality, some finals may be spaced far apart while others may fall on the same

Table 4 Sample time management calendar

Sunday	Monday	Tuesday	Wednesday	Thursday	Friday	Saturday
1	2 START TERM PAPER CRITICAL THINKING 101	3	4	5 9 a.m. SCIENCE 101 QUIZ CHP 7–8	6	7 EXAM REVIEW 1: SCI 101
8 EXAM REVIEW 2: SCI 101	9 EXAM REVIEW 3: SCI 101	10 9 a.m. SCI 101 MIDTERM p.m. ECON 101 EXAM REVIEW 1	11 ECON 101 EXAM REVIEW 2 sleep early for a.m. review	12 a.m. ECON 101 EXAM REVIEW 3 1:15 p.m. ECON 101 MIDTERM	13 WRITE SPEECH FOR PUB SPKG 101	14 TERM PAPER Revision 1 CRITICAL THINKING 101
15	16	17	18	19	20	21 TERM PAPER Revision 2 CRITICAL THINKING 101
22	23 PRACTICE SPEECH	24 PRACTICE SPEECH	25 PRACTICE SPEECH	26 9 a.m. SCI 101 QUIZ CHP 9–10 11 a.m. PUB SPKG 101 SPEECH	27	28 TERM PAPER Revision 3 CRITICAL THINKING 101
29	30	31 TERM PAPER DUE CRITICAL THINKING 101				

Note: Speech preparation is explained in Chapter 9, writing approaches in Chapter 10, and 3-day staged exam reviews in Chapter 11.

day. Although you shouldn't worry about final exams during the first week of class, it's important to calendar their dates to see how much study time you'll have between each one. In addition, note the percentage weights of your finals. It is best to know beforehand what awaits you. The spacing and percentage weights will affect your entire semester strategy. Final exam dates are disclosed by your instructor or in your college's course schedule.

For example, if a final exam constitutes 50% of your course grade, you'll really need to keep pace throughout the semester—come-from-behind learning on the cusp of finals week will be risky and create undue pressure. Conversely, if a course's final test is only 10% of your grade, you'll know that its midsemester assignments are more crucial. But less pressure on this final means you'll have more time and energy to devote to others.

Some finals may be on consecutive days. Some may occur nearly a week apart. One semester I saw that two classes (C and Q) gave final exams on the same date. I found it hard to retain a wealth of information for two finals administered just 15 minutes apart. Accordingly, I sought to score high from early through midsemester in these two courses. In writing-intensive class C, keeping pace with frequent assignments paid off: my score going into the final was 97%. With an A semester grade and a final exam weighted at 35%, I would've had to score less than 74 points on the test to be pushed down to a B course grade. This would happen only if I was very negligent. (Grade calculations are explained in Chapter 13.) With less pressure to perform in class C, I allocated more energy to prepare for class Q. That tough course's final exam was comprehensive, worth 35% of our grade, and the class average score was in the mid sixties!

Also determine the kind of final exams you'll face. Note whether they're multiple-choice, essay, open book, or other, and factor this into your strategies.

It is common practice to focus on final exams during the last several weeks of a term. However, discovering at the last minute that you have two finals back to back, or several nearly butted up against each other, is an unwelcome surprise. Looking ahead allows you to see which finals will be isolated, giving you more breathing room. In other cases, you'll be fore-warned of the importance of scoring strongly early in the semester. This provides a cushion when your divided efforts may result in less-than-great test scores. You'll also have advance notice to structure your review sessions during this intensive period.

Table 5 Sample final exam calendar

Sunday	Monday	Tuesday	Wednesday	Thursday	Friday	Saturday
1	2	3 Review 1 Class A	4 Review 2 Class A	5 Review 3 Class A	6 Class A FINAL 9:00–11:00a Go celebrate	7 a.m. Review 1 Class B p.m. Review 1 Class C
8 a.m. Review 2 Class B p.m. Review 2 Class C	9 a.m. Review 3 Class B p.m. Review 3 Class C	10 9:45–11:45a Class B FINAL 12n–2:00p Class C FINAL Break p.m. Review 1 Class D	11 a.m. Review 2 Class D Break p.m. Review 3 Class D	12 early a.m. Review 3 Class D Class D FINAL 9:45–11:45a	13	14 Deadline to leave dorm

Note: Whether you schedule the third review for Class D for the evening prior or the morning of depends on your best study time and absorption capacity.

Textbook Readings and Class Handouts

Reading is to the mind what exercise is to the body.
—Sir Richard Steele, 1672–1729[36]

Part of my strategy included highlighting text readings. I did not rely on this technique exclusively but I used it often.

The drawback of highlighting is not the method itself, but if and when a reader highlights superfluous information. Highlighting is a time-saving measure. In its most streamlined form, one highlights the minimum words needed to understand chapter information and rereads only these areas during exam reviews. There's nothing wrong with writing your own summary notes based on text readings; this is also an effective method for test preparation and a strategy endorsed in this book. However, rather than present a this-not-that scenario, you are encouraged to adapt various techniques according to what works for you. Your study approach need not be limited to only one routine.

Instructors lecture on their preferred topics from given chapters. Provided you take good notes in class, your notebook should be an adequate supplement to your highlighted texts for purposes of exam review. With fast paced academic schedules and information-intensive courses, I often found writing summaries for every chapter too time consuming. Hence, I present the technique of highlighting as a viable alternative, should you find yourself subject to similar time constraints.

Used books cost less than new ones. So as not to waste money, I bought used textbooks as long as they were in good condition and had clean pages. If the pages were already marked, I spent the extra money to buy a new textbook. With your learning and grades predicated on reading comprehension, avoid purchasing books that have been extensively highlighted by previous readers. It's highly unlikely that every page of every chapter highlighted will match your comprehension and streamline pattern—so in this case, buying a new textbook is preferable.

Highlighting your textbook will lower its resale value, but the quality of your learning and overall intellectual growth are far more important than trying to save a few bucks this way. I didn't worry about the resale value of my books because I used them first and foremost for learning. In one reader, I even wrote notes adjacent to important paragraphs as my teacher lectured.

Once you have a new or used text with clean pages, I endorse highlighting your assigned readings. Highlighting is simple, neat, fast, and more readable than underlining with pen or pencil. Pencils may also be too light or they may smear and dirty pages. Highlighting makes it easy to search for and piece together important points. You avoid having to reread and sift through unnecessary information, thereby streamlining your study process. You are less likely to overlook these areas during exam reviews. Note, however, that the strength of your using this technique is dependent on how well and carefully you select information from your text.

Choose a single color that helps you comprehend with the least distraction and visual fatigue after extensive reading. I found green highlighters preferable to bright yellow, pink, or blue. (Some students prefer using multiple colors for highlighting—choose whichever method maximizes your learning efficiency.) I used the same color on all notebooks, texts, syllabi, and handouts. Using up three to five highlighters per semester isn't unusual.

The technique is to highlight the absolute minimum words necessary for your learning. For example, if I were to highlight the previous paragraph as if it were part of a text, I would do something like:

Choose a single color that helps you comprehend with the least distraction and visual fatigue after extensive reading. I found green highlighters preferable to bright yellow, pink, or blue. (Some students prefer using multiple colors for highlighting—choose whichever method maximizes your learning efficiency.) I used the same color on all notebooks, texts, syllabi, and handouts. Using up three to five highlighters per semester isn't unusual.

Your highlighting does not need to be in complete sentences. In many cases, highlighting key words and phrases will suffice. Highlighting only parts of words to expedite rereading is acceptable provided it does not significantly alter the meaning of the author's message. It's also important not to memorize highlighted sections by rote but to understand the reasons behind the information. This is especially pertinent when you prepare for essay tests that reveal how well you analyze and apply new material.

Try the following method:

Step 1. Read the chapters or sections assigned by your instructor *before* the scheduled lecture. If a chapter is long and you cannot complete it in a single sitting, break it up into several portions. This is an example of the goal-setting model. You could read several chapters over several days or in one sitting, according to what works for you. Having read the text positions you to make immediate sense of lectures, frame more precise questions, take stronger notes, and be better prepared for exams. Don't fall behind in readings assigned by your teachers. I used to read and highlight my entire week's chapters before my first class meeting each week.

Step 2. Read the chapter title and subtitle.

Step 3. Read a chapter summary first, but not as a substitute, to gain an overview of contents.

Step 4. Read the chapter's headings and subheadings to gain a sense of direction.

Step 5. Read the learning goal statements if included.

Step 6. As you read the main text, highlight only the minimum number of words necessary to understand important points. Not every book is written with complete word economy.

Pay careful attention to highlighting. *What you highlight is all that you'll study from your text for exam reviews.* Excessive highlighting means you'll have needless elements to sort out and digest. *Seek not to highlight one unnecessary word.* You may have to read some sentences in their entirety before determining which words to omit. This will be the most time-consuming stage of the process, but this effort will pay off during reviews.

This kind of highlighting is tailored specifically to your comprehension pattern and is why buying already highlighted textbooks is counterproductive. Don't try to selectively highlight only what you think is going to be on the exam. If you highlight primarily to learn thoroughly, the test topics will be included somewhere in your colored sections. If an instructor specifies the information on which you'll be tested—for example, a comparison of opposing views held by historical experts—you'll be able to factor this into what you highlight.

Step 7. Note any areas you don't understand even after careful reading. (I used to write these questions in my notebook on the first page for the next scheduled lecture.) Afterward, ask your teacher in class or at his or her office for clarification. Some chapters build on previous information. Not comprehending a topic can create roadblocks to understanding subsequent chapters.

Attend Every Class

Simply stated, going to class is the backbone of your learning. Hearing lectures solidifies your silent reading, provides answers to questions from experts in the field, and supplies notes for understanding test material. Attending class is your most basic means to passing a course, and graduating.

In addition, teachers may deduct points for absences. My Class E had an unusual approach to attendance. Attendance wasn't taken daily, but students were called on to answer questions in class three to five times during the semester. Our professor recognized, by sight, who of the forty-six students were missing. More than coincidence, she would call on those who were absent that day. Not being present to answer meant no credit, which translated into up to 5 points off your total grade. Class N pegged class participation at 33% of our course grade, so absence considerably affected your score. Class O gave students an F for the course upon their fourth absence. This was quite significant because the course met thrice a week, or 46 days during the semester.

By attending each class, you can ask questions and glean insight from discussions and your teachers' feedback. At times, certain lecture topics won't be in your text, but they'll be on the exam. At other times, teachers may tell you what topics will be on the test. Students who skip class won't get this information unless they have a friend to relay it. I wasn't one to stake my grades on secondhand information. I do not suggest cutting class, relying on copying others' notes, and taking exams just to get by. Attending every class is fundamental to being a self-reliant student.

Sit at the Front of the Class

Sit at or near the front of the room, not at its perimeter or in the rear. The goal is to absorb lecture information free from interference. Your mind is less likely to wander with your instructor standing close by and making frequent eye contact. You see blackboard notes and hear the teacher more clearly, and can ask questions without having to shout across a room. You can clearly hear the dialogue between other students and your teacher as you take notes.

Sitting on the perimeter creates sharper viewing angles and makes it difficult to see chalkboard writing, especially if there is reflective glare. In large rooms, sitting toward the back makes it harder for you to hear unless the instructor has a microphone or a voice that carries well. And when you're sitting toward the rear, especially in auditorium-sized classrooms, students are facing away from you, so you can't hear their questions or comments unless a teacher repeats them. The rear of class can also have distractions and annoyances: other students chatting, fidgeting, sleeping, doing homework for another class, and arriving late or leaving early. The distraction of students arriving late or leaving early was why I wouldn't sit near the door, either.

Class Participation

There are times when your grade is determined partially by participation in class discussions. Initially, speaking openly in class was difficult for me because I come from a cultural tradition that discourages individual expression. But with my grades at stake, I was forced to compete with students who didn't originate from repressive backgrounds and, hence, didn't view discussions as a competition. I did, for two reasons: (1) I had to muster the courage to speak up amidst outspoken students and (2) seeking top scores required that I be more assertive in speaking up when teachers allotted limited time for discussions. It became a matter of comprehending, analyzing, and relating things faster and raising my hand more often to fulfill this portion of my grade.

Based on my observations, instructors welcome open dialogue with students to enhance learning. In many settings, such discussion is expected. The substance of your remarks or questions is more important than speaking frequently without depth, dominating class discussions, or depriving others of sharing their thoughts. If your thoughts are solid, you needn't fear appearing silly in front of anyone. By having read your text beforehand and relating your own experiences to a lecture topic, you'll be able to answer on-the-spot questions accurately, volunteer to answer a question, add a thought or two to other classmates' remarks, form more reasoned opinions, and learn more comprehensively. You'll lose any anxiety about participating in class and will earn your points in the process. This is significant for students who are shy or apprehensive about speaking up. It will be apparent to others if you contribute to class discussions without having prepared ahead of time. Unless it is an impromptu discussion, your remarks will appear misguided or behind those of other classmates. Your teacher will notice this, and you may not earn top scores. Hence, it is essential to read class material beforehand rather than trying to wing it.

Some of my classmates dominated discussions, while others simply remained silent. Unless your statements are blatantly mistaken, withholding your remarks from graded class discussions will work against you. Not all students participate, and this costs them points. If you want top grades, you must go the distance, regardless of others who merely want to get a class out of the way and don't care about maximizing their learning and grades.

Don't Be Shy about Asking Questions

A prudent question is one-half of wisdom.
—Francis Bacon, 1561–1626[37]

Asking questions is part of the learning process. Some students learn better through questions, answers, and paraphrasing, as opposed to straight listening. Good questions may simultaneously fulfill your participation score. If you're serious about learning, your questions will reflect it. It's important to read your text assignments beforehand, lest your questions reveal how behind or ill-informed you are, thus compromising your image and points with the teacher. If you've read the text and hear something during a lecture that you don't understand, don't hesitate to ask for clarification. It's nothing to be embarrassed about.

"It never hurts to ask" is generally a good policy, both inside and outside the classroom. Asking concise questions can be difficult, but they help you understand topics more accurately, not just for test-taking but for making better decisions at large. The classroom is your opportunity to develop this skill. Incomplete information can lead to flawed premises, flawed conclusions, false starts, and wasted efforts. Your learning, homework, and test scores can thus be jeopardized.

Teachers may unintentionally omit things from their syllabi, lectures, or instructions. Querying this helps you understand your material or what's expected on an assignment. Adding a teacher's verbal clarifications to your notes is a good practice. This gives classroom attendance an added advantage over straight text readings at home.

Like anyone learned in their field, some instructors may unintentionally take certain knowledge for granted. Subjects that are second nature to an expert may be alien to other people. Even seasoned professors know it's not easy to explain a specialized topic concisely to a first-time learner. When unclear on certain topics or expectations, I asked teachers for clarification. In other cases, I would paraphrase what appeared vague to me to see whether or not my teachers agreed. Sometimes they did, sometimes they followed up with additional clarification, which I would indicate in my notes. For example, one lecturer spoke of "industry standards." I asked whether such standards were based on a national scale or prevailing regional practices. In that particular context, the term referred to the latter. As an example of clarifying expectations, one course syllabus didn't state the technical criteria for our term paper. I asked whether the paper was to be single or double spaced, its minimum and maximum length, its margin widths, and so on. Because these criteria had a bearing on my grade, I wanted to know them before starting my paper.

Sometimes there was no chance to ask questions during lectures, so I would approach the teacher at the end of class. As he or she was erasing the blackboard or collecting his or her notes, I would ask my questions. If my questions couldn't be answered within a brief span of time (since other students had questions and the room needed to be cleared for an incoming class), I would arrange to meet the teacher during office hours.

Being shy about asking questions is not uncommon among students. In light of my prior failures, I thought my questions might be stupid; but I forced myself to ask anyway. None of my teachers looked at me as though I was some sweet, dumb thing. Some remarked that other students often had the same questions, were too timid to speak up, and were relieved when someone else asked. Ignore students who express dissatisfaction at your questions. Some classmates laughed at me when I asked questions or expressed my opinion. None of these people were on stage with me at the Honors Convocation or the Phi Beta Kappa initiation. Whether such students are eager to finish a lecture so they can leave early or whether they think you're asking a stupid question is immaterial. Regardless of your grade level, you're there to learn. You paid tuition, you qualified for the class, and you're clarifying a point that helps you piece together the big puzzle. Furthermore, you're ensuring that your notes are complete for your exam reviews. If some students don't care about doing their best to learn, or if they have an elitist attitude, don't be dragged down with them.

For your writing, you can ask your teacher to enumerate the characteristics of an A paper or A answer to an essay question. In either case, you'll gain a more definitive idea of how to prepare. Remember, however, that you are ascertaining criteria, not content. You can even state this, so as to avoid any misunderstanding by your teacher in class. If you are a D or C student, it is still reasonable to ask your instructor to list the criteria for a C or B essay. You needn't be embarrassed about asking, or bothered by how any smart-aleck classmates may react. You're aiming for grades that are

commensurate with your abilities and are merely ascertaining the requirements to achieve those acceptable goals. If a teacher knows you're trying
your utmost, he or she won't take a dim view of such a question.

7

Note-Taking

He listens well who takes notes.
—Dante Alighieri, 1265–1321[38]

Type of Notebook

Since I usually consolidated classes into several days a week, I used a four- or five-subject spiral notebook with a moisture-resistant cover and heavy-duty double pockets separating each section. Thus my notes for an entire semester were consolidated into one notebook. To me, several notebooks were cumbersome, required more time for finding the right one, and were easier to misplace. Double pockets allow you to keep your course syllabi, handouts, and homework organized, handy, and in good shape. For days with only one class, I sometimes used a single-subject notebook, still with a heavy-duty cover and double pockets. Given a choice, select the kind of notebook (and color of your pen) that gives you greatest readability and comprehension while causing the least visual fatigue after prolonged rereading. The choices are matt recycled or bright white paper with college or narrow rules. Off-white, matt recycled paper (for example, that which contains 50% post-consumer fiber) has less glare, and its greater opacity minimizes show-through from text written on the back side of the pages. Notebooks which contain pale green, college-ruled paper are an alternative when those with matt, off-white recycled stock are not available. Avoid notebooks with flimsy covers and pockets; they crease, curl, and tear more easily.

If you opt to use one multi-subject notebook per semester, you'll need to ensure that you don't lose it. A major part of your learning, exams, and grade-point average will hinge on your notes. Some students leave their

79

bags unattended at the cafeteria or other public place only to return and find them stolen. One student had a habit of forgetting his notebook on the bus! In seeking your potential in school, by all means avoid losing your notebook.

There are also different kinds of spiral notebooks. Some include the spirals within the 8.5-inch width of their pages. This kind of notebook doesn't give you enough room for writing in the margin; your pen hits the spiral when writing most words (see Figure 1A). The preferred notebook has 9 x 11 inch pages, so its spiral is outside of the 8.5-inch page width. You gain an additional half inch of writing space per line per page, and wider margins for adjunct notes, so that note-taking is easier, faster, and more effective (see Figure 1B). Another type of 8.5 x 11 inch notebook comes with a 3-inch margin preprinted (for example, the Law Margin notebook by Comet School Supplies, Inc.), but may only be available in a single-subject format. However, this design is worth considering if it increases your note-taking and learning efficiency. The product may be available either at campus bookstores or law schools. Alternatively, should you desire a wider margin in your notebook, you could draw your own on each page using a ruler.

In an emergency, almost any paper will suffice, though loose papers are easier to misorder or lose. Margin-gummed notebook pages are also easily detached and lost. I also didn't use top-bound notebooks. Turning over an entire tablet to write on the back of each page takes time that's needed to keep up with lectures and also breaks your train of thought. Twice the amount of time is spent flipping pages than with book-type formats, both during note-taking and exam reviews. Some of my single-subject notebooks were completely full of double-sided text. Other course lectures filled entire sections of multi-subject notebooks.

Keep your course syllabus in the appropriate section pocket of your notebook.

General Tips on Taking Notes

The examples of note-taking (see Figures 2–9) are not limited to specific subjects. The techniques can be used in any combination for a given course, depending on how your teacher structures his or her lecture:

8.5 inches

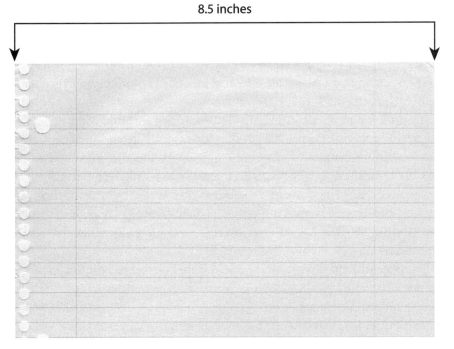

Figure 1A:
Spiral notebook
with little usable
writing space in
the margins.
This format is
not preferred.

8.5 inches

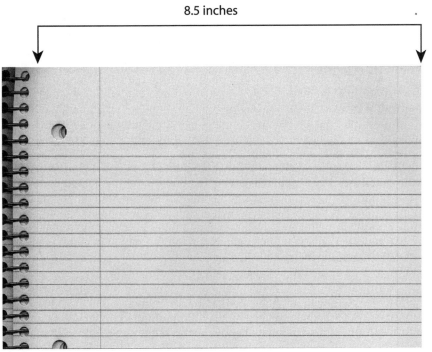

Figure 1B:
9 × 11 inch
spiral notebook
format with
maximum
marginal writing
space on each
page. This type
is preferred.

1. Notes are a major source of learning and are often the backbone of your test preparations. It is important to use good techniques starting on the first day of class.

2. Taking good notes requires careful listening, concentration, retention, writing as quickly and neatly as you can, and sometimes asking your teacher to repeat certain information.

3. Use a ballpoint pen with a color you find most comfortable when rereading notes for long spans of time. Black ink is more readable and much less visually fatiguing and distracting than blue ink. (When was the last time you saw books at the store or library printed entirely in blue ink?) The idea is to use every nuance you can to maximize your progress. I wouldn't bother with fountain pens or markers. The gauge of ballpoint tip (fine, medium, or broad) should be whatever gives you greatest writing ease, readability, and comprehension.

4. The first page of each notebook section should be reserved exclusively for:
   - General class information
   - Teacher's contact information
   - Class policies for matters such as
     - attendance
     - make-up exams
     - late work
   - Procedures for
     - submitting drafts
     - extra-credit assignments
   - Major deadlines
   - Changes to deadlines
   - Dates and chapters for each midterm, exam, and quiz
   - Exam type(s)—i.e., essays, definitions, fill-in-the-blanks, true or false, multiple choice, comprehensive, or take-home
   - Criteria for
     - term papers
     - homework
     - group presentations (see Figure 2)

5. The second page should be reserved for documenting your class's scores for quizzes, tests, term projects, and other major assignments. Test results may be disclosed verbally in class, written on the blackboard, listed on an instructor's office door, or posted on a class web site. If they're disclosed verbally in

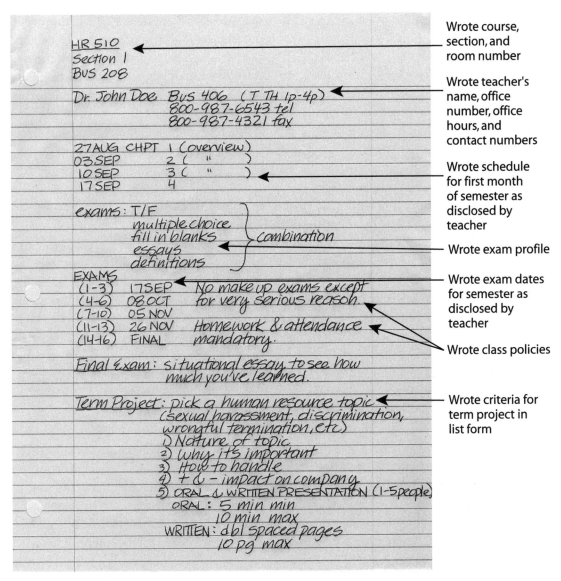

Figure 2: First page of each notebook section reserved for course particulars:

- course, section, room number
- teacher's contact
- class policies
- important dates
- homework criteria

class, be ready to write them down immediately. If posted on the office door, jot the scores down in your notebook. Web site printouts can be kept in your files at home. You will use these data later to gauge yourself in relation to others during the term, going into the final exam, and throughout your academic career. Feel free to write your class's exam results in any format, so long as it gives you complete information (see Figure 3).

6. Pay close attention to your teacher's lectures. Block out distractions from other students.

7. As you listen to your instructors, learn to use the fewest words needed to document your message.

8. The more thorough your notes, the better. Document your lecture topics in adequate detail and depth. Writing three to five pages of notes per class isn't uncommon for an A student. Include examples, key points, situations from life cited during discussions, pertinent questions, and insightful comments.

9. Some teachers lecture at hurricane speed. To keep up, train yourself to be able to listen to and comprehend the lecturer while writing one or two sentences behind what he or she is saying.

10. For diagrams, don't write a component's name twice. Draw a letter or number within a circle at the component. In the text section of the page, write the name and description next to the respective letter or number (see Figures 4 and 5).

11. Writing things in list form is faster—and easier to comprehend when rereading (see Figures 4 and 6).

12. Don't doodle. Though spontaneous and possibly artistic, doodling distracts you from comprehending your teachers' messages. This is in contrast to sketches that assist your learning. In certain subjects, instructional diagrams or pictures enhance your learning when combined with word-economical notes. Draw yourself a picture if needed (see Figures 5, 6, and 7).

13. Don't worry if you misspell one or two everyday words. Keeping up with lectures has priority. As long as you understand the message when rereading your notes, you can always correct spelling later. Exception: Formal names, technical terms, and study topics should be spelled properly from the outset.

14. Invent your own abbreviations or shorthand to write the same lecture information in less time. Such abbreviations are simple, quick, and immediately understood, because you yourself create them. You may use familiar symbols or even write a process in equation form.

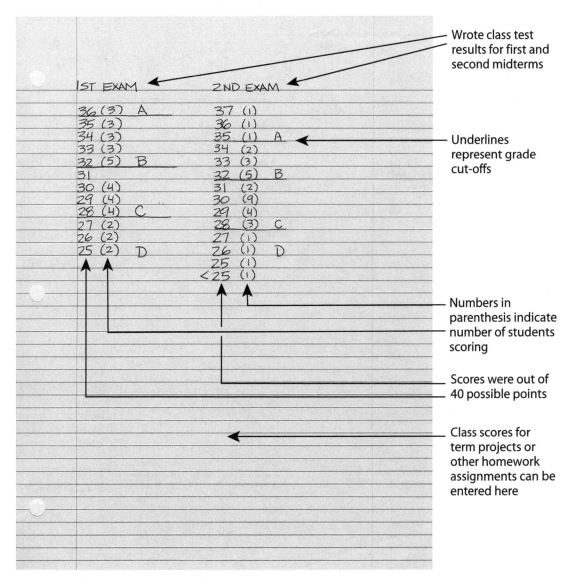

Figure 3: Second page of notes used to write class exam results to gauge your performance.

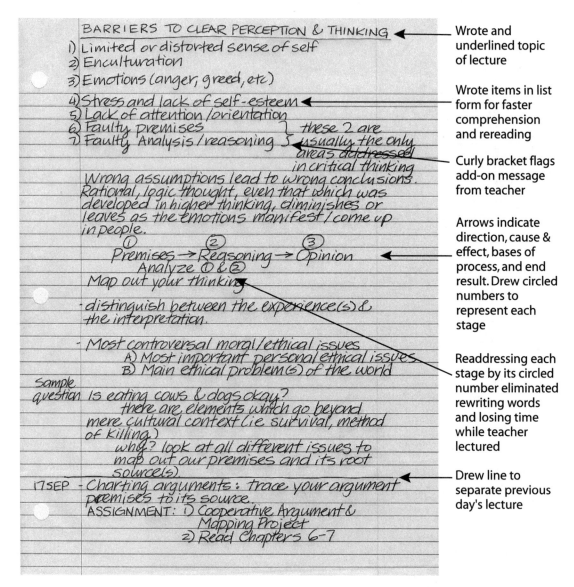

The following annotations appear alongside the notes:

- Wrote and underlined topic of lecture
- Wrote items in list form for faster comprehension and rereading
- Curly bracket flags add-on message from teacher
- Arrows indicate direction, cause & effect, bases of process, and end result. Drew circled numbers to represent each stage
- Readdressing each stage by its circled number eliminated rewriting words and losing time while teacher lectured
- Drew line to separate previous day's lecture

The notes read:

BARRIERS TO CLEAR PERCEPTION & THINKING
1) Limited or distorted sense of self
2) Enculturation
3) Emotions (anger, greed, etc)
4) Stress and lack of self-esteem
5) Lack of attention /orientation
6) Faulty premises
7) Faulty Analysis /reasoning } these 2 are usually the only areas addressed in critical thinking

Wrong assumptions lead to wrong conclusions. Rational, logic thought, even that which was developed in higher thinking, diminishes or leaves as the emotions manifest /come up in people.

① Premises → ② Reasoning → ③ Opinion
Analyze ① & ②
Map out your thinking

· distinguish between the experience(s) & the interpretation.

- Most controversial moral /ethical issues
   A) Most important personal ethical issues
   B) Main ethical problem(s) of the world

Sample question Is eating cows & dogs okay?
   there are elements which go beyond mere cultural context (ie survival, method of killing.)
      why? look at all different issues to map out our premises and its root source(s)

17 SEP - Charting arguments: trace your argument premises to its source.
   ASSIGNMENT: 1) Cooperative Argument & Mapping Project
            2) Read Chapters 6-7

Figure 4: Notes made during lecture
Wrote items in list form to speed note-taking, comprehension, and rereading. Used curly bracket to flag adjunct message. Drew circled numbers to represent stages of a process. Rewrote each stage by its circled letter to save time during lecture. (Original subject was Critical Thinking.)

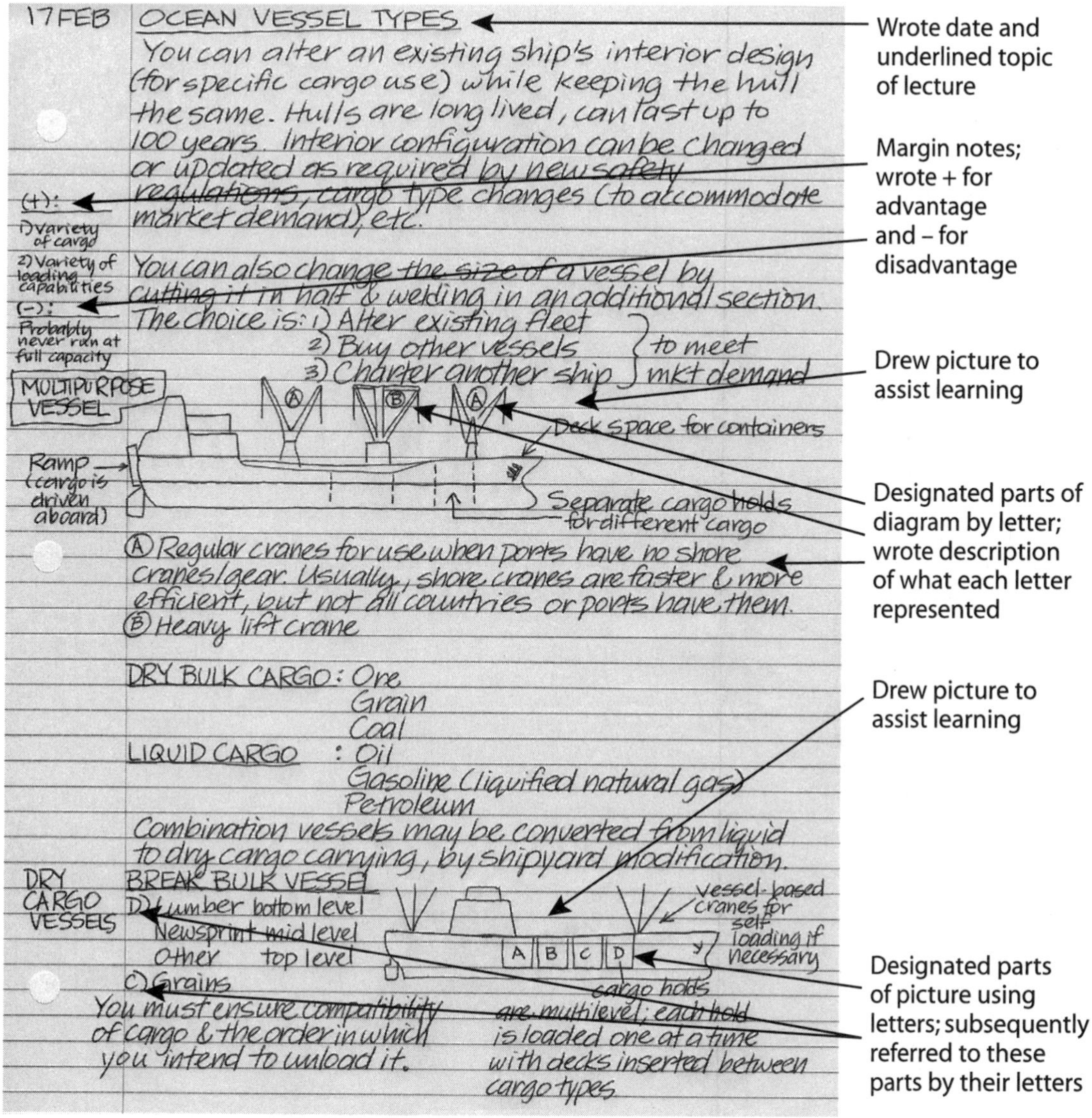
17 FEB
OCEAN VESSEL TYPES
You can alter an existing ship's interior design (for specific cargo use) while keeping the hull the same. Hulls are long lived, can last up to 100 years. Interior configuration can be changed or updated as required by new safety regulations, cargo type changes (to accommodate market demand), etc.
(+): 1) Variety of cargo 2) Variety of loading capabilities
(–): Probably never run at full capacity
You can also change the size of a vessel by cutting it in half & welding in an additional section.
The choice is: 1) Alter existing fleet 2) Buy other vessels 3) Charter another ship } to meet mkt demand
MULTIPURPOSE VESSEL
Ramp (cargo is driven aboard)
Deck space for containers
Separate cargo holds for different cargo
Ⓐ Regular cranes for use when ports have no shore cranes/gear. Usually, shore cranes are faster & more efficient, but not all countries or ports have them.
Ⓑ Heavy lift crane
DRY BULK CARGO: Ore Grain Coal
LIQUID CARGO: Oil Gasoline (liquified natural gas) Petroleum
Combination vessels may be converted from liquid to dry cargo carrying, by shipyard modification.
DRY CARGO VESSELS
BREAK BULK VESSEL
D) Lumber bottom level
Newsprint mid level
Other top level
C) Grains
A B C D
vessel-based cranes for self loading if necessary
cargo holds are multilevel; each hold is loaded one at a time with decks inserted between cargo types.
You must ensure compatibility of cargo & the order in which you intend to unload it.
Wrote date and underlined topic of lecture
Margin notes; wrote + for advantage and – for disadvantage
Drew picture to assist learning
Designated parts of diagram by letter; wrote description of what each letter represented
Drew picture to assist learning
Designated parts of picture using letters; subsequently referred to these parts by their letters

Figure 5: Notes made during lecture
Drew pictures to assist learning. Designated parts of a diagram by letter.

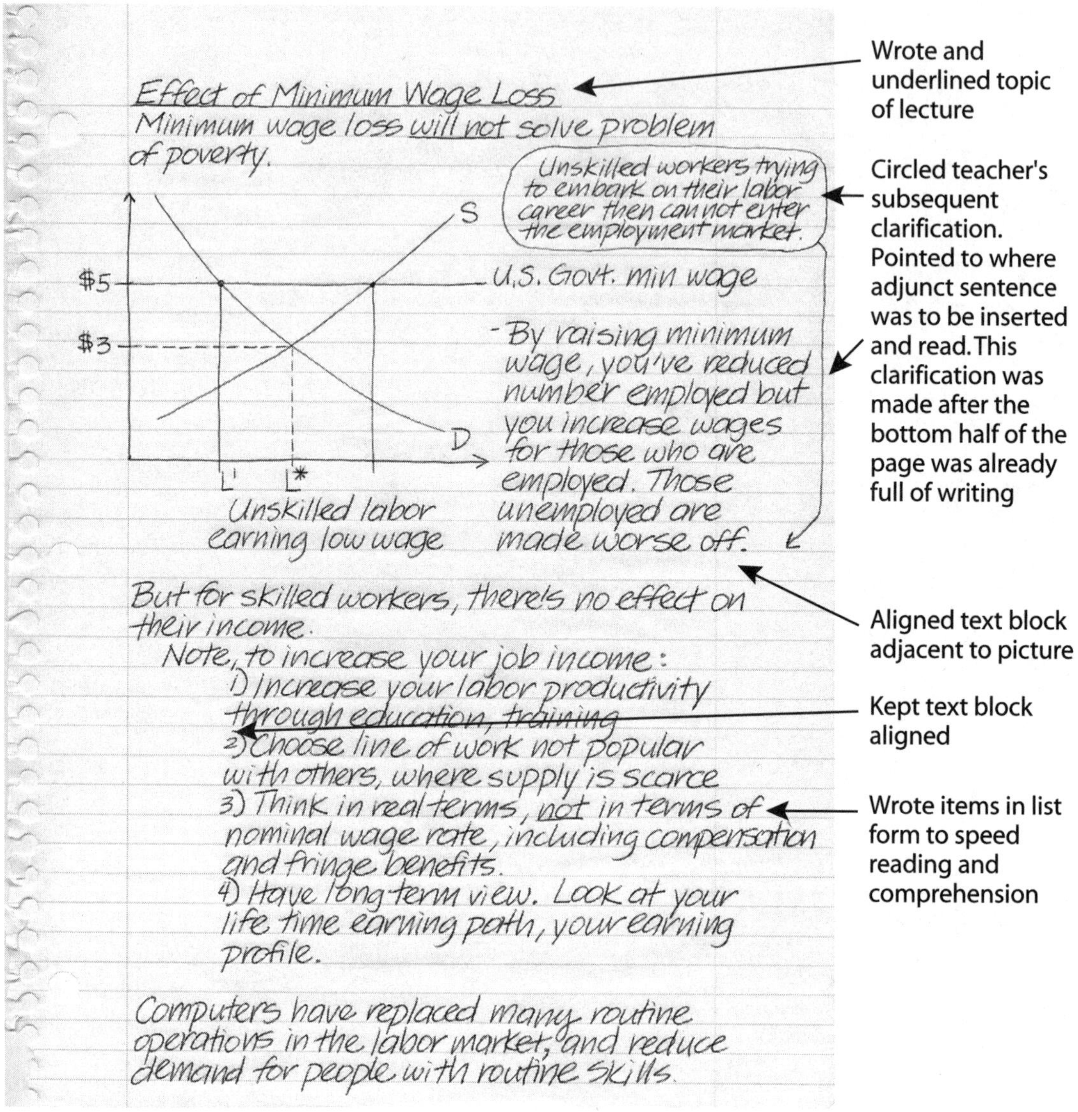
Effect of Minimum Wage Loss
Minimum wage loss will not solve problem of poverty.
Unskilled workers trying to embark on their labor career then can not enter the employment market.
S
$5
U.S. Govt. min wage
$3
D
L' L*
Unskilled labor earning low wage
- By raising minimum wage, you've reduced number employed but you increase wages for those who are employed. Those unemployed are made worse off.
But for skilled workers, there's no effect on their income.
Note, to increase your job income:
1) Increase your labor productivity through education, training
2) Choose line of work not popular with others, where supply is scarce
3) Think in real terms, not in terms of nominal wage rate, including compensation and fringe benefits.
4) Have long term view. Look at your life time earning path, your earning profile.
Computers have replaced many routine operations in the labor market, and reduce demand for people with routine skills.
Wrote and underlined topic of lecture
Circled teacher's subsequent clarification. Pointed to where adjunct sentence was to be inserted and read. This clarification was made after the bottom half of the page was already full of writing
Aligned text block adjacent to picture
Kept text block aligned
Wrote items in list form to speed reading and comprehension

Figure 6: Notes made during lecture

Drew a circle around sentences to be read at a different part of the page. This is done when a teacher makes an important subsequent remark. (Original subject was Micro Economics.)

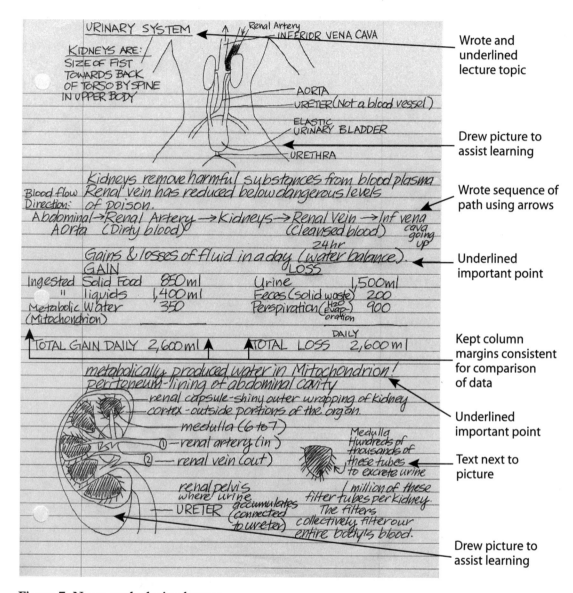

Figure 7: Notes made during lecture
Drew pictures to assist learning. (Original subject was Human Biology.)

Note: Beware of using personalized abbreviations on essay exams. If a teacher cannot make sense of your word or message, you may lose points. One of my professors was livid over some students writing "B4" and "2U" on their midterm essays. He roared, "This isn't the back of a music album!" But legitimate and designated abbreviations can be on your essay tests. For example, on a long essay you might write "Dietary Supplement Health and Education Act" where it first appears, followed by "(hereinafter DSHEA)." All subsequent uses would be written as DSHEA.

Some examples of abbreviations include

aka	also known as	NE	Northeast
gov	government	NW	Northwest
max	maximum	SE	Southeast
min	minimum	SW	Southwest
mkt	market	US	United States
qty	quantity	LAX	Los Angeles
re	regarding	NYC	New York City
w/	with	SFO	San Francisco
w/o	without		

(Adopt three-digit city codes used by airlines and abbreviations used by U.S. Post Office for states)

=	equal to, the same as	≠	does not equal; not the same as
~	approximately equal to; analogous to	$	money, expensive
		%	percentage
@	at; located at; rate	&	and
#	number of something	△	changes in quantity or price
→	causes, leads to	+	plus, positive, pro, advantage
↑	increase	↓	decrease
>	greater than, superior to	−	minus, negative, con, disadvantage (use a hyphen for a bullet when listing notes)
<	less than, inferior to	lbs	pounds
m	meters (standard abbreviations used for weights and measures)		

15. Aligning text blocks (vertically and horizontally) on an imaginary grid provides better reading (see Figure 6). You could experiment with using notebooks with graph paper, but I've only seen them in a single-subject format, without matt, opaque, recycled paper.

16. Lecture remarks aren't always in perfect sequential order. The teacher may give subsequent clarification. I sometimes heard classmates moan when they had to amend their notes. A quick and simple remedy is to circle and point to connect relevant elements that appear at separate places on a page (see Figures 6 and 8).

17. Writing in the margins is very useful both for learning and test preparations (see Figures 5 and 9). The following examples could be margin prompts to yourself:
    - Date of class. This allows you to distinguish and separate a given day's lecture.
    - "TEST" flags a specific item that you'll need to know for the test.
    - "LOOK UP" points out a lecture topic you don't immediately understand but know is explained in the textbook. If not explained fully in the textbook, you can use this prompt to ask your teacher for clarification.
    - Remarks combined with arrows indicate the differences and similarities between two topics on the same page.
    - "END MIDTERM 1" or "BEGIN MIDTERM 2" tells you where a section cutoff is for a test, so you'll know precisely where to begin and end your exam reviews (see Figure 9).

18. Write the date and time for test reviews given by your instructor or teacher assistant if it's different from regular class. With so many obligations in college, it's easy to forget things unless you have written reminders. You may wish to transfer this information to your calendar or datebook.

19. Notebooks are your personal property. Their contents should be shared selectively. As a rule, I didn't lend my notebook to anyone. Notebooks lent are either seldom returned or only retrieved after great inconvenience or frustration. The same problem applies to lending books.

    Lending your notebook carries another risk: unwanted photocopying by others. In one course, two students never spoke to me until the last class before our final, when they asked for a copy of my notes for the entire semester. Very crass.

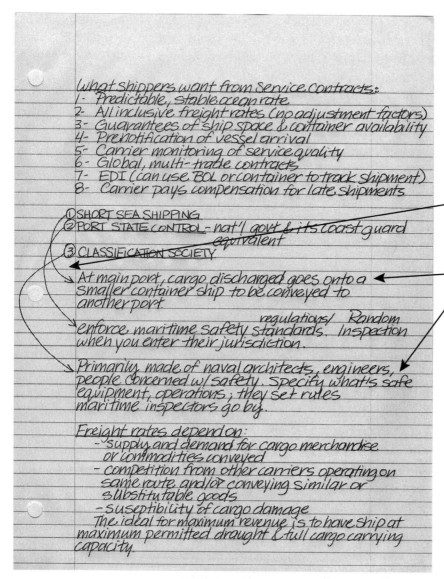

What shippers want from service contracts:
1- Predictable, stable ocean rate.
2- All inclusive freight rates (no adjustment factors)
3- Guarantees of ship space & container availability
4- Prenotification of vessel arrival
5- Carrier monitoring of service quality
6- Global, multi-trade contracts.
7- EDI (can use BOL or container to track shipment)
8- Carrier pays compensation for late shipments

① SHORT SEA SHIPPING
② PORT STATE CONTROL - nat'l govt & its coast guard equivalent
③ CLASSIFICATION SOCIETY

→ At main port, cargo discharged goes onto a smaller container ship to be conveyed to another port

                                        regulations/ Random
enforce maritime safety standards. Inspection when you enter their jurisdiction.

→ Primarily made of naval architects, engineers, people concerned w/ safety. Specify what's safe equipment, operations; they set rules maritime inspectors go by.

Freight rates depend on:
    - supply and demand for cargo merchandise or commodities conveyed
    - competition from other carriers operating on same route and/or conveying similar or substitutable goods
    - suseptibility of cargo damage
The ideal for maximum revenue is to have ship at maximum permitted draught & full cargo carrying capacity.

Drew arrows to connect subsequent explanations after having written list of topics. Saved time during lecture and connected relevant information to aid learning and exam review

Figure 8: Notes made during lecture
Lecture remarks aren't always in perfect sequential order. A teacher may give subsequent clarification. A simple remedy is to use arrows to connect relevant elements appearing at separate places on a page. (Original subject was Transportation Management.)

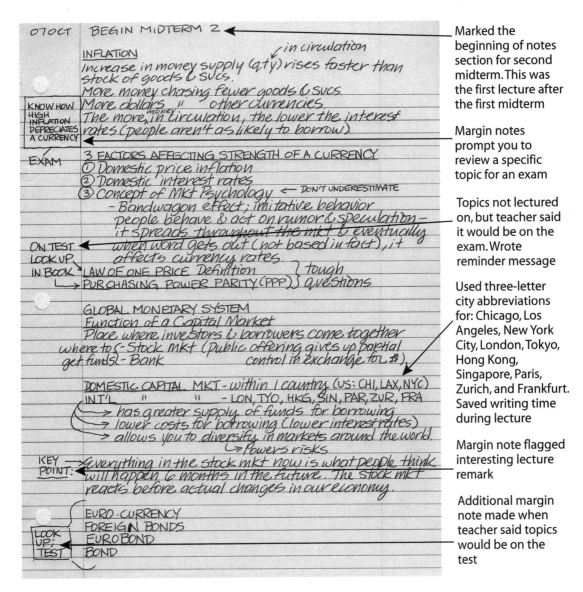

Marked the beginning of notes section for second midterm. This was the first lecture after the first midterm

Margin notes prompt you to review a specific topic for an exam

Topics not lectured on, but teacher said it would be on the exam. Wrote reminder message

Used three-letter city abbreviations for: Chicago, Los Angeles, New York City, London, Tokyo, Hong Kong, Singapore, Paris, Zurich, and Frankfurt. Saved writing time during lecture

Margin note flagged interesting lecture remark

Additional margin note made when teacher said topics would be on the test

Figure 9: Notes made during lecture
Margin notes flag important messages, especially when a teacher emphasizes that something will be on an exam. (Original subject was International Business.)

I would be cautious if a classmate asks for a copy of your notes unless you know the person very well. Photocopying notes has greater significance when a course is graded on a curve—your competitor gains your notes, combines them with his or her own, those from others, or both, and can use the information to potentially outscore you on the exam. Compound this individual's increased competitiveness with the number of other students also taking the test. When you let someone else copy your notes under these circumstances, you make it harder for yourself to achieve a good grade. You didn't attend every class and painstakingly compile your notes for the convenience of freeloaders or calculating competitors. Each student is responsible for doing his or her own work. There may be exceptions for friends in a genuine emergency, such as when they miss class due to severe illness. But "an emergency" is not an excuse for habitual neglect or for evading personal responsibility. I've been known to show up to class even when sick. On rare occasions (as in three times in three years), I asked a classmate to fill me in on what I had missed.

If I ever let a classmate photocopy a section of my notes, I accompanied that person to the copy machine and took back my notebook immediately afterward.

One student had a novel approach to collecting my classmates' notes. Before our midterm exam, he hosted everyone at his house for lunch and a study session. People had a good time with all the food and socializing while he obtained their notes. His reassurance to me was that he was graduating one semester ahead and wouldn't be competing with us in the job market. I did not attend the party but also noticed that he actually graduated at the same time we did. If you do not approve of indirect tactics that others use to gain an advantage, at least be aware that you may, at some time, be a potential target.

Note-Taking during Lectures

Notes are useful for learning because lectures can be easier to understand than the wording in textbooks. Also important, instructors may test you on lecture information that is not in your text. However, errors in transcribing lectures can occur if you're not careful. This may cause misunderstandings, mistakes on exams, and a potentially lower grade. I've seen classmates approach professors after they lost points on exams. For some, these errors pushed their scores just below the cut-off for the next higher grade. They opened their notebooks and cited the parts used as bases for their answers. The professors replied that these students had inferred inaccurately or had written down incorrect information. The classmates' test scores remained unchanged, and they were upset. Accuracy is paramount in note-taking.

The summa cum laude student I mentioned earlier went home after each lecture and typed out her notes. Her rationale was that (a) typing was neater than handwriting, (b) while her memory was fresh she could recall things her teachers had said that she hadn't written down, and (c) she could further clarify or expand on certain items during the typing stage. She'd then use these typewritten notes for studying rather than her notebook. Two friends, who eventually went to medical school, also rewrote their lecture notes saying that the process reinforced their memory for content and spelling of complex terminology. Because I had a full plate of classes and outside obligations, I didn't rewrite my notes; instead, I ensured that they were clearly written during actual lectures. Combined with margin notes and occasional adjunct sentences added after lectures, all the information was complete for exam review. All I had to do was highlight and study. (Notebook highlighting is covered in Chapter 11.) But if rewriting notes helps you learn and retain lecture material more efficiently, by all means incorporate this into your strategy.

Also, listen to your classmates' questions during lectures. Some of their questions may elicit remarks from your teacher that will enhance your test reviews and learning.

Note-Taking during Class Presentations and Videos

Unless your teacher says you don't need to, take notes during videos and student presentations. You have nothing to lose. You learn from a broader scope of topics and perspectives, and may also need these notes for exams.

Many classmates don't take thorough notes during student presentations. More than a third of the courses I attended after resuming college required speeches. Of these, some gave exams with questions derived from students' speeches. Two teachers announced this before our presentations began. The third never told us—we found out on the test. That particular essay question was worth 15 points. Students who had neglected note-taking during the presentations lost their A grade on this question alone. Most of us took quite a hit on that test. And although the presentations hadn't been covered during our in-class midterm review, I later noticed a clause on our syllabus stating that "students are responsible for everything found in assigned readings and everything discussed in class." This goes back to heeding your course syllabus thoroughly from the first day of class on out.

It's not uncommon for students, who were asleep at the switch, to ask you for a copy of your notes when they discover that presentations will be included on an exam.

8

Pick Your Group Project Members Carefully

Team projects hinge on the work of each and every member. Teachers vary in their grading of group projects. Some instructors give individual grades, while others give all members the same grade.

Because group projects are predicated on mutual dependence, you'll want to avoid teaming up with students with counterproductive attitudes and work habits whenever possible. Unless you're assigned a partner or partners by your instructor, you'll benefit most by selecting classmates who are reliable and at least as driven and resourceful as you are. A team progresses farther when it doesn't have to pull along dead weight. If you receive individual grades, you'll be drawn to perform better with top-notch students. If you receive a shared grade, everyone pushes one another to perform well.

When the grade is shared among a grossly mismatched team, the most highly motivated student incurs the greatest liability. Unmotivated students need constant prodding, contribute less work, may force you to assume more than your fair share of duties, and can cause your grade to be lower. Time and energy are taken up by negotiating rather than working. There may be added frustration from teammates submitting substandard work behind schedule. If a high grade is ultimately received, it's because the top student has done most of the work while inept members reap the benefits without having shouldered responsibility. Without sounding curt, no member should drag the team down.

Some of my classmates complained about unproductive team members. One became so disenchanted with her classmates' indifference that she asked the professor for a team change in midsemester. In such cases, motivated classmates felt that shared grading was unfair. Two of my teachers said, in essence, that that's the way life is in the world, so "get used to it." I did not, and still do not, agree with this cold response. I believe that when such disputes occur, teachers should act as arbiters. It is true that flaky people exist in the workplace, but let these lessons take place on the job. The classroom is foremost a place to help a student reach his or her individual learning potential.

As soon as you discover that a team project is on the horizon, begin observing your classmates to distinguish the earnest from the unmotivated. You probably won't be assigned to pick your partners until later in the term. In the meantime, notice who sits at the front, asks intelligent questions, attends every class, pays full attention during lectures, and is punctual. (If your instructor does not disclose course criteria in advance, observe your classmates anyway and take note just in case you do get assigned a group project.)

Some teachers give you a choice between doing a term project as a group or on your own. When the pickings of ambitious team members are slim and you are a self-reliant A student, going solo is preferable. You'll have more control over the quality of your work and the resultant grade.

Structure your group strategy with two principles in mind: to move your team forward in its most efficient capacity and to achieve your target grade. Here are tips for organizing your group:

1. Have a group meeting the day the team is formed. At this meeting, address the following points.
2. Establish basic policies and goals to foster mutual understanding.

Everyone should be on the same page, in agreement, and clear on their tasks and what's expected of them. Such a team will out-perform those whose members are sifting through confusion, ambiguity, and misunderstandings as work is being done. Avoid duplicating each other's work due to poor communication. Certain ideas may appear obvious to some, but in a newly formed group, it is important not to assume too much. Communication is paramount. Group projects are also very good testing grounds for developing your interpersonal skills. Newly formed groups can be problematic if opinionated individuals become caught up in spatting instead of focusing on the tasks ahead. Group coherence is key, and this is where establishing basic policies and goals can help smooth things out.

3. Agree to move together as a group.

4. Target the same grade to provide a central goal.

5. Clearly understand your group's mission and where each member fits in.

6. Assess all criteria for the project (such as formatting, features, whether charts, images, or binding are required, minimum overall length, margin widths, line spacing, font, and point sizing, etc.).

7. Forecast the overall time required to meet the project deadline. Starting from your due date and working backward, calculate the total time needed from start to finish. This is where your team determines the tasks that need to be done. This may include but not be limited to the following:

- everyone to research information at the library, lab, Internet, or other sources;
- obtaining literature, reports, and published reference materials;
- members to write their respective sections and hand in their interim work via paper, diskette, or e-mail;
- (if applicable) constructing tables, graphs, charts, or submitting images for scanning into the report, (note: image research can be a time-consuming task);
- your designated graphics person to consolidate all text and images into one computer file;
- printing out and distributing the first draft among the group. Your final paper will be more polished and contain fewer flaws if your team reads paper printouts instead of attempting to copyedit on screen for convenience. Aim to make at least two revisions.
- reading the first draft, critiquing, and editing;
- your graphics person to make revision #1 on the master file (allow one week's turnaround time between group critique and corrections made on computer);
- assembling your group to critique and revise the second draft;
- your graphics person to make revision #2 on the master file (allow another week's time);
- assembling the group to evaluate the third draft (there should be no extensive changes necessary if everyone paid close attention during the two prior revisions);

- newly acquired information that's regularly exchanged via diskettes or e-mails throughout the semester;
- adding, proofreading, and editing new information;
- time factored in for delays in any of the preceding points (for example, somebody's floppy disk files or attachments may not be opened, or a member may be running behind schedule); and
- purchasing paper stock and binding services, if applicable.

8. Determine and divide duties fairly. Appoint a member to consolidate group-compiled data onto one computer file and design your team's paper. This individual will play a pivotal role, so he or she should be reliable, have good aesthetic design judgment, and be skilled with computer graphics and word processing programs. Either appoint a person to be your project editor or plan to read your drafts together at meetings.

9. Encourage open communication. State that everyone is to be treated equally and to feel comfortable speaking freely at all times. At meetings, everyone should have his or her say in all matters. The leader should ensure that everyone has good morale so the team functions at its best. Disgruntled members will erode team cooperation and overall performance.

10. There should be no put-downs. If constructive feedback is in order, speak objectively.

11. Members are to agree on all interim deadlines.

12. Agree that meetings can be called at any time by a member, as needed. This member would merely tell your group in class. The group could convene briefly after class to set up a mutually suitable time to meet later that same day or week.

13. Agree that members be punctual for all meetings.

14. State that, at any time, a member should feel free to suggest how work in progress could be improved; such ideas should be evaluated and adopted, or declined, by group consensus.

15. Exchange phone numbers, e-mail addresses, and note the best times to contact each person.

16. Monitor and accomplish your work in stages. Also, members are to update each other in class or via phone calls or e-mails.

17. Phone messages and e-mails should be returned within 24 hours. Telephone conversations are more expedient for trouble-shooting problems than e-mailing.

18. Group meetings should be regularly scheduled. At each meeting, evaluate your team's work-in-progress and consider how to improve it.
19. Each member should complete his or her interim work on time, as agreed upon at the previous meeting.
20. Make sure your graphics person saves your group file on a back-up disc.
21. Appoint a member to keep your team abreast of interim deadlines, time constraints, and remaining days before due date. Time management throughout every stage is important. This is where less experienced members need reminders. Being exacting about keeping pace and making revisions might seem excessive to inexperienced students, but the results benefit everyone.

The preceding steps were used in a class where our group of five competed with twenty-four other teams. Not only did our time management, constant communications, and meticulous revisions result in a 95 for the project, but it helped two members pass the course with a full letter grade (C to B) higher than they would've received from their test scores alone.

When forecasting your overall start-to-finish time, it's better to err on the side of too much rather than too little time for a group project. If you're given two months for your project, use the full eight weeks to produce superior work at a comfortable pace rather than waiting until 2–3 weeks prior to the deadline to begin your work. If you plan to make two revisions to your paper, you would need to allow at least three weeks merely for proofing and revising alone. *Communicating the importance of time and ensuring that every member is entirely clear on this is sometimes difficult, but if time is underestimated, there can be a mad rush toward the due date to squeeze in remaining work.* This can have a number of undesirable consequences. First, a well-begun project can be weakened by hasty completion, resulting in a lower grade that could have been avoided by allowing an extra week or two. Second, team members may have scheduled other course assignments around your leader's original time forecast. If so, even if they try their best to take up the slack on short notice, their portion of work may be beneath their full capabilities. Multiply this by however many members have the same circumstances and you can see that a team project, even if well begun, becomes eroded. Third, not every student responds well to the urgency and stress of producing good work fast. Some students may not see that everyone else is suddenly diving in due to the emergency. They may respond with displeasure and blame. Time and energy will be consumed arbitrating interpersonal problems rather than being allocated to the project. If you find yourself caught between a difficult member and an approaching deadline, try to find ways for people to complete the project instead of focusing on personality issues.

9

Speeches and Class Presentations

No one can make you feel inferior without your consent.
—Anna Eleanor Roosevelt, 1884–1962[39]

The first and great commandment is, Don't let them scare you.
—Elmer Davis, 1890–1958[40]

A public speaking course early in your academic career is helpful because the skills you'll learn in it are useful both in subsequent courses and beyond college. If you're after top scores in other courses, delivering speeches effectively will be essential.

Giving presentations in class was something I dreaded. However, if you're determined enough, you can compensate for a deficiency. Have you heard people say that a certain skill was originally their weakness and that they simply worked at it long and hard enough that it became a strength? The same applies to writing, speech, or presentation skills. Learning all the rules and guidelines combined with organized, solid content and frequent practice are your best remedies.

Your instructor and text will illuminate the fine points of delivering speeches. Other course instructors may stipulate criteria verbally or through handouts. Following your teachers' guidelines is your first step to scoring well. Add to this what you learn from lectures, text readings, guest speakers, and practice, and your speeches will be as smooth as they can be.

My teachers typically allotted 5 to 8 minutes for speeches. This isn't a long time. In fact, you may discover that your speeches easily run over the allotted time during your practice sessions. Do not exceed the time limit set by your teacher. It won't earn you strong scores. (Students in the classroom and professionals outside school often exceed their speech times, but this is either inept or rude and not something to emulate.) I've seen class-mates go beyond time limits due to lack of planning and preparation. When teachers cut them off in midstream, they had to pause to fast-for-ward through their notes. Their topics weren't adequately developed, so they couldn't make smooth transitions into their conclusions or final editori-als. The jump from underdeveloped topic to abrupt ending meant the audience couldn't grasp the full picture. This defeats the purpose of a speech.

To ace speeches and presentations requires advance preparation, as with everything else. The actual speech is only 10% of your overall task. Every-thing about your presentation should be tailored to your audience. Accordingly, it is important to assess your audience beforehand. Contents need to be specific, organized, well developed, and free of logical fallacies. Include only what strengthens your message; omit whatever detracts. Avoid redundancy. Shorter sentences are more easily digested than long ones. Your audience will only hear your speech once, so it has to be good. On the day you speak, you want everything to proceed at a pace that's comfortable for your audience, so that your messages are sound and clear.

I did not ad-lib my speeches in class because I wanted to say everything correctly. If you're apprehensive about giving a speech in the first place, it's torture to say something in error and then not know where to pick up your train of thought and continue smoothly. *A written speech keeps you on track, even during unexpected interruptions, because you can easily mark the spot where you leave off.* A friend who had addressed large audiences, ranging from college commencements to foreign crowds on behalf of the U.S. State Department preferred a written speech over ad-libbing because (a) she didn't want to say anything incorrect or misleading, and (b) she did not want to be misquoted. An impromptu speech can be problematic for a beginner. Since you've never rehearsed, you won't know whether you'll be able to develop your points smoothly or say everything needed, in the order needed, within the time needed, in the way most appropriate for your audience—all while your grade is on the line. *If you're apprehensive, it's best to prepare and practice from a written speech.* There are people with a definite gift for impromptu speeches, but developing these skills is best deferred to more advanced studies in speech communication.

When preparing speeches, first write your draft a week beforehand. After it's complete, read it out loud. Some words or sentences that appear fine in written form may sound unnatural when spoken. Keeping your audience in mind, reword or rephrase these areas for sharpness, then use a variation of the 3-Day Method described in Chapter 11. This means practicing your speech in three daily sessions leading up to the actual day in class. Each time you practice, including handling all props, transparencies, and exhibits as you would during the real presentation. Use a digital watch to gauge your pace and to finish your presentation within 20 seconds of the time limit. If you exceed the time limit, edit your speech to convey the same information in less time. It's important not to compensate by speaking faster; an audience will have difficulty following and comprehending. Avoid information overload even though you feel there's lots of information to cover. Content should be reduced to the bare essentials.

Practice until there are no hesitations and everything is said, paced, and finished within the time limit and with no mistakes. When you no longer improve during practice, you're ready. I used to practice my short speeches six times per day. Yes, it was tiring, but this saved a lot of headaches when I faced the audience.

For longer speeches, such as those spanning 20 to 50 minutes, memorizing them entirely may be unnecessary. It may also be more productive to practice them only two to three times a day over four to five days leading up to your presentation. However many times you practice per day, take breaks between sessions to give your mind relief and a chance for the information to sink in.

In Singapore, I used a slightly different strategy to overcome apprehension. I would memorize my speeches and practice them in the same classroom in which I would be speaking. The rationale was that all variables would remain constant except for the people looking at me on speech day. The practice sessions took place in afternoons after classes had ended. Two teachers and an administrator often noticed me talking in an empty room. Memorizing the speech meant that I didn't have to look back and forth between the audience and my notes, amidst a silent room of eyes aimed at me. It allowed me to focus on their reactions and facial expressions, while getting accustomed to people looking at me. Whereas I was initially too nervous to look at people, eventually I made eye contact and saw that they were genuinely interested. This helped me relax and be more enthusiastic about delivering my messages.

None of this was easy; it took time, practice, sweating in front of classmates, even stuttering once or twice, and feeling my legs buckling underneath me one time while standing at the podium. But things only became easier from there.

Before your practice sessions, it's good to visit the room in which you'll be giving your speech. You'll see the spatial characteristics of your venue, whether your audience will be seated above or beneath you, whether your closest listeners will be right at your feet gazing up at you, or whether you'll have lots of space around you. You'll gain a better idea of where you'll be positioned and how your line of sight will need to be adjusted to maintain eye contact with your listeners. You'll know how to tailor your volume during practice sessions and prepare your visual aids properly. These variables are easy to evaluate if your presentation will be done in class.

Here's a good point related to me by the friend who once represented the State Department. She remarked that as nervous as some may be, people don't die from giving speeches. "Nobody knows you're nervous inside but you. If you don't reveal it, nobody knows." I asked another friend who'd been in show business on Broadway in New York whether she became apprehensive before a performance. Her reply was, "Sure you get nervous. But once you're on stage, you have to recite your lines, remember how to move around, and ensure you don't fall into the orchestra below. You're so focused on technical requirements, you're too busy to think about being nervous." Another useful perspective came from monologue actress and writer Cornelia Otis Skinner, who related her opinion to my State Department friend. Skinner said that being nervous before a speech was good. It shows you care; you wouldn't do a good job otherwise. One guest speaker in my course reassured that being nervous was the best way to motivate ourselves to prepare and perform well. He also thought speeches were great opportunities for a single mind to influence large numbers of people. If your speech is backed by solid information and you believe in what you're saying, you won't be so anxious because you'll be engrossed in conveying what you feel is genuinely important.

One of my spirited classmates tape-recorded her practice speeches while looking at herself in a large mirror. She said that watching your own facial expressions and body language and listening to your voice recordings helps you evaluate your visual and auditory messages to the audience. I joked with her, saying that this was an excuse to admire herself in the mirror, that she was her own best audience, and that she was the only one I knew who had worn out several mirrors from overuse. With a smile she replied, "Don't quit your day job, Lance." Actually, she was very astute in gauging her appearance, voice, and diction. Body language, facial expressions, posture, hand gestures, eye contact (which are nonverbal messages), and tone of voice converge with your words to make a total impression on the audience. Since she didn't have a video camera, a mirror was a simple, sensible substitute. However, a video camera allows you to tape your practice sessions at venues outside the home and view yourself from a third-person perspective. If you have no video camera, tape recorder, or large mirror immediately accessible, ask friends, roommates, or family members to watch and listen during your practice speech. This evaluative session would ideally occur after you've gained basic fluency of your speech but still have a few sessions remaining to incorporate their suggestions.

Your public speaking text will elaborate on the principles and major pitfalls. As a suggestion of what to avoid, here are the most common mistakes I've seen among classmates, from freshmen to seniors: not telling the audience the subject of the speech; jumping into procedural explanations without first explaining the topic; speaking too quickly to cram in too much information within the allotted time; overloading the audience with information they couldn't fully absorb; speaking too softly; sitting instead of standing; reading the speech instead of looking at the audience; using tape recorders with poor sound; using visual aids that weren't clearly visible from a distance (such as 4 x 6-inch photos mounted on boards or placards written with thin markers or in colors with poor contrast); holding a tape recorder up to the audience with a shaky hand (which I found more distracting than placing the recorder on the desk or podium instead); and introducing new information during concluding remarks. Last but not least, avoid saying "um," "uh," or "you know" during speeches.

I list these problems because I've seen them repeatedly, not just in speech class but also in business, philosophy, management, and foreign language courses, and even in the workplace. In addition, some students placed sensationalism above substance. While sensationalism may grab the attention of classmates, speeches lacking in substance won't receive high marks. Sensationalism combined with substance can work, but if it's not your forte (some students have a knack for it, others don't), concentrating primarily on content is a safer bet.

Even though I memorized my speeches, I always wrote them well in advance. When I read them, I would write in bold parentheses the time it took (1 Minute, 2 Minutes, 3 Minutes, and so on) to reach a certain spot on the page. These notations served as guideposts when I practiced and memorized newly created speeches. The minute guideposts were also useful when editing and shortening sections was necessary. After memorizing, I focused on pace, tone, volume of voice, and staying relaxed. I then abandoned the time posts, noting instead whether I finished my speech within 20 seconds of my teacher's time limit.

Figures 10 and 11 (see following pages) are examples of a two-minute speech. The assignment was to introduce a classmate based on her personal and academic interests and how she envisioned herself in the future as a professional. Figure 10 shows handwritten revisions to improve flow and decrease overall speech time by 20 seconds.

In my class, one guest speaker made the following points:

■ Your delivery begins as soon as you're visible to the audience.
■ Avoid negative communications, verbal or nonverbal, in your opening or introduction.
■ Eyes are your main visual link to the audience. Don't look over their heads; look at them.
■ After an interruption, such as people laughing or someone entering or leaving the room, pause for a moment to allow everyone to refocus their attention.
■ It's okay to move around moderately to alleviate anxiety, but be sure that you still communicate to, and maintain eye contact with, the whole audience.
■ Coordinate every verbal and nonverbal communication to supplement each other and reinforce your message. Avoid conveying irrelevant nonverbal messages, such as looking at the clock, tapping your fingers, or twirling your pen; these will weaken your presentation. A well-prepared message will naturally produce the right gestures and facial expressions.
■ Don't leave the podium the moment you finish; stay poised, calm, and relaxed.

Using Visual Aids

A picture shows me at a glance what it
takes dozens of pages of a book to expound.
—Ivan Sergeyevich Turgenev, 1818–1883[41]

One of the best first-semester level speeches I recall included videotaped interviews with other students. Visually, the tape was quite well done. Composition and cropping were good, image clarity sharp, lighting good, no harsh shadows, interview subjects up close and in focus, their body language natural, not stiff or expressionless, and dialogue lively and interesting. It was as if the tape had been edited. The audio portion was also good. (I used to be an audiophile, so I notice sound quality.) The only factor that detracted from the presentation was that some of the interviews had been conducted adjacent to a construction zone so that background noise from a bulldozer and jackhammer made it hard to hear what interviewees were saying at times. Noise interferes. I include this anecdote so you can apply this lesson to your own projects and avoid any barriers to communication in your presentations.

Whether the medium is graphic design or public speaking, a key element in communication is audience retention of your message. This is particularly important for persuasive or educational speeches. And for classroom speeches, visual aids make a more lasting impression than audio aids.

Besides reinforcing your messages, visual aids communicate faster and more graphically than spoken words, thus saving you the time needed to describe points during your speech. Images contain so much information that even computers require lots of memory to store them as compared to text files. However, discretion is necessary. One classmates' group presentation included color photos of the symptoms of sexually transmitted diseases. While definitely a reality and constructively educational, the shock value of these images had an effect unanticipated by the speakers. Our teacher acknowledged the strengths of their presentation but cautioned them with some sound advice. Certain pictures, if shocking to an audience, may actually cause people to remain psychologically fixed on the images so that they don't hear or follow your subsequent messages.

Images and projected word lists should not distract your audience from what you're saying. Both should only contain essential information. They *our guest speaker on*

"I am pleased to introduce Ms. [Jane Doe], ~~who will be speaking to you about~~ developmental psychology for children. Many of you have children in the first, second, and third grades. ~~In recent years,~~ *R*research has shown that assistance in a timely manner is important before children develop poor self-image and poor work habits. [Jane] is here to ensure that parents *don't* ~~do not~~ mistake a temporary ~~developmental~~ issue with a permanent personality or cognitive trait.

Before [Jane] speaks, I'd like to tell you a little about her. [Jane] was born in [Saratoga] and grew up in our Bay Area. Her early interests include bicycle riding, shopping at malls, and spending quality time with her friends and family. She obtained her ~~Bachelor of Arts~~ *B.A.* in Psychology from San Francisco State University, *and* ~~placing on the Dean's list four consecutive years and graduating summa cum laude. Shortly thereafter, [Jane] went on to~~ ~~acquire~~ her Ph.D. in Child Psychology from the *USF* ~~University of San Francisco~~, our city's oldest school for higher education.

[Jane] now has her own private practice in San Francisco. Her volunteer professional services for various ~~local young~~ children's organizations earned her an Award of Merit for Outstanding Public Service by the City and County of San Francisco. Her studies have been widely discussed in her profession and she is nationally recognized as an expert on Child Psychology. In spite of her impressive achievements ~~and contributions,~~ what [Jane] enjoys most is returning to her family of four everyday.

We are extremely fortunate to have *Jane* ~~her~~ share her expertise with us. On the other hand, [Jane] is not overly technical. *and* ~~Therefore,~~ you as parents can go home with some ideas *on* ~~as to~~ how to apply her advice to your own family context. Ladies and gentlemen, it gives me great pleasure to introduce to you Ms. [Jane Doe]."

Annotations (right margin):
- Changed wording to sound more conversational
- Eliminated wordiness
- Used contraction
- Changed "Bachelor of Arts" to "B.A." for parallel construction with Ph.D.
- Eliminated wordiness
- Changed name of school to its abbreviation. Audience knew what USF meant. Using the abbreviation shortened the sentence, making the speech smoother while reducing overall time

Figure 10: Sample draft of a two-minute speech.
Needed to reduce time by 20 seconds. Made handwritten revisions for smoothness and to shorten speech time. Revisions were made to appeal to a student audience in the classroom. Words in [ ] have been changed from their original. (Original subject was Public Speaking.)

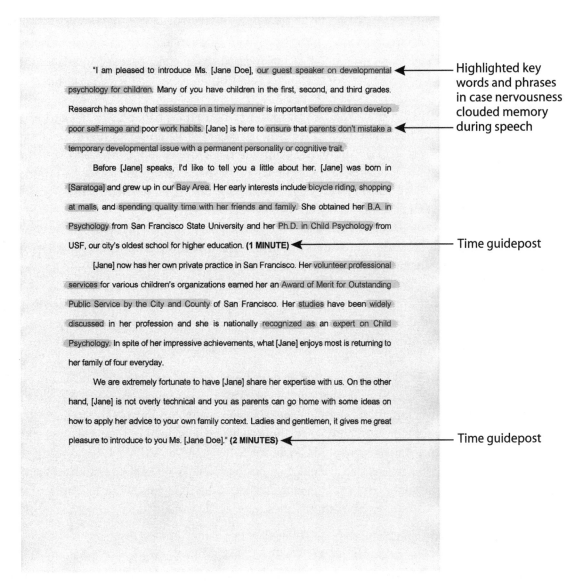

"I am pleased to introduce Ms. [Jane Doe], our guest speaker on developmental ◄——— Highlighted key
words and phrases
psychology for children. Many of you have children in the first, second, and third grades.   in case nervousness
clouded memory
Research has shown that assistance in a timely manner is important before children develop   during speech

poor self-image and poor work habits. [Jane] is here to ensure that parents don't mistake a ◄———

temporary developmental issue with a permanent personality or cognitive trait.

   Before [Jane] speaks, I'd like to tell you a little about her. [Jane] was born in

[Saratoga] and grew up in our Bay Area. Her early interests include bicycle riding, shopping

at malls, and spending quality time with her friends and family. She obtained her B.A. in

Psychology from San Francisco State University and her Ph.D. in Child Psychology from

USF, our city's oldest school for higher education. (1 MINUTE) ◄——————— Time guidepost

   [Jane] now has her own private practice in San Francisco. Her volunteer professional

services for various children's organizations earned her an Award of Merit for Outstanding

Public Service by the City and County of San Francisco. Her studies have been widely

discussed in her profession and she is nationally recognized as an expert on Child

Psychology. In spite of her impressive achievements, what [Jane] enjoys most is returning to

her family of four everyday.

   We are extremely fortunate to have [Jane] share her expertise with us. On the other

hand, [Jane] is not overly technical and you as parents can go home with some ideas on

how to apply her advice to your own family context. Ladies and gentlemen, it gives me great

pleasure to introduce to you Ms. [Jane Doe]." (2 MINUTES) ◄——————— Time guidepost

Figure 11: Sample of a revised two-minute speech.
This version was used for 3-Day practice sessions. Time guideposts are determined
by reading aloud at the pace you'd use for your audience, then writing the times on
your draft. Guideposts serve as markers when practicing a speech from memory.
Although the speech is memorized, taking a written backup with you to the
podium is helpful in case of interruptions or nervousness.

must be understandable, high contrast, and large enough to be seen easily from the farthest viewing point of your audience. Text on transparencies may need to be 18 to 24 point size. Fonts should be easy to read, not ornate. The adage "Form follows function" is your best guideline. Keep it simple, big, clear, and effective.

I noticed that when a transparency contained too lengthy a word list, students became glued to reading it instead of listening. Either give them some time to read your list completely or break it up into two shorter transparencies instead. It can be tricky to give a handout because students can become fascinated with flipping through its pages or viewing its pictures at the expense of listening to your speech.

In *Essentials of Human Communication*, J. A. DeVito advises that your speech rehearsals include your visual aids, including the timing, order of appearance, and length of exposure for each one. A visual aid should appear when you want your audience to focus on it. As appropriate, explain the image that you display. Remove your visual aid once the audience has digested it or when you're ready to address your next issue; this keeps your audience focused on you instead of your picture. As you speak, face your audience and not your visual aid—turning your head away at such time makes it difficult for audience members to hear you clearly. DeVito even suggests that you "know your aids so well that you can point to what you want without breaking eye contact with your audience. Or, at the least, break audience eye contact for only very short periods of time."[42]

On your written speech, write "VA 1," "REMOVE VA 1," and so on at the spots you believe are most strategic. "VA" is short for "visual aid" and can represent either a transparency or slide. The following example of a written classroom speech includes such guideposts:

I. Introduction
A. Attention Step [TRANSPARENCY 1—image]

As [name of team member] demonstrated, the Internet allows you to book your own flight reservations and order air tickets. Generally, we all want to find the lowest airfares possible. But what do you really need to know to ensure you receive the lowest fare? I will tell you the main criteria behind airfares to ensure that you get what you pay for when using the Internet.

B. Establish Credibility

This information was obtained from a variety of travel industry resources (verbal message citing references and experience of the speaker)....

[REMOVE TRANSPARENCY 1]

C. Preview Body of Speech [TRANSPARENCY 2—word list]

(verbal message...)

[REMOVE TRANSPARENCY 2]

II. Body

[TRANSPARENCY 3—word list]

A. Understand the Criteria for the Lowest Airfares

Before buying an air ticket, every customer should know these seven points about airfares:

1. Advance purchase (verbal message...)
2. Date and time restrictions (verbal message...)
3. Routing and connections (verbal message...)
4. Availability (verbal message...)
5. Refund policy (verbal message...)
6. Changes to reservations (verbal message...)
7. Penalty fees (verbal message...)

[REMOVE TRANSPARENCY 3]

B. How to Find the Lowest Fare [TRANSPARENCY 4—image]

Question: Given the aforementioned, how do you find the best airfare? **Answer:** You must determine what is most important to you: time, money, or both. The goal is to maximize your vacation at your final destination and not waste time in transit. Nonstop is usually everyone's first choice. But suppose your ideal nonstop flight is sold out. What then? Here are your options (verbal message)....

Note: It's a good practice to include both minute and visual-aid guideposts on your written speech.

For visual aids, I preferred transparencies for their simplicity. First, they allowed me to practice my speeches thoroughly at home. I couldn't have done this had I chosen computer-projected programs, and I wasn't fond of executing something for the first time on the day of a speech. Second, they were lightweight and convenient to carry in my notebook. Third, I had greater control over the contents projected to my audience. I chose strong black and white line drawings or high-contrast halftones. Black and white communicates without the distractions associated with using color. With black and white, what you see is closer to what you get. Fourth, I had no video camera.

There are two ways you can transfer images onto transparency: by computer printer (using an image from disc, download, or scanner) or by photocopy machine. Different transparencies are made specifically for laser printers and photocopy machines. Both types are generally available at campus bookstores.

If you have an image on disc or computer file, you can resize, crop, and print it out onto a transparency. Images remain sharp after repeated resizing, and can be rotated or enhanced. A note of warning, though: working with high-bit color images requires lots of computer memory, is time-consuming, and can be susceptible to crashing unless you save often (as in every few minutes).

Assuming you have no computer photo-edit program or scanner, a standby method is to use a photocopy machine. Ordinary photocopiers, however, cannot retain image clarity with each successive resizing. You have less control over image quality because copy machines have limited capabilities. But photocopied transparency images will suffice if needed, and this method can be much less time-consuming than using a computer that's subject to memory limits or crashing.

Cropping Pictures

Form ever follows function.
—Louis Henri Sullivan, 1856–1924[43]

Cropping of images affects what you communicate (see Figures 12–14). Cropping includes enlarging certain portions and discarding others. *Choose what you want your viewers to focus on and leave out the rest.* Think of this as economy of visual elements. If you wish to take your visual-aid strategies to a higher level, you can enroll in a graphic design course or contact one of your school's communication art teachers for advice. If you wish to use a border in your visual aids, black, white, or warm grey provide the most neutral backgrounds.

If using transparencies, determine your cropping before calculating your enlargement percentage. If you cannot crop your image on computer, there is an alternative. An easy way is to take four sheets of blank white paper and lay them over your original to create a frame. The area within this mock frame is what you wish your audience to focus on, whereas the image areas outside of the frame will be removed. By playing with different positions of each piece of paper and shifting your frame over various areas of your original, you'll see how cropping changes the character and strength of your visual aid. As an option, you could tape the papers together to create a fixed frame (or tape two papers together and make a pair of L-shaped frames) that will be easier to shift. You can decide whether a vertical, horizontal, or square format presents your picture most effectively. Once you arrive at your ideal cropping, measure the dimensions of this frame.

To calculate your enlargement percentage: take the size you want, divide it by the size of your cropped original, and multiply the result by 100. The biggest dimension will govern your enlargement percentage. For example, suppose the cropped portion of your original image measures 2 inches wide x 3 inches high and you wish to enlarge it to 7.5 x 10 inches (to allow a half-inch border on an 8.5 x 11 inch transparency) respectively. 7.5 ÷ 2 = 3.75; 3.75 x 100 is 375%. However, 10 ÷ 3 = 3.33; 3.33 x 100 is 333%. Using 375% would cause your image to exceed 10 inches in height, so you would use 333%.

A photocopier may feature stepped percentage increments (i.e., 121%, 129%, or 200%) or offer variable percentages selected manually by you. Depending on circumstances, you may be able to achieve your desired enlargement size in one copy. If the size you need exceeds your machine's maximum capability, you can make two successive copies (an enlargement of an enlargement). For example, if you want a 333% enlargement but your machine only goes up to 200%, you'd make two copies: the first at 200%, the second at 167% (333 ÷ 200 = 1.665, or 167%). During these enlargements, adjust the contrast controls for image clarity.

Depending on the size of the cropped portion of your original, your desired presentation size, and your machine's maximum enlargement

Figure 12: Examples of cropping
(A) Original photo. Note the differences between (B) and (C).
(B) emphasizes double figures, whereas (C) emphasizes hieroglyphics.
Photo © Lance O. Ong.

Figure 13: Examples of cropping
(A) Original photo.
(B) Image cropping enhances viewer focus on subject.
(C) Further cropping maximizes viewer focus on subject.
President Taft speaking at Manassas Court House. Photo courtesy of Library of Congress, Prints and Photographs Division [reproduction number LC-USZ62-38780]

A

B

Figure 14: Example of cropping
(A) Original photo.
(B) Image cropping maximizes viewer focus on subjects.
Cindy Parlow Playing Soccer. Photo © Duomo/CORBIS.

increments, you may need to make three generations of copies. There will be some loss of clarity each time you photocopy, which is why it's important to choose an original picture that isn't too busy or detailed.

Once you're satisfied with your enlarged photocopy, use this as your "master." Make a photocopy of this master to see how it reproduces, adjusting the machine's contrast levels as desired. All copies up to this point have been made on paper. If results are satisfactory, photocopy the same master but this time feed your transparency through your photocopy machine. The transparency is now ready for your presentation.

Whether you use a computer or photocopier, evaluate your images on paper printouts until you arrive at your optimum size, cropping, position, and contrast, to avoid wasting transparencies.

Last but Not Least

Remember how you wrote your deadlines for all your courses in your notebook? When given a choice of the date on which to give a speech, try to select a day that's at least several days to a week from your other course deadlines. This will give you more undivided time and attention to construct and practice your presentation.

A finishing touch to your speeches is your physical appearance. Appearance affects your credibility as a speaker because your audience judges you in part by how you look and dress. You want an audience to take you and your message seriously. One sure way is to be clean and well groomed. Dress to appeal to your audience, be they students, faculty, or professionals. Evaluate the circumstances, such as your audience's age, level of education, cultural norms and mores, political sensitivities, attitudes, and interests, in relation to you, your age, and how you think you can best relate to them. You don't need to wear a suit (though some business courses may require such attire for presentations), but do dress to suit your audience, the context of your speech, and the occasion.

10

Writing Papers

Grasp the subject; the words will follow.
—Marcus Porcius Cato, the Elder, 234–149 B.C.E.[44]

Writing well is part of your intellectual potential and will be an asset throughout your life. It is a skill many do not possess. Writing demands discipline, creativity, time, and endurance for revising your piece until it is polished. Strong writing skills strengthen your job qualifications and increase your worth to a company. You will use them for your cover letters, reports, correspondence, customer service grievances, and documenting incidents for personal, legal, or insurance purposes.

First-generation immigrant classmates often told me how hard writing English was for them. I told them that they faced two challenges: (1) technical criteria, and (2) expressing their individual critical thinking, something that is often new to those who come from cultures that emphasize rote learning. Actually, writing good English isn't easy even for native English speakers in America. Like any acquired skill, writing well takes practice.

On the one hand, writing assignments give you a great deal of control over your grades because you create and shape what goes onto the blank pages. On the other hand, readers can't ask you questions or paraphrase your points as they can during verbal communication, so your messages need to be clear the first time around.

If you find writing difficult, don't try to write in an elaborate or jargon-filled way. You can still gain high marks using plain words. Simply write what you mean. The depth and breadth of content that show through your simple words are what counts. That's why it's necessary to think out your paper carefully so that your words will convey sound research, analysis, and insight, and not just a succession of empty phrases.

The Barron's guide to the Graduate Management Admission Test (GMAT) states that using plain words is

> a principle easy to say but hard to live by when you're hoping to impress readers with your intellect and sophistication. Nothing, truly nothing, conveys your erudition (learnedness) better than plain words. . . . There's always a risk, in fact, that words that sound profound to you may seem pompous (pretentious) to your readers. Or worse, they could make you appear foolish. . . .
>
> The student who wrote, "I am of the opinion that a prerequisite to parenthood includes disbursement of penal adjudication among siblings with an even, dispassionate hand," needs a basic lesson in plain writing. How much clearer to have written, "I think that good parents should know how to be fair in disciplining their children" or "I think that being equally strict with all their children is a prerequisite of being good parents." Words should be like gifts, carefully chosen to give pleasure to someone you like. High gloss is not a measure of value. You won't gain much by dressing ordinary ideas in fancy robes or from trying to appear more impressive than you already are.[45]

William Strunk and E. B. White's *The Elements of Style** is a classic reference for every student. The book is short and concisely explains rules of grammar, composition guidelines, and commonly misused words. Strunk advises that writers "Omit needless words!" and that

> Vigorous writing is concise. A sentence should contain no unnecessary words, a paragraph no unnecessary sentences, for the same reason that a drawing should have no unnecessary lines and a machine no unnecessary parts. This requires not that the writer make all sentences short, or avoid all detail and treat subjects only in outline, but that every word tell.[46]

"You can't dance fancy until you dance plain," one of my professors remarked. Write in simple and direct English so readers clearly understand you. Generally, using fewer words to convey your message is superior to being wordy. For example, instead of writing "owing to the fact that," write "because"; instead of using "did not pay any attention to," use

---

* From Strunk, William Jr. & White, E. B. Elements of Style 4/e (c) 2000. Published by Allyn and Bacon, Boston, MA. Copyright (c) 2000 by Pearson Education. Reprinted by permission of the publisher.

"ignored."[47] Choose your words to convey what you really mean. One student wrote "economic justification" when he really meant "court-awarded money damages." Another thought "commercial law" was synonymous to "written contracts for TV commercials."

You may want to write your first outline or draft as you would express yourself verbally to a colleague or acquaintance. This will help you get your basic thoughts down on paper. Some students have difficulty stating their thesis. One remedy is to imagine your closest friend asking you "What's your main point to all this?" and "Why is this so important?" and "Can you give me examples to substantiate your assertions?" Your succinct verbal answers could then be transferred to paper and revised as necessary. Avoid slang and clichés unless they're the focus of your paper.

Jade Snow Wong, author of *Fifth Chinese Daughter*,[48] recalled her college English teacher stating "Just as a dog has a head and tail, so should your writing."[49] Papers should proceed from the What (your topic or thesis) to the Why and How (the body developing your points). They should also have a definite ending. Waiting for a punch line that never appears will leave your readers feeling cheated. One of my professors referred to this as "academic weaseling." A writer's purpose should be clear in his or her work. The Barron's guide concurs:

> A good essay can easily be spoiled by an ill-fitting ending. . . . The best endings grow organically out of the essay's content. . . . A catchy conclusion isn't always needed, but some sort of ending is necessary to make readers feel they've arrived somewhere. They won't be satisfied with an essay that just evaporates.[50]

It's also worthwhile to verify your teacher's technical criteria because these can affect your grade. Technical criteria include minimum and maximum page or word count, margin widths, font size, line spacing, indentations, form of citations, gender-neutral wording, binding or stapling, cover pages, and positioning of your name, subject title, course, section number, page numbers, date, and assignment name. Neglecting this will give the impression that you ignored directions, which can adversely affect your score. If criteria are not given, ask your instructor.

If a teacher expects you to include pictures, select them to reinforce your messages. Incorporating images adds to your overall project time, so take it into account during your planning stages. High-contrast black-and-white halftone images can be effective, but color images have a more dramatic impact. If you don't have the resources to scan and print color images, an alternative is to paste spray-mounted color photocopies onto Bristol paper. Whether you use black-and-white or color images, remember that good cropping enhances their impact; poor cropping detracts (see Chapter 9 for more details).

If you truly want to hone your writing skills—and earn top scores in the process—don't expect to complete your paper in one draft. You'll need to revise it several times to transform it into your strongest work. However, each successive revision should entail fewer corrections. You may make changes to content, sentence structure, grammar, spelling, word choice, formatting, or delete certain parts. As Strunk states, "Few writers are so expert that they can produce what they are after on the first try. . . . Remember, it is no sign of weakness or defeat that your manuscript ends up in need of major surgery. This is a common occurrence in all writing, and among the best writers."[51]

Going through two to three revisions will noticeably improve the quality of your paper. Imagine yourself in a teacher's place, reading ten to over one hundred student papers. Multiply this by however many classes that teacher has. Other students' papers may be hastily written, wordy, unrevised, and a chore to read. Yours, however, having been well planned, written, and revised several times, will stand out. The teacher may actually gain relief and enjoy reading it. My papers did not start out strong; I was simply willing to revise again and again until I got things right. I revised some of my term papers six times before handing them in. Teachers may agree to review your drafts prior to deadline and provide feedback on how to improve them. These are opportunities to obtain higher scores than those of first and only drafts blindly submitted on a due date.

The better your classmates write, the better you must also write. Give yourself enough time to write a good paper. After determining how much time you'll need, whenever possible, add five extra days to provide a safety zone for unexpected interruptions or writer's block. The latter can occur during both the creative phase and the revision process.

Composing the first draft is the most difficult and time-consuming stage; revisions are easier and faster to accomplish. During the creative process, you may find writing to be mercurial. You can't guarantee that you'll spend 8 hours to produce 20 pages. Writing doesn't work that way. On some days your thoughts will flow onto the page for hours on end, while on others you might sweat over a single page for an hour. Don't be discouraged by these ups and downs. A little patience goes a long way in writing. During the revision process, rereading can desensitize you to strengths and weaknesses in your work. It's similar to not being able to smell your food after cooking at the stove for a long time—you can't discern things acutely.

It helps to take a break when you're mentally exhausted. Leave a paper unread and out of mind for one hour to two days, while minding your deadline and how many more drafts you need to do. When you return, you'll be able to evaluate your paper more objectively and notice deficiencies that, if left uncorrected, will compromise your paper and grade. In some cases, you'll have new ideas for improving your paper. Read your paper aloud. Its voice, flow, strengths, and weaknesses will become apparent. When reviewing your drafts, ask yourself, "Does this paper read like a solid paper?" If not, improve it accordingly. At other times, it can help to have a friend, preferably one who writes as well or better than you do, or tutor read your draft for clarity. Managing time is crucial for your writing. Some students wait until their due date before presenting their drafts to a tutor for feedback. This is far too late to make any extensive improvements.

Computer word-processed papers are preferable to handwritten papers. Even if your teacher accepts the latter and your script is neat, the need for several revisions will be too time-consuming and frustrating. Computers allow you to save versions and cut and paste whole sentences or sections, which you can't do when writing by hand. I typically made one or two on-screen revisions before printing out my first draft.

Proofreading paper copies is superior to reading your work only on-screen. A writer should know exactly what he or she is handing in. Your teacher will probably read a paper copy. I wouldn't chance my score on a paper proofed and revised solely on-screen. Revising via paper printouts is faster, visually less fatiguing, and better for spotting weaknesses. Your viewing frame for a page is larger on paper than with an on-screen window, plus you can compare several pages side by side for content organization and juxtaposition, which is difficult on computer even if you work on a split screen. Paper copies are also more convenient and portable. You can take them with you anywhere, anytime, read a section, and leave and pick them up faster than on a computer. You can find your place more easily after an interruption or voluntary break to accommodate writers' rhythm.

Writing does not respond well to being rushed from rationed time at the campus computer center. Revise while you are focused, away from distractions, and not in a hurry. Revisions should be written by hand as you proofread your drafts. Use red ink (as opposed to using pencil or black ink) so that you're less likely to overlook these amendments when retyping on the computer.

When working on the computer, save your work frequently. To be safe, also save the large portions of work that you omit from your revised editions, in case you want to restore them later on. If you're interrupted by someone at the computer center, or by a phone call at home, save your work before diverting your attention or leaving your station.

Save each version of your paper, for example, (A), (B), (C) or (1.0), (2.0), (3.0), to indicate revision number. Keep the printout of your first draft to compare with your final draft; you should see a significant, not marginal, improvement to your paper.

Also save your work on a backup disc. Although you may never need it, such a backup is a wise form of insurance. One of the worst things that can happen, especially when your mind is on a roll, is that your computer crashes and you lose a lot of unsaved information. Not only does it take time to reconstruct, but many good spontaneous ideas may have been forgotten. Always keep a copy of your homework papers (especially take-home exams), either by photocopy, on floppy disc, or on your home computer's hard drive. I used to keep a spare disc in my school bag on general principles. Beware of macros and viruses when working on different computers for the same file. After printing out the final version of your paper, keep it in a folder or one of your notebook pockets to avoid dirt, creasing, dog-earing, and folding. A clean paper with sharp corners adds to the total image of your work.

The time and work you invest in revising and improving your writing will give you an advantage during essay exams. Because your writing skills and frame of mind are improved by frequent practice, your on-the-spot essays will read more smoothly, and stronger essays mean better grades. (You'll also perform better on your take-home exams).

When you're assigned a subject and can choose specific areas of it, avoid writing about too broad an area. (The same applies to your speeches.) There won't be enough space in a typical 8 to 10-page double-spaced term paper to provide the focus and depth needed to cover a big topic. To narrow a topic to manageable scope, try this method used by public-speaking instructor Alice Filmer. At each stage, the concern is to generate ideas, not evaluate or critique them on the spot. After compiling your list, evaluate the feasibility of each subtopic. If one isn't feasible, try another. Filmer's method is illustrated below.

Suppose that you were assigned to write something about "sex." You could start with a list of prospective areas:

Psychology
Intercourse
Orientation
Gender
Harassment
Industry

Suppose you chose "industry"; you could further subdivide "sex industry" as:

Pharmaceuticals
Employment opportunities
Laws
Strip clubs
Morality
Contraception

After choosing an area, for example, "contraception", the topic could be further narrowed down:

Benefits of
Moral issues
Forms of
Customer usage, satisfaction, and statistics
Manufacturer's research

Suppose you decided on "benefits of contraception." You started with the broad topic of sex but narrowed it down to a topic that is far more specific, would give your paper greater focus, and be enough information for you to write about. You could then begin thinking about your outline and researching reference materials.

Write Down Spontaneous Ideas

Sometimes you'll have difficulty coming up with ideas for your writing. Spontaneous thoughts can be valuable to your papers, especially when you expand upon them. These can occur while brushing your teeth, lying in bed, eating, exercising, at the library or bookstore, riding the bus, driving, bathing, walking, reflecting upon a new experience, or wherever and whenever your mind sparks.

Spontaneous ideas, however, are easily forgotten and lost. Alice Filmer suggests keeping a notepad in your pocket. You can also keep a small notepad beside your bed, on the kitchen table, or in the bathroom, car, or locker. Sometimes I took a small notepad with me on short hikes. As ideas popped up, I stopped to jot them down. These ideas were very different from those conceived at home. Being removed from your normal routine often enables you to think more unfettered, creatively, or objectively. If you have a brainstorm and are without pen and paper, repeat the idea to yourself over and over to commit it to memory. The main goal is to document your ideas before they are lost. After that, evaluating, refining, and organizing them in your paper is a matter of mechanics.

When a Writing Assignment Involves a Series of Chapter Summaries

If a teacher requires you to summarize your assigned reading, writing quality and order do matter. One instructor may want summaries in chapter numeric order, whereas another may not stipulate this. Even after your best work, some of your summaries will be stronger than others. Whatever the case, position your best writing at the front, in order of descending strength.

You want to give your finest presentation. If your best summaries are toward the end and the teacher doesn't read your paper in its entirety, you won't be graded on your best work. It is also unwise to write several good summaries followed by others that are hastily written. If the teacher reads all your summaries, the drop from good to poor writing will stand out and cause points to be deducted. Strive to write all chapter summaries well *and* order them by strength.

When You Can't Find a Good Case Analysis

If you need a real-life case for your paper and can't find a suitable one in books or in personal experience, an alternative is to call up local organizations related to the subject at hand. This can be a good learning experience and also lead to useful information for your paper. In some cases, a teacher may assign you to contact a local business firm for informational interviews.

Urban business people typically don't welcome unannounced phone soliciting. If you are in an urban area, firms may assume that you're trying to sell them a product or service. It is important to tell them that you are not looking for a job and are simply trying to obtain a case analysis for academic purposes. When contacting larger businesses, whether by phone or mail, it is generally best to contact them on Tuesdays, Wednesdays, or Thursdays. Mondays are often busy due to weekend backlogs of mail, phone messages, business matters needing immediate attention, and people having meetings. On Fridays, people are already focusing on the weekend. (The same applies to targeting your résumé and cover letter mailings after you graduate.)

Although some firms have a policy of not speaking with students, many will grant phone or face-to-face informational interviews on an individual basis. It is essential that you be very prepared and well organized. Urban business people are busy, have high standards of organization, and don't have time to burn if a student is fumbling around with his or her questions.

Determine the case topic to analyze and the appropriate companies or professionals to contact. For example, if you wish to study a business ethics dilemma, you could contact the human resources department of a local firm, a temporary job agency, or even a government organization. An opening to your phone inquiry could go something like, "Good morning (or afternoon), I'm (first and last name), a student at (your school's full name). I wonder if someone at your firm would be willing to grant an informational interview for purposes of my term paper?" The person may reply with some questions, which is why it's important that you be prepared to answer them comfortably and clearly.

Note that it is not merely what you say but how you say something that conveys a message to your listeners. Tone of voice sends a message, in many cases one stronger than the face value of your remarks. Practice your phone inquiry before actually calling your prospective interviewers. Also

- Be clear about what your assignment's objective is.
- Do a little research about the company you plan to contact. An interviewee may ask why you selected his or her organization. You need to be able to explain the connection between your course, your assignment topic, and their line of business.
- Although ignorance of etiquette and phone manners may be forgivable in a school setting, it is not during communications with business firms.
- Have all your questions prepared and written in advance. Remember, the more concisely you frame your questions, the more workable information you will obtain for your paper. Some firms may require you to fax them a list of your questions beforehand.
- *Whatever you do, don't wait until the last minute to solicit an informational interview.* One business manager told me that students waited until one to three days prior to their deadline before scheduling an appointment. A business interviewee isn't responsible for making him- or herself available on short notice simply because a student hasn't planned his or her time. It is better for interviewees to regard you with respect, not as someone who's desperate. Since most writing projects are announced months in advance, such procrastination is not only poor time management but a good way to destroy your grade as well.
- Later the same day you interview someone, mail him or her a thank-you card with a handwritten expression of your appreciation on it. (This is also a good practice when you interview for a job that you highly desire.)

Don't be disheartened by rejection. This isn't something to take personally. Businesses have their own agendas, policies, procedures, deadlines, and pressures inherent to their industry. If someone declines to be interviewed, simply thank him or her and contact another firm.

11

Exam Preparation

Knowledge is the antidote to fear.
—Ralph Waldo Emerson, 1803–1882[52]

As a general policy, don't miss exam reviews given by your teacher. This is another chance to ask questions and ensure that you're clear on everything. Also, if an exam is ever rescheduled, whether by your teacher or at your request, ensure that you have no other schedule conflict.

During Exam Reviews

Here are sixteen fundamental principles I used for all test reviews:

- Plan your studies so that your knowledge, understanding, and memory of the test material peak on the day *and* at the time of the exam.
- Don't underestimate an exam and under-prepare. This is a willful sacrifice of points and personal progress—not a good choice. It's better to be over-prepared than under-prepared.
- These are the worst times to be lazy, casual, disinterested, to make excuses about being tired, or to otherwise rationalize not remaining focused on your review.
- Thorough exam preparations always have priority over leisure activities.
- The more organized your review methodology, the less time and energy you'll waste piecing random elements together while studying. Strong organizational skills allow for clearer memory. Exams are often a race against time. Thorough preparation not only gives you the knowledge but also helps you apply it more quickly and accurately during the test.

- Leave as little to chance as possible. There is no greater insurance for exams than knowing the right answers. You'll be more confident going into the test, and less at the mercy of guessing.

- Aim to score 100%. Striving for it pushes you to study as well as you can. With that, you can be content with whatever score you get knowing it was the highest within your abilities. (If you're curious about whether I practiced what I preach, I scored 100 on one course's semester cumulative point total, 17 foreign-language quizzes, 5 homework assignments, 3 midterms, 1 term paper, and on 1 final exam on which this was the high score among 138 enrolled students—all based on an absolute scale, not a curve.)

- Study in stages. Pace yourself and digest measured doses of test information. Each stage should be manageable, not overwhelming. Several sessions are superior to a single cram.

- Each review session should coincide with your peak hours of concentration in a day.

- Allow yourself adequate time for review on each of these crucial days. Don't rush your sessions; don't cram.

- Find the best method that helps you absorb and retain the information needed. This includes time of day, time for each review session, site of review, and number of days leading up to the test.

- Select study place, position, and environment to foster concentration so that everything in your mind is reduced to just *you and your notes.*

- Eliminate distractions during reviews: no TV, radio, music, or noise from people and vehicular traffic. Exception: some students study better when they have background music or use headphones. As always, choose the method that maximizes your test preparations. But be aware that extraneous noise may impede concentration. In a comfortable position, focus on two things: you and the notes. I preferred studying in absolute silence, such as in an isolated section of the library or at home alone. Distractions include interruptions that disrupt your rhythm and rob you of time. During reviews, I would even turn off the phone ringer and let the answering machine record messages I'd later address. Cell phones and pagers are also a source of interruption during these times.

- Take breaks when you *really* need them. Highlighting, reviewing texts and notes, and compiling summaries takes time and concentration. When your brain has reached the saturation point, give yourself a break, nap, or a short walk for relief. If you find yourself in a rut, don't stay in it for long; do something to pull yourself out.

- When pressures mount, keep your composure, sense of humor, and a positive attitude. Becoming your best in anything is hard work. Have faith in the strategies you've constructed and follow through to the end.

- Be sure you have your test materials packed in your bag the night before, or double-check before leaving home. I've seen students running around class asking others for blue books, #2 pencils, or standard test sheets as teachers were on the verge of distributing our exams. The last thing you need is to be desperate on test day. Don't wager your score on luck and charity.

When Teachers Give a Study Guide

Forewarned forearmed.
—Miguel de Cervantes, 1547–1616[53]

Some teachers don't hand out study guides for a test. Because you don't know what topics will be omitted, you may actually study some information that won't be on the test. This is necessary if you want to maximize your chances for scoring well.

However, some teachers do supply handouts prior to a test that list certain topics from each chapter to study. One of my study guides for a first midterm contained 120 topics, some of which related to microscopic cycles and processes. As extensive and comprehensive as it may be, a study guide gives you greater certainty. You can focus your energies and attention on specific items and avoid memorizing unnecessary information. Study guide topics should be cross-referenced with your notebook and text when you prepare for exams.

Some teachers verbally disclose the exam breakdown beforehand. Write this in your notebook, especially noting point breakdown per section. Give review priority to the areas worth the greatest number of points, followed by others in descending order. For example, one class gave the following exam breakdown for 100 points total:

30 multiple-choice questions   (1 point each = 30 points)
25 fill-in questions   (2 points each = 50 points)
5 word definitions   (4 points each = 20 points)

I gave first priority to the word definitions, second to fill-ins. Though the test only included 5 word definitions, there were 71 words on the vocabulary list given by the teacher. This required planning well in advance. Both quality and quantity were needed for an A score. Each definition had to be 25 to 30 words. But my thorough definitions also prepared me for the exam's multiple-choice and fill-in questions.

Sample questions, practice problems, and study guides given by your teacher increase your chances of scoring well on exams. It is critical to score 100% on sample questions or problems without looking on the answer sheet. For questions you get wrong during practice, by all means learn and understand how to arrive at the right answer. If you can't understand these by yourself, seek the help of your teacher, teaching assistant, or even a classmate. Whether it's calculating the rate of return on Common Stockholders' Equity or using a Punnet square to forecast genetic characteristics of human offspring, don't walk into a test without knowing how to determine the right answers.

Mark Your Notebook for Exam Sections

Mark the beginning and end of each test section to be studied in your notebook (see Figure 9). For added efficiency, you could paperclip the previous test section to avoid flipping through pages needlessly. A course can have two to six exams in a semester. Dating your lecture notes will help you refer to a particular item when you need clarification from the teacher before an exam.

Notebook Highlighting

Imagine reading every page of your notes, word for word, top to bottom, multiplied by however many classes you're taking. Time and energy are wasted sifting through essential and nonessential information. Because you will be reviewing lots of notes, every time-saving measure (without compromising learning quality) adds up. Not everything in your notebook will be required for an exam. So why waste time reading over unnecessary parts?

A solution is to reread and highlight your notebook, which

- Gives you instant readouts of what's needed for reviews at a glance;
- Makes it faster to study only what's needed; and
- Clarifies your memory by eliminating excess information.

Depending on circumstances, highlighted sections can vary from almost an entire page to a few lines or even a few words per page. At other times, you may skip entire pages. Whatever the case, the aim is the same: highlight only what's needed for your learning and test preparation, however slight or extensive. Use care when highlighting. Concentration is important at this stage because you will read only these highlighted sections for your exam reviews (see Figures 15–18).

Draw an arrow in the margin with your highlighter next to important points (see Figure 16).

Cross Out Nonessential Pages or Sections

For purposes of the test, some large sections or whole pages of your notes may be unnecessary to review. Give yourself an immediately visible sign that this page or section has been eliminated. Using your highlighter, draw a bold diagonal line through the entire section or page. As you flip through your pages for exam study, you'll know that these portions are to be skipped. As long as you've paid special attention during rereading, you can be sure that these skipped sections or pages were not an oversight (see Figures 15, 18, and 20).

Exam Reviews: When and How Much?

To avoid repeating the follies of my freshman year, I first experimented with studying for a test one week in advance, but started to forget the material after several days. I then fine-tuned test preparation to span the three days

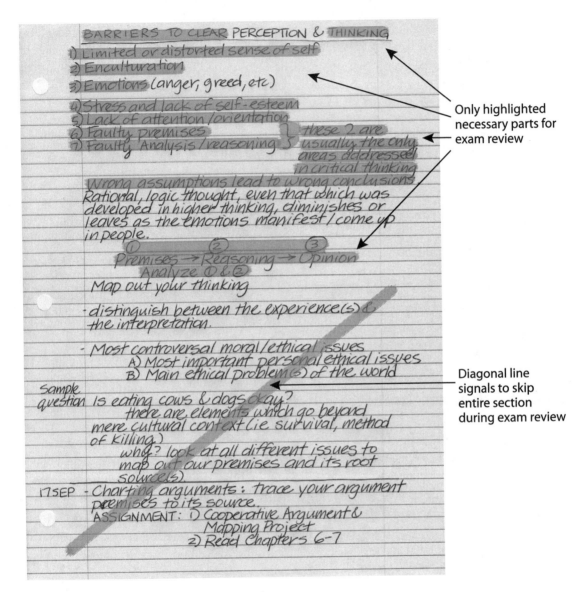

BARRIERS TO CLEAR PERCEPTION & THINKING
1) Limited or distorted sense of self
2) Enculturation
3) Emotions (anger, greed, etc)
4) Stress and lack of self-esteem
5) Lack of attention /orientation
6) Faulty premises
7) Faulty Analysis /reasoning } these 2 are usually the only areas addressed in critical thinking

Wrong assumptions lead to wrong conclusions
Rational, logic thought, even that which was developed in higher thinking, diminishes or leaves as the emotions manifest /come up in people.
① Premises → ② Reasoning → ③ Opinion
Analyze ① & ②
Map out your thinking

- distinguish between the experience(s) & the interpretation.

- Most controversial moral/ethical issues
    A) Most important personal ethical issues
    B) Main ethical problem(s) of the world
Sample question Is eating cows & dogs okay?
        there are elements which go beyond mere cultural context (ie survival, method of killing.)
        why? look at all different issues to map out our premises and its root source(s).
17SEP - Charting arguments: trace your argument premises to its source.
    ASSIGNMENT: 1) Cooperative Argument & Mapping Project
            2) Read Chapters 6-7

Only highlighted necessary parts for exam review

Diagonal line signals to skip entire section during exam review

Figure 15: Notes highlighted for exam review

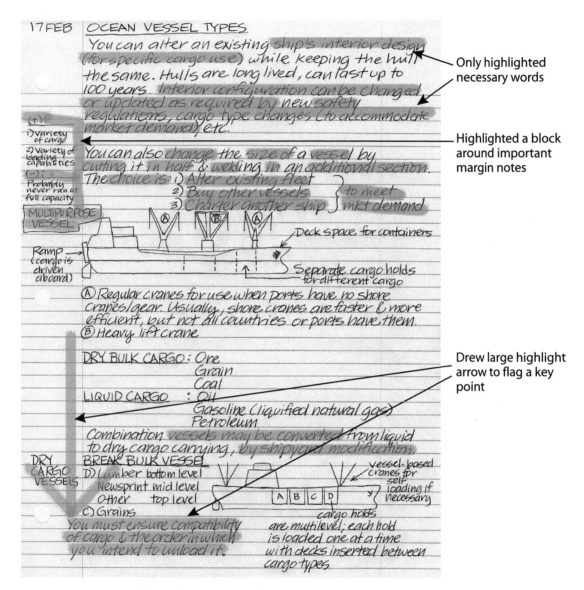

17 FEB   OCEAN VESSEL TYPES

You can alter an existing ship's interior design (for specific cargo use) while keeping the hull the same. Hulls are long lived, can last up to 100 years. Interior configuration can be changed or updated as required by new safety regulations, cargo type changes (to accommodate market demand), etc.

— Only highlighted necessary words

(+)
1) variety of cargo
2) variety of loading capabilities

(−):
Probably never run at full capacity

— Highlighted a block around important margin notes

You can also change the size of a vessel by cutting it in half & welding in an additional section. The choice is: 1) Alter existing fleet
2) Buy other vessels } to meet
3) Charter another ship } mkt demand

MULTIPURPOSE VESSEL

Ramp (cargo is driven aboard)

Deck space for containers

Separate cargo holds for different cargo

Ⓐ Regular cranes for use when ports have no shore cranes/gear. Usually, shore cranes are faster & more efficient, but not all countries or ports have them.
Ⓑ Heavy lift crane

DRY BULK CARGO: Ore
                Grain
                Coal
LIQUID CARGO   : Oil
                Gasoline (liquified natural gas)
                Petroleum

Combination vessels may be converted from liquid to dry cargo carrying, by shipyard modification.

— Drew large highlight arrow to flag a key point

DRY CARGO VESSELS

BREAK BULK VESSEL
D) Lumber bottom level
   Newsprint mid level
   Other   top level
C) Grains

vessel-based cranes for self loading if necessary

A B C D

cargo holds are multilevel; each hold is loaded one at a time with decks inserted between cargo types

You must ensure compatibility of cargo & the order in which you intend to unload it.

Figure 16: Notes highlighted for exam review

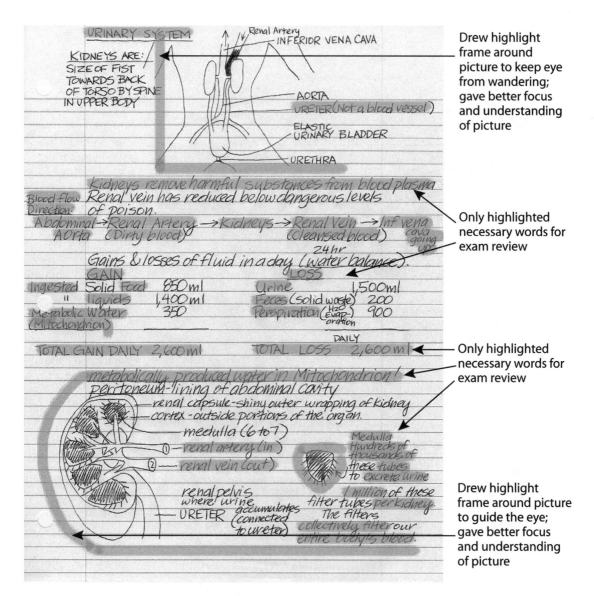

Figure 17: Notes highlighted for exam review

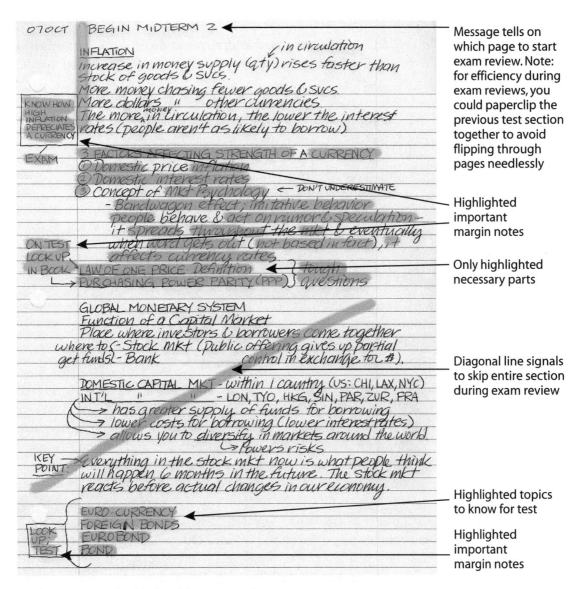

07 OCT | BEGIN MIDTERM 2 ←

INFLATION
in circulation
Increase in money supply (qty) rises faster than stock of goods & svcs.
More money chasing fewer goods & svcs.
More dollars " other currencies.
The more *money* in circulation, the lower the interest rates (people aren't as likely to borrow)

KNOW HOW HIGH INFLATION DEPRECIATES A CURRENCY

EXAM

3 FACTORS AFFECTING STRENGTH OF A CURRENCY
① Domestic price inflation
② Domestic interest rates
③ Concept of Mkt Psychology ← DON'T UNDERESTIMATE
   - Bandwagon effect; imitative behavior
     people behave & act on rumor & speculation
     it spreads throughout the mkt & eventually
     when word gets out (not based in fact), it
     affects currency rates

ON TEST
LOOK UP.
IN BOOK — LAW OF ONE PRICE Definition ← tough
   └→ PURCHASING POWER PARITY (PPP) } questions

GLOBAL MONETARY SYSTEM
Function of a Capital Market
Place where investors & borrowers come together
where to ┌ Stock mkt (public offering gives up partial
get funds└ Bank   control in exchange for $).

DOMESTIC CAPITAL MKT - within 1 country (US: CHI, LAX, NYC)
INT'L   "   "   - LON, TYO, HKG, SIN, PAR, ZUR, FRA
   ┌→ has greater supply of funds for borrowing
   ┌→ lower costs for borrowing (lower interest rates)
   ┌→ allows you to diversify in markets around the world
              └→ Lowers risks

KEY
POINT — Everything in the stock mkt now is what people think
will happen 6 months in the future. The stock mkt
reacts before actual changes in our economy.

EURO CURRENCY ←
FOREIGN BONDS
LOOK   EUROBOND
UP.
TEST   BOND

Message tells on which page to start exam review. Note: for efficiency during exam reviews, you could paperclip the previous test section together to avoid flipping through pages needlessly

Highlighted important margin notes

Only highlighted necessary parts

Diagonal line signals to skip entire section during exam review

Highlighted topics to know for test

Highlighted important margin notes

Figure 18: Notes highlighted for exam review
Highlighting included important margin notes.

up to and sometimes including the day of the exam (see the following). I used this 3-Day Method for all my midterm and final exams, both abroad and here in the States. It's also derivative of the goal-setting model described in Chapter 3:

Important: It is up to you to determine the *exact number of days* leading up to a test, which gives you optimum results.

Step 1. Start preparing three days prior to the exam.
Step 2. Divide your notes into three portions.
Step 3. Study one section each day, leading up to the exam day.
Step 4. During the second and third study sessions, review the notes from the previous day.

In other words:

Day 1: Review portion 1
Day 2: Review portions 1 and 2
Day 3: Review portions 1, 2, and 3 (exam may be late in the day on Day 3 or on Day 4, if the test is given in the early morning.)

If an exam was given in the early morning, I began preparation three days before because I don't study well at the crack of dawn. If the exam was held in the afternoon and I had no commitments for several hours beforehand, I started my review two days prior; the third and last study session was on the day of the exam. Experiment to see what works best for you.

Each study session will vary depending on the total length of your notes for a given exam. For example, my first biology midterm notes spanned thirty-four (seventeen double-sided) pages. This translated into reviewing roughly eleven pages per session. Other classes yielded as little as twenty-one pages of notes for a midterm, which meant that I only needed to study seven pages per session. Generally, exam review portions were separated into whole lecture or chapter increments.

Remain single-minded during exam reviews. Don't rush a session or be concerned about targeting a specific number of hours. As long as you continue absorbing information in a given review portion, keep going; don't break your rhythm. During intensive exam preparations, my breakfast, lunch, and restroom leisure reading was replaced by reviewing notes.

Strange as it may sound, whatever technique enhances your exam perform-ance and gets you the A is fine as long as it's honest.

When your mind is saturated, take a break. Return when you're refreshed. I took breaks at no particular set interval, just whenever I reached saturation point. Different days and subjects' intensities saw differ-ent endurance spans. Breaks can be relatively short or long but only up to the minute when you're ready to go back for more. If your absorption pat-tern responds better to a more regimented method, you can divide a given day's study session into threes and take your breaks in between (another example of the goal-setting model). Whatever the case, ensure that you complete the day's portion on that particular day. *Don't defer one day's study portion to the next day.*

Another key point to this 3-Day Method is not to subject your mind to new stimuli immediately afterwards or upon taking breaks. I would take a short walk at home, around the dorm floor, or up and down the hallway to let things sink in. (Some of the best results were achieved by taking naps or going to sleep after study sessions.) But I wouldn't immediately read aca-demic information, watch TV, look at mail order catalogs, phone someone, browse the Internet, check my e-mails, go out with friends, engage in con-versation, balance my checkbook, or even look at the homework for another class. My feeling is that instant exposure to such stimuli interferes with absorption of test material. I'm not suggesting you can't do anything at all, but merely that you give yourself a break for however long you need until you *feel* your review information has sunk in, and only then go about activities that could actually interfere with your digesting and retaining the information.

The 3-Day Method isn't the primary basis for your learning of course material, which takes place on a day-to-day basis when you read your texts, go to class, ask questions, listen to discussions, and take good notes. In fact, 3-Day exam reviews are just that: reviews and occasional clarification of a few gray areas. But several hours per session was nevertheless the norm for me!

A trickier juggling act occurs when two midterms or final exams are sched-uled on the same day. I once had two midterms within two and a half hours of each other. The final exams for these classes were only 15 minutes apart: one ended at 11:45 a.m. and the other began at noon. There was barely enough time to walk over to the next building to find a good seat, let alone have lunch. A young student with a high metabolism and low body fat will feel awful after more than four hours without food. A couple of athletic energy bars and some bottled water took the rough edges off the empty stomach. You need to be your sharpest on test day and cannot afford distraction or mood changes due to hunger.

On Days 1, 2, and 3, I had to divide my time and mental energies between two sets of exam reviews. This can be done, provided you allow yourself plenty of quiet time in a conducive atmosphere where everything in your mind is reduced to only you and your notes. Besides giving yourself the time needed for each subject, ensure that you take adequate breaks between the two. Conduct your reviews during hours when your mind is clearest. To separate the course information better, I would study one in the morning and the other in the afternoon or evening. In between parallel exam reviews, I took a refresher break or nap. Then I made sure I returned to complete the study portion that day.

Whenever possible, the less your mind must retain during an exam, the better. If I had two exams on the same day, and if there were several hours or more between the two tests, I would schedule my third study section for exam 2 after finishing exam 1:

Table 6 Review timeline for tests administered on same day

Day before Test		Test Day		
a.m.	p.m.	a.m.	—Several hours—	p.m.
Review portion 3 for Test 1	Review portion 2 for Test 2	Take Test 1	Review portion 3 for Test 2	Take Test 2

This way, your mind isn't forced to retain as much information at one time.

There are times when your exam preparations require notebook, handouts, and text review. When reviewing the textbook and handouts for exams, read only your highlighted areas. If there's any disparity between your notes and the textbook on a specific topic, clarify this with the teacher before the exam. If you discover the discrepancy late and there's no time for clarification, when in doubt, follow your textbook. Note, however, that there may be instances where instructors test you on lecture information that doesn't appear in your text. As your text may not help in this case, it's important that you take solid notes during lectures.

For comprehensive final exams, I used the same 3-Day Method. When the total amount of information is too much to review in three days, you can break a final exam review into four days instead, to yield smaller, more digestible portions. You know you're ready for the test when you can mentally recite your notes while you're lying in bed. When you can recall the relevant study material for whatever topic pops into your mind, you're fully prepared.

Defer going out to have fun until after you've mastered a given review section. It is important to put the brakes on yourself when temptations arise. You may have the urge to go out when friends ask, have a go at a favorite video game, watch a new show with dorm mates, or go to someone's party. It's very easy to say, "I'll do it just this once." Actually, such deferral will probably not be "just once" but repeated. *Sacrificing a grade or the maximum number of points you can earn isn't worth one night of fun.* If you're poised to get an A, why quit your reviewing and get a B for the sake of going out one night? If you're on the verge of a B, why settle for a C simply to play a video game? A video game is seldom one's intellectual zenith. If you're on your way to a C, why risk a D for the sake of a party? Fun as it may be at the time, such imprudent practices confine your learning and lower your grade-point average. Inopportune timing of fun curtails your growth and progress when it really counts. You can still have fun— just wait until you've thoroughly completed each review session or blitzed your exam. This same policy applies when you have a heavy-duty term paper, report, or presentation deadline looming on the horizon.

Know All Formulas by Memory

For closed-book exams, memorize your formulas. Consolidate all formulas for a given test into one set of handwritten notes. Use this list for your study guide of formulas. During review sessions, double-check yourself by writing out all formulas from memory (see Figure 19). Write them again and again until you have instant recall. Know how to use them to arrive at the correct

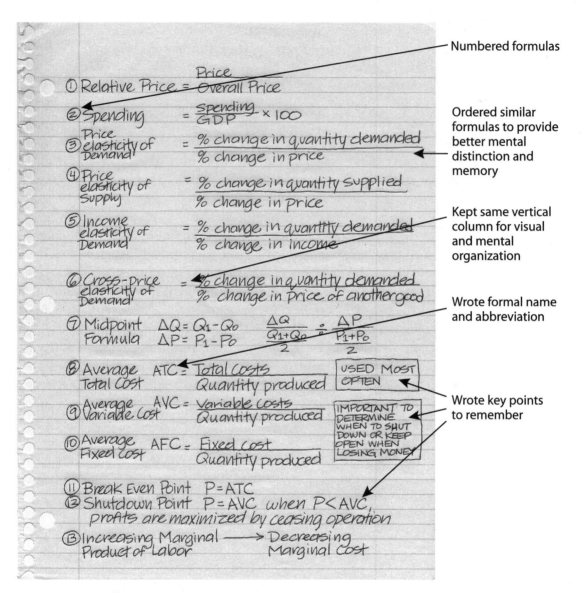

Numbered formulas

Ordered similar formulas to provide better mental distinction and memory

Kept same vertical column for visual and mental organization

Wrote formal name and abbreviation

Wrote key points to remember

① Relative Price = $\dfrac{\text{Price}}{\text{Overall Price}}$

② Spending = $\dfrac{\text{Spending}}{\text{GDP}} \times 100$

③ Price elasticity of Demand = $\dfrac{\text{\% change in quantity demanded}}{\text{\% change in price}}$

④ Price elasticity of Supply = $\dfrac{\text{\% change in quantity supplied}}{\text{\% change in price}}$

⑤ Income elasticity of Demand = $\dfrac{\text{\% change in quantity demanded}}{\text{\% change in income}}$

⑥ Cross-price elasticity of Demand = $\dfrac{\text{\% change in quantity demanded}}{\text{\% change in price of another good}}$

⑦ Midpoint Formula $\Delta Q = Q_1 - Q_0$ $\Delta P = P_1 - P_0$ $\dfrac{\Delta Q}{\frac{Q_1+Q_0}{2}} \div \dfrac{\Delta P}{\frac{P_1+P_0}{2}}$

⑧ Average Total Cost ATC = $\dfrac{\text{Total Costs}}{\text{Quantity produced}}$ [USED MOST OFTEN]

⑨ Average Variable Cost AVC = $\dfrac{\text{Variable Costs}}{\text{Quantity produced}}$ [IMPORTANT TO DETERMINE WHEN TO SHUT DOWN OR KEEP OPEN WHEN LOSING MONEY]

⑩ Average Fixed Cost AFC = $\dfrac{\text{Fixed Cost}}{\text{Quantity produced}}$

⑪ Break Even Point P = ATC

⑫ Shutdown Point P = AVC when P < AVC, profits are maximized by ceasing operation

⑬ Increasing Marginal Product of Labor ⟶ Decreasing Marginal Cost

Figure 19: Consolidated notes for exam review
Consolidated formulas for a given test in list form to aid memory. Ordered similar
formulas consecutively to distinguish them better. Also wrote important axioms.
Above information taken from John B. Taylor, *Principles of Microeconomics*
(Houghton Mifflin, 1995).

answers. Once you begin the exam, immediately write out all the formulas on scratch paper or on the inside cover of your blue book. This reduces your burden of retaining information during the test, gives you an immediate reference for your formulas, and allows you to focus more on answering questions.

What If a Test Topic Appears in Different Places of Your Notebook?

There will be cases when information on a certain exam topic appears on different pages in your notebook. You need to keep track of such dispersed information. First, find and count the number of places where a given topic appears in your notebook. On a blank spot next to the information, write your topic and number with your highlighter. For example, in one of my classes, the subject "Service Contracts" appeared five times in my lecture notes. Using a highlighter, I wrote in the margin "SVC CONTRACT 1 of 5" the first time it occurred; "SVC CONTRACT 2 of 5" where it next appeared, and so on (see Figure 20). This helps you track and mentally combine dispersed notes needed for your test. Alternatively, you could consolidate notes on the subject onto a separate sheet of paper to supplement your reviews. You can then cross out the dispersed sections in your notebook with a highlighter to avoid duplicating your efforts.

When a Test Includes Many Chapters That Weren't Covered in Class

If you've kept up with your text readings, preparation is a matter of rereading your highlighted sections. I recall one emergency. In one course, many of our chapters hadn't been covered in lectures but nonetheless would be included on our exam. Because we learned this very late in the semester, I didn't have time to highlight every chapter carefully, break, and review as I normally would. In response to the short notice, I used a different approach. The technique requires a bookmark and serious concentration because you'll only make one pass at compiling your review notes:

Step 1. Have a notebook or loose binder paper alongside as you read the chapters not covered in class.

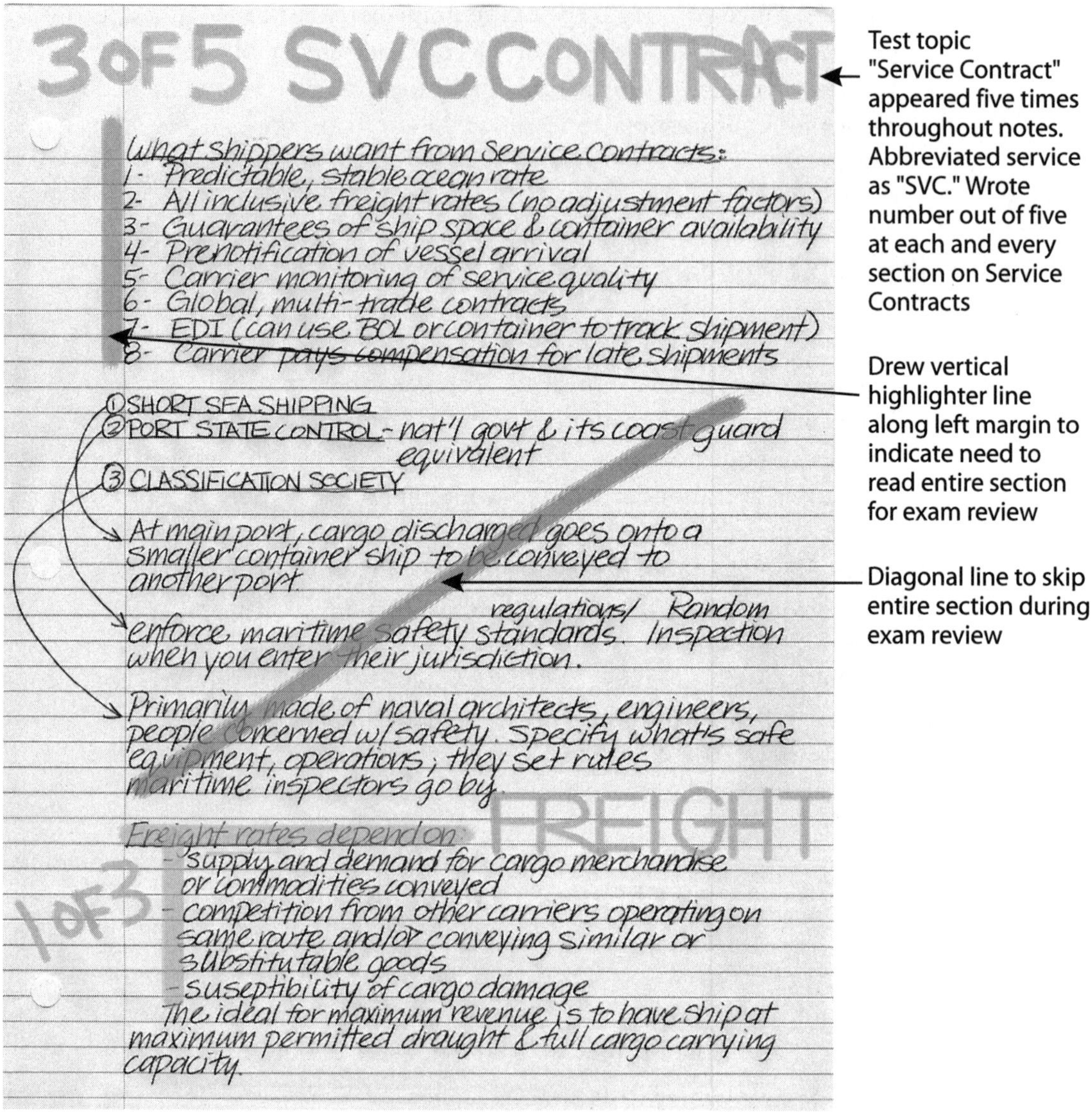

What shippers want from Service contracts:
1- Predictable, stable ocean rate
2- All inclusive freight rates (no adjustment factors)
3- Guarantees of ship space & container availability
4- Prenotification of vessel arrival
5- Carrier monitoring of service quality
6- Global, multi-trade contracts
7- EDI (can use BOL or container to track shipment)
8- Carrier pays compensation for late shipments

① SHORT SEA SHIPPING
② PORT STATE CONTROL - nat'l govt & its coast guard
                          equivalent
③ CLASSIFICATION SOCIETY

→ At main port, cargo discharged goes onto a
smaller container ship to be conveyed to
another port

→ enforce maritime safety standards. Inspection
when you enter their jurisdiction.   regulations/ Random
                                    Inspection

→ Primarily made of naval architects, engineers,
people concerned w/safety. Specify what's safe
equipment, operations; they set rules
maritime inspectors go by.

Freight rates depend on:
  - supply and demand for cargo merchandise
   or commodities conveyed
  - competition from other carriers operating on
   same route and/or conveying similar or
   substitutable goods
  - suseptibility of cargo damage
  The ideal for maximum revenue is to have ship at
maximum permitted draught & full cargo carrying
capacity.

Figure 20: Use of highlighter to track test topics dispersed throughout notebook

Test topic "Service Contract" appeared five times throughout notes. Abbreviated service as "SVC." Wrote number out of five at each and every section on Service Contracts

Drew vertical highlighter line along left margin to indicate need to read entire section for exam review

Diagonal line to skip entire section during exam review

Step 2. As you read and comprehend important points, write the topic name, its description, and main points in your own words.

Step 3. If using loose papers, staple them together.

Step 4. Use these notes for your exam review. Like your essay exam notes and vocabulary list, you'll remember the information more easily because you've written it yourself. (If the teacher has told you what topics to study for the exam, you can still use this same technique.)

When the Teacher Gives a Study Guide but the Test Covers an Entire Textbook

The goal here is to avoid flipping through pages too much in search of study topics:

Step 1. Find the topics that your teacher has specified.

Step 2. Using Post-it Brand Tape Flags or the like, flag the text pages' outside margins.

Step 3. All tape flags should be the same color and size. (If using different colors enhances your performance, experiment to find your optimum combination).

Step 4. On these tape flags, write the name of the topic. With these tabs you can flip instantly to the correct page without needless fumbling (see Figure 21). Tape flags are better here than paper Post-it notes because tape flags are more resistant to curling, keeping your label notes visible.

Step 5. Align your tape flags along your outside page margins, starting from top to bottom.

Step 6. Position the tape flags so they are aligned with each other, and print clearly and neatly so the topics are readily visible and easy to read. Use the same abbreviations or shorthand as in your notes.

Step 7. Reread your highlighted portions on the relevant pages, or apply the technique described in the preceding section.

Step 8. This page-flagging system can also help you prep for open-book exams.

Figure 21: Text prepared with tape flags for open-book exam
Used Post-it Brand tape flags to mark pages with main test topics in case needed during actual exam. Tape flagging saves time during exam because you don't flip back and forth between the table of contents or index and your page of reference. (Original topic was Ocean Shipping.)

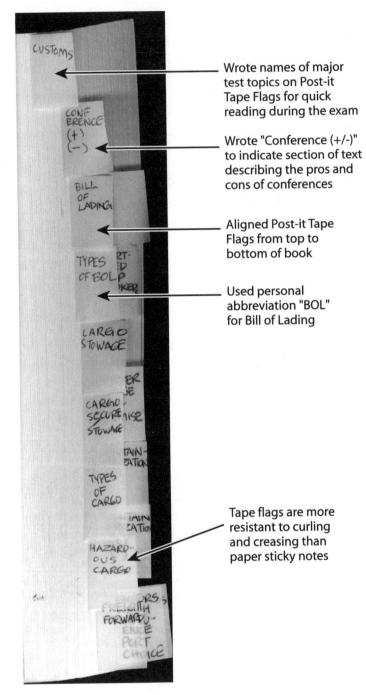

Wrote names of major test topics on Post-it Tape Flags for quick reading during the exam

Wrote "Conference (+/-)" to indicate section of text describing the pros and cons of conferences

Aligned Post-it Tape Flags from top to bottom of book

Used personal abbreviation "BOL" for Bill of Lading

Tape flags are more resistant to curling and creasing than paper sticky notes

Preparing Your Text for an Open-Book Exam

One of my professors recalled a former student opening his textbook for the first time during a final exam. There was the sound of a new book's spine and pages creaking from expansion. This is far too late to do well on any exam. Generally, your book is a back-up reference but not a substitute for prior preparation and review. You want to minimize time consumed by on-the-spot research. An exception is when you have an enormously thick text or a generous amount of time to complete the test:

1. Begin preparations several days in advance.
2. Use the tape-flagging system described in the preceding section. Advance review means you won't be nervous as time elapses during the test because you'll already be familiar with your information.

If your textbook is extremely thick and you are given lots of time to complete the exam, knowing where to find your answers in the book is more important than memorizing all your test information. One of my courses used a 561-page reader. I had already highlighted the chapters included in our assigned reading. If you find yourself in a similar situation, try this approach:

Step 1. Use paper Post-it notes here because their surface area is larger. You'll need to avoid creasing and curling these paper tabs.

Step 2. All Post-it notes used for a given textbook should be the same size (see Figure 22). I typically used yellow Post-it notes throughout. However, if color coding with several colors improves your performance, experiment to find your optimum combination.

Step 3. Tab only those pages that you feel are genuinely important. Write the main point for that page so that during the exam you won't waste time rereading page after page to locate your answers—you read what's written on your tabs. If this isn't sufficient, simply list the topics on the Post-it note and re-skim the text page to locate specifics during the test. During reviews, use your highlighter and draw arrows to important points in the margins. During the test, your eye will be drawn instantly to these areas on a given page.

Step 4. Write the page number in the top left corner of each Post-it note to safeguard against accidental removal.

Step 5. The message on each Post-it note can be your own summary sentence, the

Figure 22: Text prepared with Post-it tabs for open-book exam.
Gives immediate access to pages with main exam subjects. Eliminates flipping between table of contents or index and page of reference. Saves time during exam.

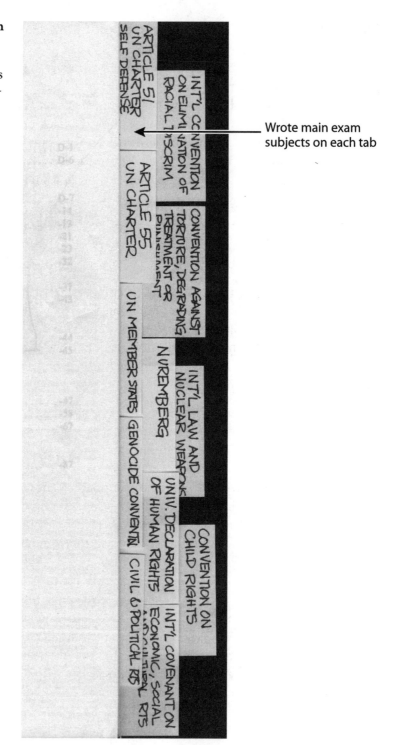

Wrote main exam subjects on each tab

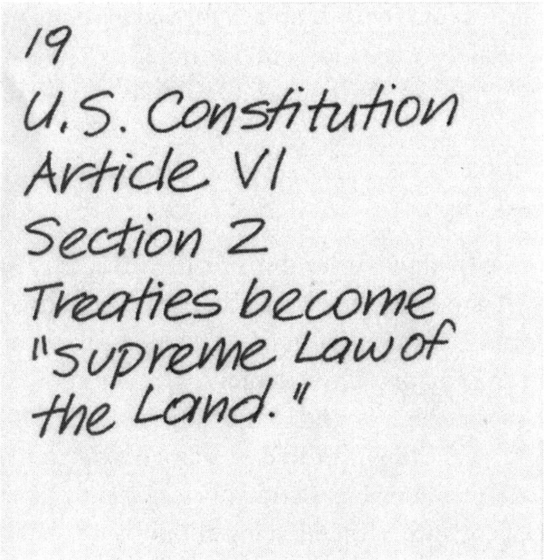

19
U.S. Constitution
Article VI
Section 2
Treaties become
"Supreme Law of
the Land."

375
PROP 209 VIOLATES
① Int'l Convention on
  Elimination of All Forms
  of Racial Discrimination
② United Nations Charter
③ Int'l Covenant on Civil
  and Political Rights
④ Universal Declaration
  of Human Rights
⑤ Beijing Declaration
  and Platform For Action

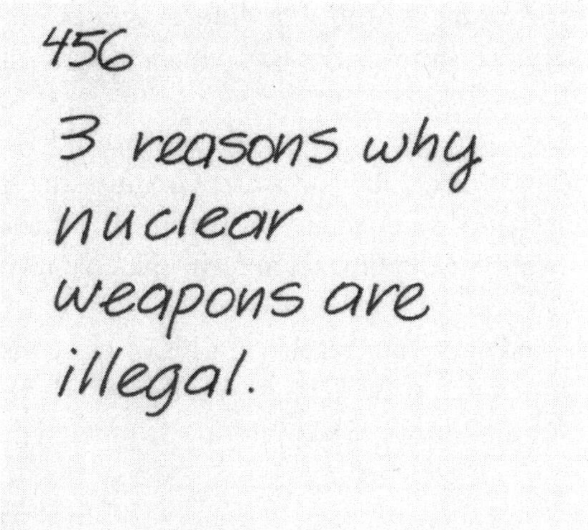

456
3 reasons why
nuclear
weapons are
illegal.

Figure 23: Examples of Post-it notes prepared for open-book exam
- Text page number written at top left of each Post-it note in case of accidental removal.
- Each Post-it note contains important message for relevant text page.
  (Original subject was Peace Law and Human Rights.)

central message of that page, an axiomatic remark, an author's key point, or other information you deem essential for the exam (see Figure 23).

Step 6. Not every highlighted page will be needed for the test. Omit flags on these pages.

Step 7. During the test, first locate your topic in the index or table of contents, flip to that section, and read your Post-it tab.

The table of contents of my 561-page reader did not list case studies that were on the test. In the last class before the exam, I had asked the professor to let us use our case handout because it contained page numbers of where cases appeared in our reader. The professor denied permission. The remedy was either to write the case names and page numbers on the reader's inside cover or to use a tab system with the case names written on them. I suppose I could have torn out the reader's table of contents to have an immediate reference in front of me rather than having to flip pages back and forth. In hindsight, this would have saved time. However, since we had several hours for the exam, the thought didn't occur to me then. This is an option you can explore should you find yourself with greater time constraints.

Whether or not this page-flagging method would violate a teacher's classroom policy depends on the particular circumstances. If it's an open-book, open-note test, I don't see any violation. If it's an open-book, no-notes test, then using flags could, technically, be a violation because they contain a student's notes, though very slight.

You could privately ask your teacher for his or her consent, well before the test. Should your request be denied, you'll have adequate time to prepare a substitute strategy at home so as not to be put at a disadvantage during the exam.

Writing Study Notes Based on Topics Disclosed by Your Teacher

When writing a new set of notes specifically for exam reviews:

1. Compile your notes a week before the test;
2. Staple these into a single consolidated set; and
3. Study these notes using the 3-Day Method leading up to the exam.

The first time a teacher gave me a study guide, I wrote my notes on the study guide itself. By keeping my writing small, I squeezed my review notes onto one or two pages, thereby giving the illusion of less information to study. However, in subsequent classes this became impossible due to the sheer volume of information to study. You'll remember your own study notes more easily than other material because they're written in your own words—an extension of your mind and thoughts—especially if you write economically without compromising content.

Suppose a teacher gives you a massive vocabulary list prior to an exam. You can't predict which words will not be on the test. Therefore, you'll need to know definitions for every word. And some exams require definitions to have a certain minimum length:

1. A week prior to the exam, use your teacher's word list to write your own definitions. This allows enough time to ask the teacher about any words with which you have difficulty.
2. Use your lecture notes, text, or class handouts as references.
3. Ensure that each definition fulfills the minimum length set by your teacher.
4. Ensure that the quality of your definition is commensurate with your target grade.
5. Writing the definitions in your own words makes it easier for you to remember them up to, and during, the exam.
6. Use the final three days before the exam for reviewing (using the 3-Day Method), not compiling.
    (A similar procedure can be followed for compiling other exam study notes).

Another class gave four midterm exams with the following profiles:

Table 7 Sample profile of four mixed–configuration exams

Question Type	Test 1	Test 2	Test 3	Test 4
Multiple choice	5 ($\times$ 2 points)	10 ($\times$ 2 points)	5 ($\times$ 5 points)	10 ($\times$ 3 points)
Definitions	—	10 ($\times$ 2 points)	3 ($\times$ 5 points)	5 ($\times$ 4 points)
Fill-in questions	15 ($\times$ 2 points)	10 ($\times$ 2 points)	5 ($\times$ 6 points)	—
Essay questions	3 ($\times$ 20 points)	2 ($\times$ 20 points)	3 ($\times$ 10 points)	2 ($\times$ 25 points)

Essay questions were by far the biggest concern. With the exception of Test 3, they constituted 60%, 40%, or 50% of each test score. However, these exam breakdowns weren't disclosed to us beforehand. Our study guides indicated there wouldn't be any dramatic changes to test topics, but we couldn't know what mix of questions would appear or, more importantly, which topics would be selected for our essays. The test patterns changed.

We only knew what we observed—namely, that each test was different but per-question point-worth typically increased, except for essays on Test 3. Because of the changes, the only way to prepare thoroughly was to know the information inside-out. With the exception of the multiple-choice sections, which constituted only 10% to 30% of our total test scores, questions could not be answered accurately by guessing.

Essay questions required detailed answers. Questions ranged from how to prepare for and conduct formal performance appraisals and interviews to the eight factors influencing job satisfaction (both what and why) to describing five interpersonal skills that team leaders need for conflict resolution in the workplace. Other questions required applying our answers to examples, describing how our decisions affected other departments, or providing hypothetical situations for each topic. To prepare thoroughly meant extensive memorization combined with grasping how many parts of a whole were interrelated. I couldn't predict which of the 99 to 132 topics appearing on our study guides would appear on tests, so I had to know all of them.

When writing my notes, I preferred to begin the descriptions on the same line as the name of the study topic. I also wrote the chapter number in the left margin, on the same line as the first topic for that chapter. This produced an illusion of less information to study and memorize, making overall review less psychologically intimidating. An exception is when a vertical format list enhances your efficiency. The total number of pages of notes you write should not be an objective in itself. It wasn't unusual for my test notes to span up to thirteen pages (six and a half papers with double-sided writing).

When Essay Test Topics Are Disclosed Beforehand and You Can Choose Among Them

This type of exam is a blessing because it involves greater certainty of content. You can focus solely on specific topics without studying superfluous information. You have control over what you write. You know exactly how much time will be allotted for your test. The key is to write everything that needs to be said within your time restrictions.

I didn't highlight my notebook for this type of exam. Instead, I used my lecture notes and textbook as the bases for writing a separate set of summary notes, which were then used exclusively for review.

The gist of this approach is the sequence: choose the topics, write up a set of notes based on lecture notes and textbook, edit these notes, memorize them, practice writing them from memory until you can do so in their entirety and without hesitation, and then repeat this at exam time, if not verbatim, then tailored to the specific question. Here's how:

Step 1. As with any essay exam, <u>ask the teacher</u> beforehand in class <u>what criteria will earn your target grade</u>.

Step 2. In the class session before your test, <u>ask the teacher how much time he or she will give</u> for your exam.

Step 3. <u>Gauge your maximum time per question</u>. Divide the total test time by the number of questions you must answer. For example, suppose you have 50 minutes to answer three questions. Allowing lag time for reading your exam sheet and finding your target questions, you'll have about 15 minutes to answer each question.

Step 4. <u>Choose your test topics</u>. Write these on a blank sheet of paper.

Step 5. <u>Write out your own set of study notes</u>. This is usually the most time-consuming part of your exam preparation. These notes should be based on the criteria stated by your teacher. You may need to cross-reference lecture notes with highlighted text information. Write out the most important points for your first topic. Also, determine whether your answer requires a sample case or facts not highlighted in your textbook. If so, skim the text to find the needed information and integrate this into your study notes.

Step 6. <u>Repeat this for each subsequent topic</u> that you've selected for the exam.

Step 7. In writing this draft, <u>ensure good organization and depth</u>. You will notice ways of improving your first draft by changing choice of words or order of sentences, or by adding new sentences for clarity or transition.

Step 8. <u>Proofread and edit the draft for smoothness</u>; both form and content should be strong and clear. Ask yourself, "Does this answer read like the paper described by the teacher?" If not, improve on content, supporting data, depth, breadth, organization, or clarity, as applicable. Proofread and revise again.

Step 9. <u>Use this compilation exclusively for your exam review</u>.

Step 10. <u>Use a variation of the 3-Day Method</u> to prepare in stages for the test (see example later in this chapter).

Step 11. On each of the three days, <u>practice writing your answers from memory</u>. I don't like taking more time than necessary to do things, so this motivated me to concentrate and memorize faster. The rest is merely a matter of writing out your answer in legible form. Writing these notes repeatedly also helps you retain the information. During this test-of-memory stage, don't worry about timing yourself.

If answers per topic are very long, you can break each topic answer into three portions to give yourself more absorbable doses, taking short breaks in between.

If test questions have been disclosed prior to the exam, you'll just need to write your answers from memory, word for word, as you've practiced them at home. This should be easy because you simply repeat your review sessions. You know the exact question and have had time to construct a great answer outside of class. Assuming your essay meets your teacher's criteria, reconstructing it during the real test should yield you top scores. Accordingly, creating your answer will be the most critical part of your test preparation; the subsequent memorization is a matter of incidental mechanics.

If questions aren't disclosed beforehand, a top student prepares for that extra element of uncertainty. Even though a teacher may have given you a choice of topics, you can't know what questions he or she will pose. You may not necessarily be able to answer verbatim per your memorized notes. Hence, it's important not only to memorize your notes but to comprehend them all as well. A test question may call for a scenario analysis, a hypothetical situation involving you, or a discussion. To respond in kind, you need to know how to connect and relate your note information to suit the question. However, you will already have memorized the backbone of your information in detail, including key sentences and phrases. Thus you'll avoid losing time associated with impromptu essays, including recalling and organizing random pieces of information, ensuring adequate development of thoughts, wondering what information you've inadvertently omitted, and, if time runs out, the need to proofread.

Whether or not the questions are disclosed beforehand, your essay will be strong because you will have prepared and developed your thoughts and written, edited, and polished your essential sentences before the exam. You'll also have an advantage over classmates who don't do well at composing spontaneous, unedited essays under pressure.

Step 12. Once you're confident that you've memorized the information, <u>test yourself under the same time constraints set by your teacher</u>. From memory, write out your summary information of the exam topic. Have a digital watch on the table next to you. Give yourself exactly the same amount of time you'll have during the real exam. Be sure that your writing is neat and legible— writing that a teacher cannot read will compromise your grade. You may discover that writing within the time allotment is not always easy. Yes, my hand became tired from writing my notes over and over to get things right, but this was the way to ensure that I could condense all the needed information into the allotted exam time.

For example, let's assume you have three topics to answer. Ideally, before Day 1, write out summary notes for all topics. Edit and revise. Double-check accuracy, depth, organization, and grammar. This is predicated on your teacher telling you the exam topics more than three days prior to the test. Depending on when your teacher discloses the test topics, you may have to compile and practice your first review portion on Day 1. Then proceed as follows:

Day 1: Memorize. Practice writing out Topic 1's summary from memory. When done, proofread to see what mistakes or omissions occurred. Repeat. This writing from memory should be done at least three times. Keep practicing until you can write Topic 1's summary from memory without mistakes or hesitation, within 1/3 of your total exam time.

Day 2: Memorize Topic 2. Practice writing out Topics 1 and 2 from memory. Keep practicing until you can write Topics 1 and 2 summaries from memory without mistakes or hesitation, within 2/3 of your total exam time.

Day 3: Memorize Topic 3. Practice writing out summaries for Topics 1, 2, and 3 from memory. Keep practicing until you can write all three summaries from memory without mistakes or hesitation, within the total exam time.

If you know you'll have four essay questions, practice until you can write the answer to each one within 1/4 of your total exam time, if five questions, within 1/5 of the total time, and so on.

Review days should be consecutive. An exception would be if you prefer to break your preparations into four instead of three days total leading up to the exam. The first day would be spent compiling your summary notes and could be done anytime before Day 2. Days 2, 3, and 4 would be reserved for memorization, practice, and mock testing. Whatever the case, your final three days of preparation leading up to the test should always be consecutive.

During your mock tests, if you exceed the time allotment, you either need to write faster, consolidate or delete certain sentences, or further economize your wording. It saves time to use as few words as possible to answer a question in the same depth.

This type of preparation tests how good your memory is, reveals what you may have overlooked or need to reexamine, and helps you time your writing. If you finish writing well before the time expires, be sure you've included everything that needs to be covered for a good grade. Also, try to factor in enough time to proofread your paper. When you haven't made any mistakes or omissions and have finished within the time limit, you're ready for the test.

On the actual test, proofread your paper before handing it in. If you've accidentally omitted a thought or two, write adjunct sentences in the left margin or other open space on the page. You can even circle the added sentence and draw an arrow to where it should be inserted into your main text (just as you would circle and point with lecture notes). On a test, it's usually fastest to write sentences in the left margin, parallel to the book spine.

If the quantity of information is enormous in relation to the time allotted to complete the exam, you might aim to make your reviews so accurate that you eliminate the need to proofread during the actual test (time foregone on proofing means more time for writing). This is a gutsy pledge of memory with your grade at stake, but it can be done. Given only 15 minutes per question, I barely had enough time to write out my answers, often finishing within seconds of the time allotment. I didn't proofread, but mock testing made accuracy consistent and my essays received As.

Another time-saving measure is to abbreviate long titles or names appearing frequently throughout your answers. For example, instead of writing "intellectual property" ten times over the course of your essay, write "intellectual property (hereinafter IP)" the first time, and "IP" the remaining nine times.

If you run out of time during a test, you can always state the remainder of your answer in outline or list form. This shows your teacher that you knew the main points and were in the process of developing them. You will receive partial credit, if not more, as opposed to leaving your essay answers incomplete or blank.

Reinforce Your Morale with Reminders

Morale is the state of mind. It is steadfastness and courage and hope.
It is confidence and zeal and loyalty. It is *élan*, *esprit de corps* and determination.
—George Catlett Marshall, 1880–1959[54]

It is important not to let yourself become psychologically overwhelmed by homework assignments and class pace. If you're pushing yourself near to your limits and receiving top grades, you can rest assured that it's also hard for your competition. Under these circumstances, you can give yourself a psychological edge by reminding yourself that you've done well in the past in response to challenge and pressure. Exerting yourself to achieve your target grades—whether A, B, or C—requires courage and drive. When you don't yet know your full capabilities, courage and motivation need to be reinforced. When you're facing formidable challenges alone, it's fine to be your own cheerleading squad. When Muhammad Ali exclaimed "I am the greatest!" before he fought Sonny Liston, he may well have been telling *himself* this as much as he was proclaiming it to the world.

In Singapore, I used to tape my weekly quizzes to the wall next to my bed. Being tested on 98 new vocabulary words per week in addition to other reading, writing, and speech assignments was no easy task, especially with such strong competitors. Eventually, the wall was lined with twenty-two A quizzes. Try this: tape each paper, report, quiz, or midterm on which you attain your target grade, be it an A, B, or C, to the wall next to your bed. You don't always need to mount your originals, especially if it's a term paper; a photocopy of the page with your grade and teacher's remarks will suffice. You'll see the best results of your work each night before going to bed, and first thing in the morning when waking up. These reminders will be tangible proof that your strategies are working, will reinforce your motivation, and will encourage perseverance.

12

On Exam Day

All activities leading up to the day of the exam should be designed to promote certainty and a clear mind. Avoid what makes you apprehensive, nervous, or distracted, and follow these guidelines:

- Sleep well the night before, both in quality and quantity. Under urgent circumstances, however, one night's partial sleep deprivation is acceptable if it nets you a higher score.
- Eat a good breakfast. This doesn't mean chips and a candy bar or a half gallon of ice cream; it means foods that are nutritious. Eat enough that you don't suffer from hunger pangs, but avoid a heavy meal so you won't feel sleepy during the test. Avoid foods with high refined sugar content, such as donuts, cakes, and pastries, just before your exam: 30–45 minutes later, you may experience tiredness from a lowered blood-sugar level that will affect your mood and energy. In case you get hungry just before a test, have some athletic energy bars and bottled water with you. They'll keep you nourished and hydrated enough to concentrate during the exam without causing a sugar crash.
- Ensure that you have all required test materials with you (e.g., correct standard test sheet, type of blue book, calculator, prepped textbook, notes, correctly rated lead pencils, and digital watch) before you leave your abode.
- If taking public transportation to school, you may use commute time for a final review of your notes. This can put the finishing touches on an otherwise very thorough test preparation, but it is not a substitute for it.
- Use the restroom before the test.

■ Plan your schedule to arrive at least 15–20 minutes before class begins. Arriving late will:

(1) Decrease your test time;

(2) Result in less than optimal seating in large classrooms, which may adversely affect your thinking; and

(3) Force you to think faster under more pressure to finish the test. Being rushed may cloud your best thinking, thereby increasing your chances of making mistakes or not writing as well as you can. Cumulatively, your exam score is jeopardized.

At the Test Room

Keep in mind:

■ Concentration is everything. Eliminate every distracting element within your control. This allows for clearer recall and faster thinking, thus reducing the chance of error.

■ Optional: Take one last skim over a topic detail not thoroughly retained.

The following guidelines are applicable to auditorium-sized classes:

■ Sit where you can easily hear the teacher's instructions, especially when there may be a correction to the exam.

■ Don't sit near the door where you'll be distracted every time students walk in late or leave early.

■ Sit away from aisles to avoid distraction and interruption from students walking to and fro or squeezing by you to hand in their tests.

■ Sit away from the front row where you're subject to more visual and auditory distraction as students hand in their papers. One possible drawback of sitting toward the rear is that you may see more students getting up to hand in tests, returning to their seats to pick up bags and books, and leaving the room, with fewer and fewer people remaining. However, if you're deep in concentration and are going all out on the exam, you probably won't even look up from your desk to notice this at all, which was often the case for me.

■ If in the beginning being one of the last test-takers is intimidating, sit where you're less likely to notice this. However, as you'll be facing exams during the remainder of your undergraduate years, it's good to train yourself to ignore those who finish ahead of you and be at ease in taking as long as you need to complete your exam—even if it means being the last student to finish.

■ Your preparations have been extensive, and you know that you've clarified everything every step of the way. Stick with what you've studied; don't be swayed by the opinions of classmates who may speak to you about test topics.

■ Focus on retaining the information you've studied. On the day of your exam, don't try to absorb new information that won't be on the test. This can be difficult if an instructor gives a test during the second half of class, following a new lecture.

■ It's not unusual for blue books to be collected by the teacher before an exam and redistributed at random. Keep your blue books unmarked prior to the test. Here as elsewhere, honesty is the best policy.

During the Exam

There's no need to be nervous as long as you've prepared well. You've never been more knowledgeable in the subject than you are now. "Could have done better" doesn't count—you're only as good as you are now. But if you've given exam reviews your all, that's sufficient.

■ Have only what's needed on your desk. Store bags and other items elsewhere.

■ Focus on the task at hand. Don't think about projects awaiting you after the exam, appointments later that day, competitions, meetings, or a special event. Deal with them afterward—they'll still be there. Worrying about external matters will detract from your concentration.

■ Don't agonize about the percentage weight of the exam. This is something you've known for a long time from analyzing your syllabus. Your energy is best applied to thinking, not to anxiety. Simply focus on doing your absolute best.

■ To give yourself more time to complete the exam:
  (1) Keep a digital watch on your desk for instant readouts to gauge the time left throughout the exam. This eliminates having to look up or

turn around to view wall-mounted clocks.

(2) <u>Have extra supplies on your desk</u> (and not in your backpack or carry bag):
- A spare pen, in case you run out of ink;
- More than one sharpened pencil, or several leads inside your mechanical pencil;
- An eraser;
- If you perceive the need, a backup calculator in case the battery in your main one runs out during the test.

Once the Test Is Distributed

- If the instructor informs you of any questions to be amended, mark these changes on your test paper immediately.
- <u>Read instructions carefully</u>.
- Assuming a closed-book exam, immediately write down all complex or hard-to-remember formulas on scratch paper or the inside cover of your blue book.
- Scan your entire exam to see the types of questions you'll need to answer. You will gain an overview of test topics, points per section, points per question, and overall level of difficulty.
- Take your time and don't rush. There is nothing wrong with taking the entire time allotted to complete your test. I was often the last student to hand in an exam.
- Don't be intimidated by those who finish first or walk up to the teacher's desk in large numbers. Keep to your work and hand in your test when you're good and ready.
- Judge which of these three approaches works best for you:
  (a) First answer the questions you know the answers to immediately. This helps build your confidence during a test and allows you to gauge the time left for the remaining ones. You can also use this approach for blue book essays; just be sure to indicate the question number before your answer.
  (b) First answer the questions worth the most points.
  (c) First answer the hardest questions, while your mind is freshest. This

was the practice of a colleague who later obtained an M.D. degree. I did not favor this approach, however. If you get hung up, you'll lose time needed to answer questions worth more points or to complete the remainder of your test. I preferred using (a) and (b) depending on the test contents.

■ Conceiving and implementing a new strategy on the spot during an exam comes too late and is risky. If a previous strategy hasn't worked, plan a new one days or weeks beforehand, as soon as you know what kind of test will be given. Unless you have to guess an answer, have nothing to lose, or are surprised by a test being highly different from what you prepared for, stick with your game plan.

■ Proofread your paper or double-check your answers.

Multiple-Choice Exams

Appearances to the mind are of four kinds. Things either are what they appear to be; or they neither are, nor appear to be; or they are, and do not appear to be; or they are not, and yet appear to be. Rightly to aim in all these cases is the wise man's task.
—Epictetus, ca. 50–120 C.E.[55]

Test questions can be worded in tricky ways. Read questions carefully. Only one answer is right. *If two answers appear to be right, choose the one that is clearly correct and best,* not the one that's vague. One answer should stand out. In one of my courses with over 125 students, several classmates contested their exam scores. Some questions had two feasible answers: one was general and vague but could be construed as correct, and the other was specific. The professor cited our test instructions, which stated, "Choose the *best* answer." The students' test scores remained unchanged, and they were miffed.

Determine whether or not there are penalties for guessing. Usually, wrong answers receive zero points rather than incurring deductions, so if you're completely uncertain about a test question, guessing gives you some chance of increasing your score. Thorough test preparations help you leave as little to chance as possible.

I've used two approaches with multiple-choice exams. Both strategies take into account the time restrictions and chances for human error inherent in standard test sheets. Method 1 is applicable when using test sheets such as a Scantron form, and consists of darkening answers as you proceed in consecutive order. Method 2 is to circle the correct answer (or letter) on the test paper itself and then, after you've answered all the questions, to fill in the rectangles or bubbles on your answer sheet. When using Method 2, ensure that you allow enough time before the end of a test period to fill in your answer sheet completely and not be rushed to the point where you make mistakes while transcribing answers.

While using Method 2, there may be some questions for which you don't know the answer but have eliminated several possibilities. Some multiple-choice exams have five possible answers with each containing similar but different combinations of circumstances; these can be very challenging and time consuming to answer. You can draw a diagonal line through the letters that you're certain are to be eliminated. This partial elimination will save you time and energy when you return to these questions later in the test.

Method 1 avoids time spent searching for the right bubble on your answer sheet after reading each test question. After you've shaded in a bubble on your answer form, keep your pencil tip on that bubble while you read your next test question. When you're ready to darken the next answer, your pencil is already positioned immediately above that line. For example, if you've darkened in the bubble for question 5, you leave your pencil tip on that answer until you've read and determined the right answer for question 6, at which point your pencil tip is already positioned immediately next to your target. However, with exam time constraints, this is not the most expedient approach when you need to skip questions. Alternatively, you could answer your questions first using Method 2 and then, when you're ready to darken all bubbles on your answer sheet, use Method 1 to save time—this was my preferred approach.

A word of caution, though: *Whenever you skip questions while filling in an answer sheet, you run the risk of filling in a right answer for the wrong question.* If you don't notice that you've done this, it can cause a domino effect on your test sheet and sabotage your grade.

■ Always ensure that you darken the right bubble for the right question. Proofread your answers to prevent inadvertent mistakes that will cost you points. This may sound like a rookie mistake, but it can happen to anyone.

■ Also note that changing an answer after you've darkened a bubble involves two risks:

(1) The first risk involves odds. Two of my professors agreed that, three times out of four, a student changes the right answer to a wrong answer or a wrong answer to another wrong answer. If you really feel a need to change an answer, follow your instincts, but realize that statistically the odds are not in your favor.

(2) The second risk relates to tests corrected by machine. A machine may not be able to distinguish between an erased bubble with a light lead residue versus a completely darkened bubble. When this occurs, the machine may mark your answer wrong even when you've darkened in the right one.

To protect yourself, after your exam sheet is returned and scored, double-check that the correcting machine didn't err on questions you erased and changed. If there's a correcting error, speak with the teacher and ensure that your amended score appears in his or her record book.

After the Exam

After an exam, reward yourself in some form or another. Go out with friends, exercise, enjoy sports or a hobby, go to a restaurant, dance—whatever refreshes you. I used to enjoy a double ice cream, a walk on the beach, or going out for my favorite sushi.

When your test is returned, if you scored 100, you are to be congratulated. If you didn't, more important than how far below 100 you scored is whether you honestly did your absolute best. If you did, you can be content with your grade. Feel good about yourself and your achievement. Recognize the results of your working hard and efficiently.

Some instructors go over exams in class. See which questions you erred on and learn from the mistake, whether in answering questions or carrying out your strategy. This is especially important when your upcoming final exam is comprehensive because the same or similar questions may appear again. Furthermore, your final exam may affect your course grade more than your midterm. If after an exam you feel that aiming for 100 was excessive, just ask yourself how you would have scored had you set your sights lower.

13

Staying Focused as Finals Approach

When you get to the end of your rope, tie a knot and hang on.
—Franklin D. Roosevelt, 1882–1945[56]

Grace under pressure.
—Ernest Hemingway, 1899–1961[57]

Thus far, we've talked about the rationale for testing your limits and pushing yourself to do your best. However, there is a point beyond which performance and morale suffer when you've been in a sink-or-swim mode for a long span of time. Some semesters are more arduous than others. After grinding out homework and tests week after week, I was sometimes taxed when final exams approached. When you feel yourself stretched too thin, calculated tactics come into play. It also helps to keep a positive attitude. Give yourself breaks to collect yourself, stay in tune with your test preparations, and meet the challenge. Getting upset will only compromise your work. You can always splurge or go hog wild on recreation the minute exams are over.

You've worked your hardest from the beginning of the term up to now. How can you best apply your energies to clinch the grades in all your courses? The bulk of course learning occurs before a final exam. However, final exam scores are usually a sizable determinant of your course grade. The last thing you want is to retrogress due to a poor last test performance.

My classmates had mixed feelings as finals approached. There was anxiety about the test combined with relief that our term was almost over and vacation was in sight. Toward the end of a tough semester, it's tempting to say, "I just want to get it over with." But it's more sensible to target your final exam scores rather than indifferently structuring test reviews and merely seeking to get them out of the way.

Usually, final exams occur on different days, which allows you to review individually for each one and have recovery time between tests. But sometimes finals are scheduled on the same day. Unless you need to rescue a course grade because you have a D going into the final, give priority to exams where you stand the greatest chance of keeping or improving your grade.

Emotional Strain

In adversity remember to keep an even mind.
—Horace [Quintus Horatius Flaccus] 65–8 B.C.E.[58]

I will digress momentarily to address emotional strain that coincides with final exams. Whenever possible, matters of the heart are best deferred until after you've completed your finals. If you're in the right relationship, there should be no dispute about putting an issue on hold for a week or two, because the time each student has to him- or herself allows each to devote full attention to finals. This is in the mutual best interest of both students, and the relationship is easily continued afterward. There's nothing constructive about ruining your mindset for finals simply because you or your partner wouldn't wait a week to address an otherwise distressing relationship issue.

Breaking up with someone when final exams are at hand is one of the toughest challenges any student can face. Both your mind and heart are under stress. Your two largest worlds are collapsing: that of your emotional relationship and that of your studies. Life becomes a roller coaster ride as you try to sort out your feelings while knowing that your grades will be threatened if you don't remain focused on exam reviews. I wouldn't wish this on anyone.

It is tempting to dwell on your emotional dilemma because it's more captivating than a stack of notes or books. Do everything you can to avoid spiraling into depression at such a critical time, otherwise your exam reviews and final scores are likely to deteriorate. Of course, it's not easy to remain outwardly unruffled when the heart has been crushed. But with a clearer picture of things, you'll be better able to roll with the waves, and your end results will be better. If you haven't experienced this before, it won't hurt to remember this in case it happens to you in the future.

You cannot control another person, but you *can* control yourself and your studies. The choice is between (a) two negatives: emotional pain and damaged grades, and (b) one minus and one plus: emotional pain and good grades. You'll be able to salvage more if you choose the second alternative. With semester grades and your permanent academic record on the line, a little composure goes a long way. I don't think less of anyone who is hurt when their sincere feelings are rejected. Nor should you think less of yourself, either. At times like these, it helps to recall your duty to yourself. This isn't the same as extinguishing your feelings or human warmth within; it's just telling yourself that you'll address an emotional problem later (but very soon) and that you'll not only survive but will emerge intact and be fine. When in doubt during the heat of turmoil, keep this in mind.

When your semester is over after such a struggle, there can be mixed feelings but also a comfort of sorts. If you keep your grades up, you won't be as emotionally devastated. Tangible intellectual achievements will cushion the common drop in self-esteem associated with personal rejection. It happened to me twice. Okay, bad timing on my part. The first time, efforts to salvage my grades resulted in my only 4.0 semester during full-time enrollment. (All other semesters had an A– somewhere.) The second one knocked me for a loop and resulted in my only two B+ grades in two and a half years. Yes, it was hard.

In the long run, you're doing yourself a big favor by hanging in there. Those who review your transcript and test scores in the future—especially your scores on a graduate school admission test—won't empathetically attribute them to emotional hardship. The system doesn't make allowances for personal problems, so it is up to you to pull yourself through—and, again, this admittedly is hard. But you must believe in yourself. You must always keep your spirit intact, no matter what happens. Personal issues can and should be addressed after exam pressures are over. If necessary, though, you can weave time in between exam reviews to speak with a friend or counselor to gain insight, support, and encouragement. Just having someone to talk to can make a world of difference.

An East Asian saying notes that "gold is tempered through fire." We don't seek emotional adversity, nor do we wish such pain upon ourselves. But involuntary emotional hardship can have unintended benefits: reinforced self-belief, wisdom born of experience, the ability to pull yourself through difficult times, and the formation of character.

Final Exams Graded on an Absolute Scale

When you feel yourself spread too thin, you need to target your test scores. The reasons are

1. To get the highest recognition you deserve;
2. To increase or protect your grade-point average by obtaining a higher grade in one or more classes to offset lesser course grades;
3. To know how feasible it will be to earn a higher course grade by aiming for a higher final exam score;
4. To know how to allocate your energies for each course's final exam review; and
5. To avoid studying excessively for a test that's unlikely to change your overall grade while ensuring that you also don't lower your grade by understudying for it.

The way to do this is as follows:

Step 1. Know the grading scale for each of your classes. Classes differ in their point cutoffs for grades. Compare the following:

Table 8 Comparison of letter grade cutoffs

	Class X	**Class Y**	**Class Z**	**Grade**
Points	92–100	95–100	90%	A
	89–91	92–94		A–
	86–88	89–91		B+
	83–85	85–88	80%	B
	80–82	82–84		B–
	78–79	80–81		C+
	72–77	75–79	66%	C
	70–71	70–74		C–
		68–69		D+
	60–69	65–67	59%	D
	0–59	0–64	0%–58%	F

Although some courses are graded on a curve, you can't know how the curve will form. You can look at your notes to see who in your class has been setting the top scores and use these as a guidepost. I wasn't comfortable with asking a professor what type of curve method he or she would use, so I aimed for my target score based on an absolute scale, or did the best I could and accepted the results.

Step 2. Based on your previous assignments, scores, and percentage weights, determine your point status and grade up to the final exam. If your grade is partially comprised of class participation, ask your teacher beforehand what your participation score is (don't be shy); you'll need this for your calculations.

Step 3. Know the percentage weight of the final exam; the heavier its percentage weight, the more it shapes your grade.

Step 4. Know the exam's point total. A 50-question multiple-choice exam, at 2 points per question, will be easier than a 30-point essay exam, with each point worth 3.33 points on a 100-point scale.

Step 5. Gauge the feasibility of improving your course grade with a high final exam score. Based on Steps 1–3 above, calculate the minimum test score you must clear to

(a) Keep your present course grade; and

(b) Push your course grade up to the next highest level.

Step 6. In either case, aim to exceed the minimum projected score because exam results are unpredictable and you want a safety margin for yourself.

Step 7. In all cases, you should be able to achieve 5(a).

Step 8. Judge in which classes you can achieve 5(b).

Step 9. Judge how much effort you must put into exam preparations to obtain 5(a).

Step 10. Judge how much effort you must put into exam preparations to obtain 5(b).

Step 11. When feasible, allocate more effort for final exams with 5(b) criteria (without allowing grades to drop in other finals).

Step 12. Allocate enough effort for exams with 5(a) criteria.

Midterm scores should be a prelude to your final exam scores and, hence, your course grade. However, because each course configures its percentage breakdown and criteria differently, and because your scores will vary among assignments, calculations must be made on a case-by-case basis. You can plan your course of action based on your own cost-benefit analysis, how adept and confident you are about meeting the challenge, how closely spaced or far apart each final is from another, and how feasible it is to boost your grade in relation to how strained you are.

The extent to which a test affects your grade varies according to its percentage weight. Attendance and class participation may be an amalgamated score assigned by your teacher. In all cases, you should be able to score 100% for this category. There's nothing hard about showing up for class every time—there's your 100% for attendance. Nor is it difficult to contribute to class discussions as long as you read the assignments and apply what you learn—and here's your 100% for participation.

Suppose you have the following hypothetical scores going into your finals for four courses:

Table 9 Grade calculation—Example 1

Class 1: A-grade work early in the semester yields less pressure on the final exam.

Assignment	Weight	Score	Composite of Grade	
Attendance	10%	100	0.1×100	= 10 (attended every class)
Term Paper	30%	95	0.3×95	= 28.5
Midterm Exam 1	25%	93	0.25×93	= 23.25
Subtotal before final				= 61.75
			Target Final Exam Score	**Course Grade**
Final Exam	35%		81 ($0.35 \times 81 = 28.35$; $28.35 + 61.75 = 90.1$)	A–
			53 ($0.35 \times 53 = 18.55$; $18.55 + 61.75 = 80.3$)	B–

This example shows how scoring well early in the term means less pressure to perform on the final. In this case, you could score a low B (81 points) on the final and still earn an A or A– in the class. Given your performance prior to the final, you'd really have to bomb the test to incur a B–. Of course, an A student would factor in a safety margin by trying to score at least in the mid to high 80s. But again, there would be less pressure than having to score in the 90s. If you are an A student, this comparatively lower required test score means you can allocate more effort to other courses whose exam scores and final grades are more critical.

Table 10 Grade calculation—Example 2

Class 2: A borderline grade requires a multifactorial cost-benefit analysis to determine your target final exam score.

Assignment	Weight	Score	Composite of Grade	
Quizzes	20%	89	0.2×89	$= 17.8$
Midterm Exam 1	25%	86	0.25×86	$= 21.5$
Midterm Exam 2	25%	88	0.25×88	$= 22$
Subtotal before final				$= 61.3$

		Target Final Exam Score	**Course Grade**
Final Exam	30%	$96\ (0.3 \times 96 = 28.8;\ 28.8 + 61.3 = 90.1)$	A–
		$89\ (0.3 \times 89 = 26.7;\ 26.7 + 61.3 = 88)$	B or B+
		$70\ (0.3 \times 70 = 21;\ 21 + 61.3 = 82.3)$	B
		$65\ (0.3 \times 65 = 19.5;\ 19.5 + 61.3 = 80.8)$	B–

Here you would calculate your quiz score average taking into account whether or not your instructor drops your lowest score. Based on these hypothetical percentages and figures, you would really need to go all out on test reviews to score 96 on the final and catapult your grade up from B to A–. Meanwhile, you'd have a healthy 30-point span that would still net you a B in the class. Obtaining an A would be much harder, though not impossible.

Suppose this was your last final and was a week after your most recent one. You'd have more time and energy to devote for stronger preparation. Perhaps you go all out on your exam review, and the test is graded on a curve. You'd stand a good chance of pulling your course grade up to the next level.

In other cases, you might have a full agenda, so aiming for the B would be more realistic in relation to the amount of attention you would need to devote to other final exams. With a safety margin of 30 points, you wouldn't have to stress much over the exam.

Table 11 Grade calculation—Example 3

Class 3: A heavily weighted term paper and perfect attendance compensate for poor test scores.

Assignment	Weight	Score	Composite of Grade	
Attendance	10%	100	0.1×100	$= 10$ (attended every class)
Class Presentation	10%	73	0.1×73	$= 7.3$
Term Paper	35%	88	0.35×88	$= 30.8$
Midterm Exam 1	15%	75	0.15×75	$= 11.25$
Midterm Exam 2	15%	70	0.15×70	$= 10.5$
Subtotal before final				$= 69.85$

		Target Final Exam Score	Course Grade
Final Exam	15%	$100 \ (0.15 \times 100 = 15; 15 + 69.85 = 84.85)$	B
		$87 \ (0.15 \times 87 = 13.05; 13.05 + 69.85 = 82.9)$	B
		$68 \ (0.15 \times 68 = 10.2; 10.2 + 69.85 = 80.05)$	B–

Suppose you write papers better than taking tests. Given this, concentrating on the 35% term paper early in the semester and scoring relatively well buffers C grade tests, though you'll still need a 68 on the final to obtain a B– for the course. Test and presentation scores have put you out of A contention. Scoring 100 is not a strong likelihood for the average student, nor will it raise the course grade to an A in this case, so don't waste your energy. Realizing this, you need not agonize over this exam; clearing a score well over 68 should be manageable and will push you up to a B– or higher.

Table 12 Grade calculation—Example 4

Class 4: A heavily weighted final exam and perfect attendance enable you to earn a higher course grade than midterm grade.

Assignment	Weight	Score	Composite of Grade	
Attendance	25%	100	0.25×100	$= 25$ (attended every class)
Midterm Exam	25%	87	0.25×87	$= 21.75$
Subtotal before final				$= 46.75$

		Target Final Exam Score	Course Grade
Final Exam	50%	$88 \ (0.5 \times 88 = 44; 44 + 46.75 = 90.75)$	A–
		$68 \ (0.5 \times 68 = 34; 34 + 46.75 = 80.75)$	B

In these four hypothetical cases, I'd aim for

Class	Final Exam Score	Course Grade
1	Above 86	Keep the A
2	Shoot for the 96	Aim for the A but accept whatever comes
3	Above 81	Aim for a B, try to avoid getting a C
4	Above 90	Try to avoid an A–

If conditions were stressful, I'd adjust my targets to

Class	Final Exam Score	Course Grade
1	Above 81	Keep the A
2	Above 69	Accept the B
3	Above 69	Get the B–
4	Above 88	Go for the A

Note that I would set my target test scores higher than required minimums because I believe that while an A– is preferable to a B+, and a B– to a C+, obtaining the solid letter grade without the minus is even more desirable because it strengthens your grade-point average. If surpassing the minus zone is within your capability, set your goals accordingly. Such calculation, hard work, and rewards are things nobody else can give you. Only you can determine how much effort is necessary compared to how badly you want a certain grade, how strained you might be, your exam schedule, and other factors.

B and C aspiring students can make similar calculations following the same procedures. The following examples all use the same breakdown percentages:

Table 13 Grade calculation—Example 5

Class 5: Shoot for the A or comfortably land the B?

Assignment	Weight	Score	Composite of Grade	
Quizzes	15%	82	0.15×82	$= 12.3$
Midterm Exam 1	25%	83	0.25×83	$= 20.75$
Midterm Exam 2	25%	86	0.25×86	$= 21.5$
Subtotal before final				$= 54.55$

		Target Final Exam Score	**Course Grade**
Final Exam	35%	$100 \ (0.35 \times 100 = 35; 35 + 54.55 = 89.55)$	A–
		$90 \ (0.35 \times 90 = 31.5; 31.5 + 54.55 = 86.05)$	B
		$80 \ (0.35 \times 80 = 28; 28 + 54.55 = 82.55)$	B
		$73 \ (0.35 \times 73 = 25.55; 25.55 + 54.55 = 80.1)$	B–

While scoring 100 would be difficult, a score in the high 90s, combined with grading on a curve and discretionary credit for perfect attendance, could result in an A–. Conversely, on an absolute scale, you'd have a 20-point margin to land a B, and a 27-point spread for a B–. In light of your performance on the two midterms, a similar test score in the 80s would suffice to net a B.

Table 14 Grade calculation—Example 6

Class 6: C student near B level

Assignment	Weight	Score	Composite of Grade	
Quizzes	15%	77	0.15×77	$= 11.55$
Midterm Exam 1	25%	78	0.25×78	$= 19.50$
Midterm Exam 2	25%	79	0.25×79	$= 19.75$
Subtotal before final				$= 50.80$

		Target Final Exam Score	**Course Grade**
Final Exam	35%	$89 \ (0.35 \times 89 = 31.15; 31.15 + 50.80 = 81.95)$	B
		$84 \ (0.35 \times 84 = 29.4; 29.4 + 50.80 = 80.20)$	B–
		$55 \ (0.35 \times 55 = 19.25; 19.25 + 50.80 = 70.05)$	C

In this case, a student would need to score between 84 and 89 to net a B. Having scored high Cs on midterms means that scoring in the low 80s would be hard. However, by studying hard to grasp more of the material, scoring well on the final is possible.

Table 15 Grade calculation—Example 7

Class 7: D student close to a C

Assignment	Weight	Score	Composite of Grade	
Quizzes	15%	65	0.15×65	= 9.75
Midterm Exam 1	25%	68	0.25×68	= 17
Midterm Exam 2	25%	70	0.25×70	= 17.5
Subtotal before final				= 44.25

		Target Final Exam Score	**Course Grade**
Final Exam	35%	74 ($0.35 \times 74 = 25.9$; $25.9 + 44.25 = 70.15$)	C–
		45 ($0.35 \times 45 = 15.75$; $15.75 + 44.25 = 60$)	D

Although this student could score anywhere from 45 to 73 to net a D, more important would be to try to score 74 or 76—a mere 4 to 6 points above his or her last midterm score. Such a final exam score would mean a class grade of at least C–, or perhaps a solid C if there were mitigating circumstances.

When instructors give more than 100 semester total points, you'll need to calculate your target scores differently. For example, suppose you had the following:

Midterm 1	50 points
Midterm 2	50 points
Final Exam	67 points
Total	167 points

Thereupon, a teacher might base your grade on a curve or as a percentage of the semester point total. If your professor used a curve to establish the cutoff for an A at 85%, you would calculate your target exam score by

$$(\text{test 1 score}) + (\text{test 2 score}) + (\text{final exam score}) = 0.85 \times 167$$

Suppose you scored 45 and 39 respectively on the midterms; your subtotal would be 84 points.

$\frac{84 + x}{167}$ = your grade (x represents your final exam score)

85% of 167 is 141.95. 141.95 − 84 = 57.95; you'd need to obtain 58 out of 67 points on your final to earn an A course grade. Similar calculations can be made for targeting a B or C provided you know their respective cutoffs. These are details you'll need to ascertain. Note that cutoffs based on actual class results may be different from those forecasted prior to the exam. Also, curving methods will vary from teacher to teacher.

In other cases, your professor may determine your grade as a percentage of your total semester points. Suppose you had the following:

Quiz	50 points
Midterm	125 points
Final Exam	250 points
Total	425 points

Here you would add your points earned on each test: 90% of 425 (or 382.5 points) would net you an A, 80% (or 340 points) a B, and so on.

Dialing in to target scores is not as easy as it may appear. There are numerous variables to consider:

1. The subject of the class may simply be difficult, making a test hard in the first place.
2. Unless you are a top performer, you cannot guarantee that you'll score as precisely as you wish. Exams are rarely that easy. Unless you can predict the difficulty of your teachers' exams, you don't want to cut things too close and gamble that, come what may, you'll hit your exact target score. Hence, thorough preparations are still vital to be safe.
3. Teachers vary in how they calculate grades.
4. Point deductions complicate matters, depending on test configuration; some questions may be worth more than others, such as a 25-point essay question mixed in with 2-point true-or-false questions.
5. Depending on total points of an exam, each point deduction may translate into several points on a 100-point scale. A 50-question multiple-choice

exam may be based on 2 points per question. If this were applicable for Class 2 (shown earlier), you could only get two questions wrong and still meet your target test score. But with Class 1, you'd have a cushion of nine questions to err on before losing your A grade. Contrast this with an exam worth 41 points total, which translates into 2.439 points per question on a 100-point scale. Just 5 points deducted from such a 41-point test would immediately pull your test score down to a B.

6. If your instructor raises the absolute grading scale, your target scores must also be raised, making your task harder.

7. If your final exam requires creative work, scoring can be more subjective than objective.

8. If you are exempted from one or more finals in the same term, you'll have more time and energy to devote to those remaining.

9. The date of each final will also factor into your deliberations. Exams that are several days to a week apart give you recovery time and the means to focus more energy, as opposed to finals that fall on the same day.

10. Comprehensive final exams are harder because you have more information to retain.

11. Exam preparations may be made easier or more challenging depending on whether or not a teacher hands out a study guide.

12. If the final is a take-home exam, you have great potential of scoring high by creating an impressive exam paper under quiet, nonstressful circumstances at home.

Variables of your present circumstances need to be factored into your calculations. But no matter what the circumstances, *take the time to calculate your course grade going into the final, the plausibility of improvement, and necessary test performance*. This is preferable to blindly preparing for final exams and haphazardly expending your energies. If the next higher course grade is within reach, it would be a shame to miss it simply because you've mistakenly allocated more attention to a course where efforts to raise your grade will be in vain. In other cases, you may find that to keep your present grade, you don't need to agonize over the final. Such a realization will help you remain calm and will lighten your stress.

The goal is to obtain as many higher grades as possible to offset your lower grades. This will help your grade-point average. An A and three Bs, or two As and two Bs, is better than all Bs. One B and three Cs, or two Bs and two Cs, is better than all Cs. A word of caution for the Ds: depending on your school, a D may or may not be a passing grade. Minimum grade-point averages for graduation are usually set above a D average. If a D is a drop in the ocean of, say, your 3.5 cumulative grade-point average (maybe you had an accident or sickness that prevented you from finishing all assignments, or maybe you had that once-in-a-blue-moon tyrannical professor who believed in flunking 40% of his or her class and assigning Ds to others), don't sweat it unless circumstances require that you repeat the course. Generally, however, Ds are to be avoided!

Give priority to the courses in which your grade is strong or in which you have greater tactical probability of raising your grade. If you're equal in more than one course, give priority to the one with the first final. If the finals for both courses are on the same day, give priority to the course in which you're more confident; you'll have a greater chance of obtaining a higher score here, and thus more assurance of getting at least one strong grade. For your remaining courses, allocate as much effort as possible to keeping the grade you already have, or aim for the next highest grade when feasible.

If you want to take these tactics a step farther, you can calculate your semester grade as you progress during the term, using the grading scale from the syllabus. I did not do this, opting instead simply to do my best on every assignment and exam. It was only when I was extremely strained at semester's end that I calculated my target scores to determine on which tests to expend the most time and energy.

Even when final exams are graded on a curve, the fact remains that the higher you score, the better. You can't predict how the class curve will form, and you may not know what curving method your teacher will use. However, your strongest competitors will be setting the stage for the class curve. You can reasonably assume that they will perform about as well as they have during the semester. Remember writing down your classmates' scores throughout the semester? Gauge where you fall in relation to these scores. If shooting for an A on the final exam, look to your strongest competitors' track records to estimate how well you, too, must perform. You can also look at the class median and set your target from there.

When Your Semester Grade Is Borderline

While remaining honest, you want a teacher to give you every legitimate consideration when you have a borderline semester-end grade. If your course is partially graded on attendance, politely ask your teacher to take into account the fact that you have attended every class (if you really did) when deliberating your final course grade. This is not my original idea; the suggestion actually came from one of my professors.

This request should be separate from that for your course rank. If the course is graded on attendance, the teacher already has a written record of your attendance. A face-to-face, honestly worded conversation will help you stand out from other anonymous students, especially if it is a large class. I believe an in-person conversation is best here because people relate more favorably when they can associate a face and personality with your name. An e-mail or voicemail message for such a purpose can project an impersonal, selfish, or even cowardly impression, depending on your wording, tone of voice, or both. Honesty is the best policy. Watch what you say so as not to give your teacher the impression you're trying to unduly influence him or her. Keep the conversation short, polite, and remember to say "thank you." Whether the teacher heeds your request is up to him or her; your concern is merely to encourage the proper attention you reasonably deserve.

I've witnessed one student ask a professor for an extra-credit assignment (within the last two weeks of a semester) to salvage a passing grade due to emergency. This may not be easy if you're already up to your ears in work or if a teacher believes that giving extra credit would be an unfair exception in relation to other students. If it's feasible for you, however, it never hurts to ask; the worst that the teacher can say is "no."

Your Rank at the End of a Course

If you really want to gauge your progress thoroughly or see how you measure up to your competition, privately ask your teachers to disclose your overall course ranking at the semester end. Not every teacher will do so, but some will. No one's private information is infringed upon, and you can use these statistics to track your record throughout your college career.

When handing in your final exam, give your teacher a self-addressed stamped envelope (not a postcard) with a small note asking *only* for the following information:

1. Your course grade
2. Class average course grade
3. Your final exam score and grade
4. Class high score on final exam
5. Class average score on final exam
6. Number of students in class (in some classes, a simple head count during the semester or name count on the class test results list is good enough)
7. Your final rank for that particular course

This request list should only be for objective, factual, statistical information. Asking for or writing anything else can incriminate you, in that an instructor may interpret certain remarks as trying to bias his or her grading. One of my professors posted the class results on a web site that contained all the above information. Others wrote the results on the note I had provided.

I would keep both your request for and information on your class rankings completely private, not disclosing them to other classmates. The reason for this is that others may soon make the same request. A teacher may find it burdensome and deny requests if several dozen enrolled students ask for this information.

The course grades and rank that you aim for should be set according to your best abilities. Keep your rank in perspective with your original goals. An F student striving for his or her best to make all Cs shouldn't be concerned with the number of classmates scoring in the B or A range. *If you achieve your target grade within your maximum capability, you have done well and should feel good about it. You are still fulfilling your particular learning potential, and that is sufficient.* Don't be disheartened over how many students ranked above you. Use these statistics to gauge how much you've accomplished in relation to your original goals. The same applies to C and B caliber students. *The main objective is to know your full capability, set your goals, achieve them, and be content.* This is your private battle and observation, just as it is for A students. Over the course of several years, or even two semesters, monitor whether or not you're improving. It is reasonable to expect that, as you increase your awareness while honing your study skills, your grades in your sophomore, junior, and senior years will be stronger than those of your freshman year.

The results from my course rankings revealed that I was not the top student in every class, though I did place first in seven of twenty-one consecutive courses (in one of which I tied for first with two other students).

Once I began achieving As, I wanted to see just how far I could get if I put in the extra effort. To strive for rank #1 in one or more of your courses is entirely a personal decision. In my opinion, just getting the A, or even A−, is quite good enough unless you have a personal mission to achieve a 4.0 grade-point average. I was keen on ranking because I wanted to prove to myself that I wasn't a failure if I really tried. I privately set out to do my best and see what would happen. For my first semester resuming college, using my strategies, I scored three As and one B, or a 3.75 grade-point average. Although this 3.75 was diluted by my previous track record, more important was the fact that I was finally making progress. Then I implemented additional strategies to try to earn straight As.

If you choose to pursue top rankings, others in- and outside school may view you as being extreme, overly serious, even a micromanager. Their inferences may be based on the questions you ask in class to ascertain course information and homework criteria with great precision or on the degree of care you exude, which is visible to people around you. There may also be times when others are in very close contention with you. This is where starting your semester strong, by maximizing every point on every assignment, puts you at an advantage. Seeing your first score as the class high will inspire you to keep your position. As long as you start with the highest score at the outset, prepare for each test and assignment thoroughly, and keep your scores on par with or above those of your competition, you will always be one step ahead and able to clinch the #1 slot even when competitors equal you on all subsequent assignments. If you're near the top of the class and are pursuing first place, you'll need to maximize all remaining test and homework scores to surpass your competitors. You'll be one of the few students really pushing themselves.

One final thought bears mentioning. Your pursuit of top rankings and results should always be kept private from your classmates. Once a teacher discloses your rank, don't let elation predispose you to conceit or bragging, even when speaking to other teachers. They'll be able to tell whether or not you're intelligent just by the way you carry yourself and speak. Your reinforced self-belief and self-confidence from your triumphs are to be distinguished from allowing yourself to become arrogant, which will render you obnoxious to instructors and peers alike. Regardless of what your ranking turns out to be, keep your personal integrity. The purpose of aiming for rank #1 and scores of 100 on assignments, quizzes, and tests is to develop yourself into your best. Your best includes your integrity. Being able to handle success with poise and discretion separates the women from the girls and the men from the boys. Divulge your success when it's really needed: at interviews; on your résumé, cover letters, and applications for employment or school admission; and in other appropriate contexts, such as when sharing the honest good news among your true friends.

14

Your Teachers

A teacher affects eternity; he can never tell where his influence stops.
—Henry Brooks Adams, 1838–1918[59]

Getting the most out of college is heavily predicated on your teachers. Bottom line: you need your teachers to learn and grow. Unless you eventually find your career niche in academia, you'll never again have access to so many learned people. As a student, you are free to contact any teacher on campus during office hours or by appointment. On a planet plagued with poverty, war, famine, political instability, economic hardship, caste systems, a shortage of schools, and limited admission to higher education, forcing many people to find menial work with only a high school education, it's surprising that students in this country take their teachers and academic opportunities for granted. For some students, how much they like an instructor affects their motivation in class. *The key is to find the teachers from whom you can learn well.* One way to do this is to meet a teacher in person the semester before you intend to enroll in his or her course.

You can gauge whether or not you like a class within the first week. If a class is not for you and an alternative is available, there's nothing wrong with dropping it. Just be careful not to put yourself at a disadvantage in your replacement class, which will already be in session. In addition, ensure that your school's official course-enrollment confirmation verifies that you've dropped the course. If you're receiving financial aid, also make sure that dropping courses doesn't violate your contract provisions.

Imagine yourself in a teacher's position. Instructors see hundreds of students each term. They can discern the eager from the unmotivated, the earnest from the indifferent. Picture teaching a class in which you knew some students didn't want to be there, acted that way, enrolled only because your course was required, wanted to know only what you'd test them on, skipped class, did other homework in the back of your classroom, fell asleep while you lectured, or habitually walked in late or left early. (Some students behave as if their mission is to bring down the class curve which, in this context, would be to your advantage.) You'd be pretty uninspired, wouldn't you?

Conversely, instructors notice good students. If you show a sincere interest in learning, as demonstrated by your homework and dialogue in class, you'll stick out from perennial also-rans. While doing your best, an incidental benefit is that teachers will remember your engaged attitude when and if deliberating your borderline grade. In other cases, they may give you some tips on how to do better on your homework or encourage you when you need it. Most teachers are willing to help if they see you're motivated.

After graduating, I once told a professor about my having had a few teachers with whom parroting their lessons and ideas was the only way to obtain a good grade. She understood my contention but also said to appreciate that a professor may want you to learn what he or she believes is important.

I did not enroll in courses primarily based on grade curving, lenient attendance policies, or whether or not their final exams were cumulative. Such a path of least resistance could have boosted my grade-point average, but it wouldn't have challenged me with a variety of instructors and levels of difficulty, so I wouldn't have reached my full potential. More important was the quality of instruction I would receive.

Teachers who do not necessarily instruct in an organized, concise way nonetheless have valuable information to share with you. Though you may work harder to learn from these people, focus on the knowledge that you can acquire rather than on their personal habits or styles.

It's a bad idea to criticize a teacher in his or her classroom or office. What could be more personal than having someone fault you in your own classroom where you're trying to teach your life's work? It's the next worst thing to criticizing someone in his or her own home. This is just a matter of common courtesy; aggravating your grader will likely work against you. You don't need to agree with everything an instructor says but you do need to avoid an adversarial relationship by eschewing open verbal jousting. The last thing you need is to diminish the value of your learning, time, and money by creating friction between you and your teachers.

Disagreeing is to be distinguished from being disagreeable. Remember, you're trying to learn from teachers, not debate them. Focus on facts, not personalities. If you sincerely question the validity of something a teacher says, ask for clarification or politely give your reasons for your reservation about it. Don't get caught up in trying to prove who's right and who's wrong; simply understand the teacher's view and move on. You can evaluate the differences later.

Open defiance, in the self-perceived name of individual expression, isn't a good idea either. Unless something is blatantly improper, such conduct interferes with class continuity and creates a bad impression in class. One of my classmates insisted on running over his allotted speech time. The professor was patient for the first several minutes of overtime and then told the student that his time was up. The student replied that he had something important to say to classmates because they'd someday face an issue on which he was elaborating. Several more minutes elapsed. Several times the professor politely told the student that his time was up; several times he stubbornly continued, until the teacher stepped up to the front and ousted him from the podium. This won't help your grade nor make a good impression on your teacher!

In one of my required courses, few students liked the professor. One incident that may have rubbed classmates the wrong way was the teacher refusing to allow a disabled student to tape-record lectures. The student said he had difficulty keeping up with the professor during note-writing. He dropped the course and transferred to another instructor the following week. The professor was, in fact, highly knowledgeable; classmates simply had a hard time adjusting to his personality. He was also intellectually eccentric, but it takes a student who has dealt with a variety of people to see this and not be intimidated or bewildered.

When conditions are less than ideal, remain focused on learning your course material and don't get hung up on personality differences. Other students' were turned off by this professor, and their body language and tone of voice during class discussions reflected it. I recall the professor asking me a question on the text. The answer could have been legitimately answered with circumstance A, B, or C (each condition predicated on the preceding one). I knew C but answered A, thinking this would lead my discussion from the first of several logical progressions and thus be more thorough. The teacher said, rather brusquely, "Wouldn't it have been more direct to say C?" He was thinking several steps ahead for answering the question.

I realized early in the semester that this teacher had his rough edges. Although in the past I would have resented being corrected in front of the entire class, I now chose to focus more on the content of his statements than on his unvarnished manners. One of my classmates said I was a brown noser. Was I brown nosing? No. Brown nosing, as I define it, is proactively cultivating a teacher's favor for ulterior motives. I merely remained indifferent to the instructor's obtrusive mannerisms, but I did not massage, praise, or flatter. The point is, the teacher was overbearing at times, and most classmates couldn't handle it. Was my behavior duplicitous? I don't think so. What's duplicitous about indifference? For the same subject and teacher, you could let dislike color your attitude and diminish your learning. Or you could remain indifferent to shield yourself from dreading every minute of forty-eight semester hours with a teacher, while learning as much as you can from the course. To me, this approach is worthwhile, given your time, brain power, nerves, maturity, and money invested.

Even though you (or your parents) have paid your tuition, having regard for your teachers is only proper. The central goal is to learn all you can from a particular course, whether or not you like the teacher. Naturally, you'll want to seek out those teachers from whom you can learn well.

Almost all of my teachers have been highly competent and fair. I believe your experiences will be similar. Of the 110 teachers I've had since kindergarten, 65 have been at the college level. Of these, only three were truly bad. Two courses were dropped, the other I endured out of necessity, garnering an A-. As an example of what I considered bad, in one nonprerequisite course, the professor asked how I thought I could compete in his class (which had only two other enrolled students) and roared three times during our conversation that I had every right to remain as long as I didn't mind receiving a D or an F! How silly. But these three negatives were very minor in comparison to the other professors and instructors to whom I am very grateful.

Teachers' Office Hours

Visiting teachers at their offices is a good practice. It can help you

- Develop face-to-face interpersonal skills;
- Improve your communication skills;
- See what teachers are like before you enroll in a course;
- Learn information applicable to life outside school that isn't stated in the classroom or text;
- Clarify questions from your text or lecture notes;
- Develop rapport with the people chiefly contributing to your education;
- Obtain advice about your term paper; and
- Gain perspective on other projects.

After some meetings, I wrote in my notebook what we'd discussed before I forgot all the details.

E-mail is another way to communicate with teachers outside of class. E-mail can save a lot of time for simple questions or dialogue but is not, of course, a substitute for face-to-face in-depth discussions or for going to class. Three of my professors said that some students would e-mail them and ask what had been included in an entire lecture. Their reply would be to read the book and go to class.

Good face-to-face interpersonal skills are something many people lack. Having these skills in place will help when you graduate and look for a job. Your teachers are more educated than the average person and, if they are receptive, will be easier to practice these skills with than the population at large. For example, be sure to address your teachers as Doctor, Professor, Mr., or Mrs.—whatever highest title is applicable. This is not only a sign of respect but shows that you know proper manners, which can set you apart from other students. Calling a teacher by his or her first name is inappropriate unless or until he or she specifically requests it.

Phone etiquette and personal image are important, too. When leaving voicemail messages for your teachers, state your full name, course name, and section number. Instructors often teach more than one course per term and may well have more than one student with the same first name. When leaving a return telephone number, I prefer to state it twice in succession. Anyone who has retrieved voicemail messages knows the aggravation and inconvenience of having to play them back several times to accurately catch a phone number. By speaking clearly and not too quickly, and by repeating your phone number a second time, your teacher will note that you've made a conscientious effort to facilitate your communications.

Also, it's not just what you say that counts, it's how you say it—namely, your tone of voice. When a teacher isn't familiar with you, your tone of voice, choice of words, and message content will be his or her sole impression of you. I'm not suggesting donning a façade but simply remembering that tone of voice—whether upbeat, professional, lethargic, or rambunctious—is a big part of any verbal message. Separate yourself from run-of-the-mill classmates and present yourself favorably.

Letters of Recommendation

There was one semester when I knew I was going to transfer to another college. In my highest-scoring course at the time, I asked the teacher to provide me with a letter of recommendation, which she graciously did. The letter proved most helpful for my school transfer and even for subsequent job applications.

It never hurts to have good references in your files. Pick the course in which you are doing best and ask your professor or instructor if he or she will write one for you. It's even more helpful if the subject of the course is relevant to the job or study program for which you apply. A laudatory letter or two can be strategic during your last year of college attendance because potential employers prefer current year references. As long as you've been a strong student, the letter is an earned recognition that will strengthen your qualifications and help you stand out from other applicants.

Such a letter can also boost your determination and morale during arduous semesters. At one point, I posted a copy of my letter by the door so I would be reminded that I was capable of meeting my challenges. When you're facing hard courses alone, every healthy psychological edge you can give yourself is acceptable.

KEEPING A BALANCED PERSPECTIVE

15

Connect and Relate

It is not enough to have a good mind. The main thing is to use it well.
—René Descartes, 1596–1650[60]

I integrated my study strategies with some philosophies as a way of life. These philosophies are not complex, but applying them on an ongoing basis is easier said than done. The key is practice—and suiting them to your circumstances. Although for a time I sacrificed other activities to restore my grade-point average, in general, I believe it's important to have a balanced life outside of studies.

The phrase "connect and relate" was coined by J. A. DeVito in his *Essentials of Human Communication*.[61] DeVito advises readers to combine information on nonverbal communication that comes from separate parts of their text and lectures. I expanded the principle to aid lifelong learning. You receive information at different times and places, but you can blend ideas together to enhance your knowledge. "Connect and relate" can be applied during lectures, student presentations, reading, studying, watching films, reflecting on life, even looking within yourself.

Theories in their original forms need not be applied literally; they can be adapted to suit personal circumstances. For example, the concept of "continuous improvement" was adopted from a business management philosophy to strengthen my study strategies. The principle works in tandem with "connect and relate" to foster continuous learning. In Chapter 3, we saw that the notion of study efficiency was derived from a weight training philosophy.

My outlook on papers and speeches was influenced by a graphic design course taken in my sophomore year. We learned that a trademark design must fulfill three criteria: be simple, distinct, and tell something about the organization. Economy (simplicity) was emphasized. Every design element was included and organized only to communicate a message in the most effective way. Some sign ads are seen for only a split second, when you're driving on a freeway or see them on a passing bus. The rationale is that every superfluous element, however slight, makes it harder for viewers to interpret the ad, and that retention of the message is paramount. We saw the theories in actual use when viewing designs on television, in shopping malls, magazines, corporate publications, and at gas stations.

This theory of efficient communication can be adapted to your papers, speeches, and presentations. In college, your readers and audience will, of course, have longer to receive your message than with a public ad. But the content and quality of your message remain just as crucial—perhaps even more so—because your teachers and fellow students devote more undivided time and attention to scrutinizing what you have to say. When someone reads your work or hears your speech for the first time, you want to be crystal clear and distinctly remembered. Similarly, wordiness dilutes the strength of your writing. Lack of organization forces an audience to juggle fragmented information. The more ordered your message, the better. Feed people chaos and they will leave with chaos (plus your grade will be affected). Choose your words and order every statement to present your thoughts in their strongest form. Omit all unnecessary elements, however slight.

Speech and English Composition are two of the most valuable courses you'll take. Many course assignments are predicated on these acquired skills. Advanced courses build on the basics. *If you do not understand the basics, your ability to excel in college will be compromised to a large extent.*

You might also note the differences between how your professors solve problems. For example, my teacher who stressed design economy was a stickler for following rules and guidelines to the letter. Yet, an equally successful graphics instructor demonstrated to me that one need not always be rigid, that in many cases it paid to be flexible by using any approach that was honest and effective. Each approach suited each instructor. However, equally important was to see how their philosophies extended beyond the context of art assignments. Throughout my college career, there were definitely courses where highly structured work was mandatory (problems only had one correct answer), while others allowed for more than one right answer. The same may be said for situations that you'll encounter outside the classroom. Know when to be strict and when to be flexible.

As a finishing touch to your learning, during your last week of a regular semester, try asking your teacher, "If there's one thing you would like us to take beyond the classroom, what would it be?" Your teachers' replies will reflect interesting minds while providing you with potentially valuable ideas. As part of a "connect and relate" exercise, you could write their axiomatic editorials in your notebook. Even if an idea does not have apparent immediate application, it won't hurt to remember it; sometime in the future, you may find an interesting connection between a teacher's parting remarks and a new circumstance.

You Become What You Think

Ideals are like stars; you will not succeed in touching them with your hands. But like the seafaring man on the desert of waters, you choose them as your guides, and following them you will reach your destiny.
—Carl Schurz, 1829–1906[62]

Olympic world-record-holder Billy Mills once remarked, "You become what you think."[63] During his high school sophomore year, Billy Mills lived in the back seat of a car. He was a three-time college All-American star. Yet he could not join a college fraternity and was asked to stay out of his team's All-American photo because he was Native American. Mills's training, discipline, and fortitude led him to the Olympics where he competed in the 10,000-meter run. Midway through the race, he moved up from fourth place to run next to the world record-holder. He looked into the stadium and saw his wife crying for him. Then a competitor pushed him into the third lane and still another made a break between them, positioning Mills back into third place. Mills became so angry that he sought to catch up with the leader to hit him. But he then recalled that the mind, body, and spirit work as one—and in the last 100 meters, his thoughts changed from "one more try" to "I can win! I can win! I can win!"[64] Mills became the only American ever to win a gold medal in the Olympic 10,000-meter run, a record that has stood since 1964.

Mills recalled a quote from a psychology textbook that stated: "The subconscious cannot distinguish between reality and fantasy." "That hit me. From then on, as I trained, I told myself over and over, 'You can win! You can win! You can win!' I literally programmed myself."[65] Mills interpreted the quote to mean that one's mind records everything, good or bad. One becomes what one's mind dwells upon. Hence, one becomes what one thinks, great or small. Mills also said that for every hurtful comment people made to him, he'd go to his room or to a mountain where he'd tell himself hundreds of positive things to erase it.

Even if you are not subject to such harsh criticisms and discrimination, Mill's remark is a good guideline. A person is a composite of all his or her thoughts, good, bad, and in between. You can use this idea to spot certain aspects within yourself that you feel need to be developed or corrected. You may notice recurrent harmful thoughts that detract from your total progress. You may use the concept to reinforce your self-determination during tough times. While using wise tactics and discipline, tell yourself: You can succeed! You can do it! You can win! And, of course, don't let others degrade your sense of self-worth.

I'm not advising you to ignore your emotional needs. I'm reminded of an amusing discussion between one of my older, self-assured classmates and our Critical Thinking professor. During their dialogue, student's heads were turning back and forth as if we were at a tennis match. The professor had stated that emotions cloud critical thinking. My classmate voiced concern that this might lead students to deny their emotions and base all decisions entirely on logical thought. She said that to know what it is to be human, one should be able to experience the emotions. Fulfilling emotional needs is important in order to be a balanced person. To take Mills' remark a step farther, you become what you think *and* feel. Balance your practice of self-illumination by being realistic about your expectations, both intellectually and emotionally.

When Nothing Less Than 100% Is Acceptable

The best is good enough.
—Johann Wolfgang Von Goethe, 1749–1832[66]

So far, my discussion on striving for 100% has been based primarily on self-determination. You decide to push yourself to score 100. However, there are some cases when a parent, mentor, or elder pressures a student to perform to perfection. This is much different. I've experienced such demands and share my perspective on them.

Pleasing parents, mentors, or elders can motivate a student to behave in certain ways. Perfect test scores can be one criterion for pleasing them. John Naber, 1976 Olympic gold medalist in the men's backstroke, recalled a remark he believed reflected the wrong attitude—namely, "You don't win silver, you lose gold."[67]

This remark is significant for students from perfectionist environments where nothing less than "gold," or 100%, is acceptable. In these circumstances, enormous pressure is imposed on a student. Often, rather than being commended for scoring 95% on an exam, a student is berated for being 5% flawed. This is like constantly emphasizing the tiny empty portion of an almost overflowing cup.

My exposure to perfectionist standards came from Chinese Confucian elders. In Confucianism, one behaves according to social code, not individual autonomy. Subordinates are to respect and comply with their superiors—namely, parents, teachers, elders, and others who have greater authority according to the social code. Apparently there are disparities between what's stated in the Confucian classics and how some Confucian doctrines were actually practiced in China. But one thing is certain: how Confucianism was practiced in China shaped our first-generation Chinese immigrant elders in America.[68] These people were products of their place and time, and Confucianism was the basis for their child-rearing attitudes here.

To explain the conflict of perfectionism, I've cross-referenced several Confucian principles with Abraham Maslow's "hierarchy of needs," a Western motivational theory developed in 1943. Several fundamental Confucian principles govern student behavior. "Harmony is precious" instructs subordinates to accept unfair demands imposed by their "superiors." This is practicing ideal behavior.[69] "Pleasing superiors" means that "one not only submits to persons having authority, but actually acquires a sense of satisfaction and reward by pleasing them."[70] The "Golden Mean" instructs one to avoid confrontation and behave moderately.[71]

These Confucian principles were woven into a motivational system designed to make subordinates try their utmost in all endeavors. Perfectionism is a common Chinese Confucian value. The way to please superiors was by fulfilling their demands to achieve perfect scores in school.

A common penalty for imperfect scores was criticism, often scathing, derogatory, or humiliating in nature. Some Confucian students were not praised even after achieving perfect scores. Praise built ego and arrogance. Lack of humility was imperfect. In the quest for perfection, flaws were emphasized much more than achievements. Falling short of perfection motivated a subordinate to keep trying. What seemed unfair was to be tolerated.

Displeasing superiors became associated with pain of two kinds: the pain of rejection from those important to you, and the psychological wound from their criticism. Both animals and people instinctively seek to avoid pain. Hence part of a student's motivation also stems from pain avoidance.

Maslow's hierarchy of needs is a motivational theory that is studied in psychology and business management courses, but I've applied it to this subject. In *Management*, Robert Kreitner points to a chief message of the theory: "A fulfilled need does not motivate an individual."[72] If so, then it is the unfulfilled need that motivates. Perfect test scores are so intensely emphasized that a student begins to perceive them as a need. Thus multiple forces compel and impel a student: the universal human desire to be accepted by parents and superiors, the socialized need to please them, and the instinct to avoid the pain of rejection and psychological injury—all converge in the drive for perfect scores.

The rationale for this harsh system is to make you determined to achieve. Besides "gold is tempered through fire," another saying states, "batted down 7 times, you rise 8." Some people stay down (that is, their spirit becomes cowed or inhibited) while others get up and become angry. It takes some maturity to understand why you're being batted down, and such realization may occur only after long-term exposure has worn on you. The system pushes you to perform to your utmost. You learn humility and respect. You can develop strength of mind, fortitude, and tenacity as well as exceptional discipline, focus, and skill in a particular activity that can lead to outstanding achievement.

Unfortunately, there can also be side effects from this motivational system. Years of criticism can make a "subordinate" hot tempered or bitter from being treated unfairly. In other cases, your self-esteem may become debilitated if all you hear for years is negative feedback about what you didn't do or what you're not. You keep trying, but unless you get 100, you're criticized. You don't feel good about trying your best. Through repeated criticism, a big chunk of your worth is defined not by you but by your "elders and betters." Under sustained pressure, the scope of your world is greatly reduced as your bases for victory or defeat become narrowed, leading to continuous mental unrest in the quest to satisfy your "superiors."

There is additional significance. After long-term socialization, you habitually fault yourself for imperfection. Nobody may be nagging you, but inside you note with great unrest where or how you fell short. You may grow intolerant for things that can reasonably be considered good enough. In extreme cases, you may perceive that what you do imperfectly is a total failure, that minor flaws negate everything else positive from your work, or, worse yet, that every minor flaw is a glaring reflection of your incompetence. In effect, this system can teach you to torture yourself.

Based on my experiences, I can attest to the fact that you're pushed to your limits to excel. Your skills develop dramatically, but at the cost of peace of mind. You may be significantly more skilled or disciplined than others in a trade, but your self-perception may be below average from perpetual put-downs. This can place you at a disadvantage in certain contexts, such as during job interviews, when you need to confidently state your strengths. If you appear uncertain in your abilities, an employer isn't likely to evaluate you favorably.

Now consider that none of the aforementioned dynamics are explained to you in direct language: you discover all of these mechanics through trial and error. You need to be very perceptive about what's happening before you can conceive of remedial modifications. Psychological health can take a beating in the process.

Ironically, those most crucial to a student's morale can actually be tearing him or her down. Parents and mentors may mean well but not realize the harm in perpetuating such a tradition. A student is constantly compelled to do his or her utmost, but at what cost? If 100% was something every student was capable of, I could see the value in such strictness. But not every student can achieve perfect scores. They may try—and this is commendable—but faulting them for subperfect scores after their best efforts can cause them psychological conflict.

Perfect achievement is a noble ideal, but its means, as practiced, are painful. My intent is not to encourage you to despise your elders nor rebel against your mother culture, but merely to encourage you to be wise to what's happening so you can become your best without accumulating the baggage that will take years to undo. To achieve balance, my conclusion was to aim for 100, do my absolute best, and accept the results. I would work myself, face the exam, and then let the chips fall where they may. Never mind the remarks—know and enjoy the fact that that you *are* doing *and becoming* your best.

Accepting the results of your genuine best efforts is healthier than intolerant perfectionism. You're still extracting the maximum benefit from each experience, expanding your knowledge, developing discipline, using good work habits, and receiving good grades that will allow you to graduate and qualify for graduate school or a good job. Your discipline will also help set you apart from others in the workplace.

It's counterproductive to berate a student, who works hard, for the empty portion of his or her cup of achievement. Applying Mills' concept and seeing each person in totality, the "imperfect" student is not merely the product of subperfect achievements but of many concerted efforts and accomplishments as well. This doesn't condone deliberate mediocrity but highlights the fact that such negative thinking can damage your self-esteem. Seeing the full portion of your cup allows you to be content and move forward with less psychological turmoil. You'll be more at peace with yourself than those who are on an endless quest for perfection.

After I resumed U.S. college studies, I scored 100 points on only four exams. Does this subperfect test record really matter in light of an A grade-point average and six academic honors? Let the reader be the judge.

To sum up my opinion in one sentence: *Your best is good enough.*

Perfectionism: Know What You May Sacrifice

Although aiming for 100 is something that I used as a goal, I didn't agonize about falling short of it after trying my best. This is what I would call "tolerant perfectionism." There are times, however, when perfectionist standards are necessary, such as when you participate in high-stake competitions or truly wish to reach your full potential in a specific activity. An international athlete perfects his or her form to maximize performance down to hundredths of a point. A ceramist's hand-thrown eggcups are cut in half by a teacher to measure their symmetry. Any competitor striving to become #1 goes all out in training and performing. Achieving perfection can become your primary daily focus under such a regimen.

One potential cost of perfectionism is regret about sacrifices made en route, however. Whether you seek perfection primarily for yourself or for your parents, consider the pros and cons and understand any sacrifices you make. Although perfectionism will push you to improve skills to your limits, you may concentrate a disproportionate amount of time and energy each day to practice and compete. As a result, other activities in your life may need to be deferred or passed by completely.

Certain activities can only be done while you're young and free from commitment. Certain personal issues will be more difficult to correct later on. Look deep within yourself and be sure that what you forego is something you can do without. Also, consider what new personal conflicts might be created by a lifestyle of perfectionism. Feedback from friends or others who have been there can be very helpful.

I endorse your keeping your dreams in front of you. But part of your duty to yourself is being clear about why you are pursuing something, what it entails, and what you're sacrificing in the process. Factoring this into your decision may help you avoid regret in the future.

Reward Yourself

Success can be its own reward. You've gone through hours of reading, note-taking, studying, creative writing, exam reviews, test-taking, critical thinking exercises, expanding your memory, practicing new problem-solving skills, formulating strategies, framing questions to understand situations more precisely, rising to interpersonal challenges in group projects, surmounting whatever your teachers threw at you, developing communication skills, increasing your awareness of the world around you, reaching your intellectual potential, and learning how to make better decisions—all through self-discipline and determination. You sought, you achieved. See these changes within. Hey, you did it—congratulations! Why shouldn't you feel good about yourself? Reward yourself after each stage fulfilled, each target grade achieved, and each difficult assignment.

Notice whether or not you've really tried your best, though—which goes back to being honest with yourself. Undeserved rewards associated with poor performance will decrease your incentive to work hard, discipline yourself, and try your best. This confines your overall progress. Please don't do this to yourself.

Learn from Your Errors

A strong and well-constituted man digests his experiences (deeds and misdeeds all included) just as he digests his meats, even when he has some tough morsels to swallow.
—Friedrich Wilhelm Nietzsche, 1844–1900[73]

The ability to learn from mistakes, academic or personal, is a good habit and will improve life for you and those around you. Ironically, learning from errors can be a big stumbling block for some, inviting trouble again and again. Breaking a bad habit is hard, but it's much easier when you're young. While older people have the wisdom of experience, your youth is your advantage: it's easier for you to change and form good habits.

Good planning helps prevent many errors. Yet mistakes can still happen. No matter how self-confident or eloquent a person may be, no one is above committing an error. A mistake is a mistake. But you can accept it and clean things up. When they occur, view errors as an opportunity for progress. The wisdom you gain from the experience will give you greater foresight for improving your strategies the next time. You may even perceive potential errors before they occur.

After an assignment or test is scored, learn how to improve your work for the next time. Meanwhile, be content with the results; don't kick yourself for the errors if you've tried your best.

Develop a Good Memory

Those who cannot remember the past are condemned to repeat it.
—George Santayana, 1863–1952[74]

Memory substantially affects your progress in- and outside of the classroom. Pay special attention to developing your memory. A good memory helps when you're writing one or two sentences behind a teacher who is lecturing. Memory helps piece together dispersed and varied parts of a whole during problem-solving. Exams are based on what you've learned and retained and they shape a huge chunk of your grades. A good memory helps address unresolved conflicts and is an aid to learning from errors. Some lessons take longer than others to correct, and this is not always by choice. Not all personal mistakes are perceived at the time. When reflecting within yourself, a good memory allows you to recall incidents and understand them from your present perspective (another form of connect and relate). You can see them and break a particular pattern of error. If you cannot understand a past incident, a good memory provides the basis for articulating recollections to a friend or counselor. If needed, research the exercises and techniques that will help you strengthen your memory.

Don't Let Others Douse Your Glow

You become your best for your own sake, not to make others feel insecure. But there will be some people who feel insecure when they see you surpassing them, or because they can't grasp the concept of developing one's individual potential. Everyone has a potential within him- or herself, but not everyone has the vision or fortitude to fulfill it. I never rubbed my accomplishments in anyone's face, but I also wouldn't let others drag me down.

Keep your poise and dignity. Ridicule or rudeness aimed at you only reveals someone's jealousy or ignorance. Others may try to inhibit your progress or break your spirit. Be wise to it and don't let this affect you. Seek your niche among those who respect you and what you stand for, not among those who feel threatened and contemptuous.

A Healthy Mind in a Healthy Body

Health and intellect are the two blessings of life.
—Menander, ca. 342–292 B.C.E.[75]

Mens sana in corpore sano is Latin for "a sound mind in a sound body." Body and mind are your responsibility for life. The physical body is part of everyone's potential, but few develop it. To develop the body does not require competition-grade athletic training but proper diet and exercise, so that your mind and body are a balanced whole. Like your mind, you want to shape your health into the best state you can. The option is there for just about every student.

You're already building your mind, big time. Ironically, developing and maintaining your body is not promoted much in college. When was the last time you saw units in physical education, nutrition, and health studies required for all majors? People tend to place great emphasis on mental pursuits but little on physical health and fitness. Take a look at people outside your school, and I'm sure you'll see many who are overweight or out of shape.

We should all be concerned about the future because we will have to spend the rest of our lives there.
—Charles Franklin Kettering, 1876–1958[76]

We want to live as long as possible with a sharp mind and healthy body. We cannot predict our individual life span, nor does exercise guarantee its extension. But we have the choice to maximize our quality of life within that time through voluntary education, diet, and exercise. There's no impediment to making yourself smart and healthy simultaneously.

Within ten years after college, one's view changes as the first effects of aging begin to appear. Wisdom gained but youth lost through age is one of life's fundamental ironies. Quite often, I've seen older people's bodies deteriorate faster than their minds. As you age, you may find that your limitations become more physical than mental—a complete opposite from youth. Physical aging cannot be stopped, but the good news is that it can be slowed down.

The same body is going to be with you until your last day. To live a life as long as possible in good health requires taking care of your body while you're young so you can age more gracefully and avoid common health and mobility problems associated with aging. Health is a long-term issue.

Although it's all too easy to take physical health for granted in the peak of youth, it's wiser to cultivate healthful practices, starting now, as a way of life that will carry you through into later years. *If you're healthy now, stay healthy. If you're not in the best of health now, your youth is still an advantage*: your habits aren't yet fixed, an existing condition probably hasn't reached chronic proportions, and you have the time, energy, metabolism, and freedom to correct your health pattern and state. Make restoring your health a top priority. The sooner you address this, the better. There's no reason not to give yourself every advantage to remain healthy over the years.

Forming good health habits when young places you ahead of those who seek to compensate for long-term neglect in midlife. Poor health practices will eventually catch up with you, and when you're older, you may be more set in your ways. The longer health is ignored, the longer it takes to recover, restore, and maintain. Basic health cannot be bought with money after years of neglect, nor can it be maintained solely by medications. In many cases, people merely address their symptoms and not the root cause of their health problems. Their fundamental problems persist, due to lack of proper diet, exercise, or lifestyle, yet they rely on pills to mask symptoms. Perhaps they have let their bodies decline too far for too long and are at the mercy of medical intervention and continued degeneration. This is not the way to go with your whole life ahead of you.

To educate yourself on self-reliant health practices, I endorse a study in human biology, health science, and nutrition, especially if these courses simultaneously fulfill your general education requirements. These courses will give you insight into your body's intricately balanced inner workings, its basic needs, and ways to sustain good health. You'll gain an appreciation for an astonishing biological wonder that everyone is born with but that few appreciate.

Exercise is an important part of maintaining health. Exercise can help alleviate stress, heighten your self-confidence, provide a refreshing break from a monotonous study routine, enhance health, manage your weight, and help you age more gracefully.

The most common concern about exercise may be finding the time to do so outside of your studies. Other obligations of modern life may consume much of your "extra" time and energy. However, the human body has daily biological needs and cannot retain its good state of health without exercise. *Only you can find the balance between study and time for exercise over the course of your undergraduate years.*

Managing and achieving your ideal body weight is far easier when you're young because your metabolism is naturally high. Weight management is achieved by ensuring that your caloric intake doesn't exceed your body's requirements. Your body has two general caloric requirements: that to sustain basal metabolism, and that to replenish what you expend from physical activity. Basal metabolism is what your body consumes in calories each day to sustain itself at rest—to maintain your heart, respiration, nervous system, immune system, digestion, excretion, and basic biological functions. Exercise, walking, or doing work consumes calories above your basal metabolic rate; such physical activity varies according to the frequency, duration, and intensity of your movements. For example, running 7 miles a day five times a week will burn more calories than swimming 20 minutes once a week. Eat what you need to sustain your basal metabolism and replenish what you burn off from physical activity. When your intake exceeds these caloric requirements, your liver turns excess food calories into fat. Within this range of caloric requirements, the quality of your daily food (i.e., a balanced diet versus junk food) will be a key determinant of your overall health.

You might investigate the athletic programs open for enrollment at your school. You may find it easier to discipline yourself to exercise regularly each week if you do so with a friend, classmate, or training partner.

Understanding a particular exercise before you undertake it is only sound thinking. Know the fundamental purpose, criteria, risks, and benefits of a given form of exercise. For example, if you plan to bicycle long distances, make sure your handlebar stem, seat height, and seat angle fore and aft are correct for your body proportions. If you plan to weight train, familiarize yourself with common hazards and take any needed safety precautions.

Always know the proper techniques to your exercises to avoid injury. One typically does not realize the value of body health, flexibility, and mobility when young. The realization may come at an older age, after sustaining injuries in youth that may be debilitating. Learning the correct biomechanical motions reduces the chance of injury and ensures that your energy is used most efficiently to yield optimum results, for both athletic performance and health benefits. As an example of the former, despite the wealth of public information available, I've seen people at gyms executing free weight dead-lifts and bent-over rows with their lower backs arched. These were accidents waiting to happen. Such improper technique invites injury to either the spinal discs or surrounding soft tissue.

Learning the fundamental principles of warming up and stretching will also be one of your best investments. Both play an important role in athletic performance while simultaneously reducing the likelihood of injury. Injuries are not entirely avoidable in exercise, but they can be minimized relative to the hazards inherent to your activity of choice. Injuries can be a nuisance and are expensive due to the cost of medication, treatment, rehabilitation, and lost productivity. At a nuisance level, injuries cause pain or temporarily limit your physical activity. In a worst-case scenario, they linger to affect you into old age, impede your agility, and cause recurrent pain.

The last thing you need is to walk into a lecture, or even worse an exam, dazed by painkillers. I remember taking a prescription painkiller for a sports injury when in Singapore. Since missing one class would cause me to fall behind, I had to attend. I was so drowsy I had difficulty answering the teacher's questions. I felt embarrassed for appearing out of it, and my classmates were turning around in their seats to look at me because I was uncharacteristically muddled.

Such advice is not intended to discourage participation in your favorite sports but a suggestion to understand what you're doing in order to minimize unnecessary injury, pain, and inconvenience. If injuries occur, learn from them and seek not to repeat the error.

It is widely held among athletes that the three factors of an effective training program are *frequency*, *intensity*, and *duration*. Adapted to a reasonable regimen of exercise, frequency or consistency (number of times per week) is the most important aspect for sustaining your health. Besides providing health benefits that schoolwork does not, exercise strengthens your mind, thus reinforcing your determination to remain focused on your goals.

Educate yourself first by speaking with or reading books written by athletic teachers, coaches, sport physicians, physiologists, kinesiologists, or physical therapists who will steer you in the right direction. Your school may offer physical education courses that will enable you get your exercise for the day while receiving proper instruction and supervision for newly learned techniques. Also, consult with your medical doctor for his or her direction before you embark on an exercise regimen.

Today Shapes Tomorrow

What many people fail to realize is that today is in your grasp.
—Anonymous

While planning for the future is important, many people lose sight of what's in front of them—namely, today. Present experiences shape you into who you are today and will become tomorrow. You either keep what you are today or use it as a basis for change.

Think of your most successful peers. Now think of your least successful peers. With a few exceptions, these people have one thing in common: they evolved into their state one day at a time.

Everybody has 24 hours a day; it's what you make of them that shapes your life. Likewise, people have the same amount of time to go through college, but not everyone has a productive experience in doing so. If the time is frittered away, what will you have afterward? Similarly, some focus mainly on grabbing the degree and overlook their present learning opportunities. Realize the true value of time. A day wasted is a day gone forever.

In addition, take the time to reflect on what's happening to you personally, academically, and professionally. Quite often, people rush to keep up with the rat race but don't have the presence of mind to step off the treadmill and think of their blessings or ponder life's deeper meanings. Reflecting and smelling the roses are a part of maintaining balance.

Yesterday is gone. But you have the ability and choice to improve your circumstances or address long-term conflicts today. You can continue building your achievements. Today is a new day; live your life well.

See the Map That You're Charting

Take calculated risks. That is quite different from being rash.
—George Smith Patton, 1885–1945[77]

Each day can bring you challenges that you haven't encountered before, with no precedent or solution set by others. To be creative and forge ahead requires calculated experimentation to see what works and what doesn't. Public speaking instructor Alice Filmer has said that although no one is born with a road map to navigate his or her life, the path before you lights up at each step. When faced with an untried, non-life-threatening solution, my State Department friend has said, "Try it, and if it doesn't work you can always go back to the way you were before." Consider getting a few A grades—if you don't like it you can go back to your Cs and Bs, though I doubt that you'll want to revert.

There is a wealth of information accessible in the public domain by others who have journeyed, experimented, dared, erred, succeeded, and documented their experiences. Sources include our libraries, the Internet, counselors, professors, friends, mentors, elder classmates, and alumni. Though there may not be identical precedents for your situation, you can look for similarities and differences, combine such evaluation with your best judgment, and then act. There's no set formula for shaping your life as you go along, but this is part of its excitement. Isn't this a delightful prospect for those embracing individuality and plotting their direction through their own creativity and wit? Of course, individuality should be balanced with acting responsibly.

It's not always possible to see great distances ahead to determine whether or not to change your present course. In many cases, you have the option to turn back and retrace your steps. Perhaps retracing one step is sufficient, or perhaps you'll need to retrace half a dozen steps or more. In other instances a simple change of direction or other modifications will suffice.

It is said that in hindsight we all have perfect vision. When stepping in new directions or facing unique circumstances, we do not have the wisdom of hindsight. Sometimes you can go back to the way you were before, with a new appreciation of advantages. At other times, you may err or have an unpleasant experience. Sometimes you'll have both, sometimes neither. But don't be discouraged from acting according to your best judgment. You cannot do more than that, and in any case you will gain the wisdom of experience by which to improve your subsequent decisions. Experiences can be happy or sad, stressful or exhilarating, but they'll seldom be boring. See the map that you're charting and chart it wisely. Observe and learn as you go along, while keeping your heart intact.

16

Give Yourself the Chance to Study Abroad

In today's jet age, with its plethora of school cooperative programs, a well-rounded college education wouldn't be complete without one foreign academic experience. Spending a semester or a year in a foreign country develops you in a way that reading books or staying in America never could. A foreign culture has to be directly experienced in daily life. Just as the smell of bacon frying or coffee brewing is indescribable, so you simply have to experience the feeling of studying abroad to see what it is like. It'll be one of the best things you'll ever do for yourself.

Studying abroad matures you and dramatically expands your perspective on the world and life at large, far beyond that of the average student. You return to America a more globally enlightened person. Your overseas experiences affect your life for years in ways that are unimaginable at the time. You have the opportunity to observe a host country's educational, social, political, housing, medical, economic, legal, and transportation systems, its cultural norms and mores, its peoples' thinking, religion, daily behavior, philosophies, and how these affect business conduct and costs. This is an especially good opportunity for those interested in the social sciences, history, cultural anthropology, language studies, international business, and international relations. However, any student with any major will benefit from studying abroad. You'll see how other cultures, faced with some of the same problems as those of your home country, address them in completely different ways. You can compare America with other nations with your own eyes and not have to rely on what's selectively conveyed by mainstream media.

Offered and coordinated through your college at little financial cost, a foreign life experience will never be within easier reach, unless your relatives have direct contacts or roots abroad. Even so, you can expand your multicultural exposures by studying in a country in which you've not yet resided. Assuming you've never done it before, studying overseas is strategic at this time in your life because

1. You won't have more freedom from commitment to go see the world than you do now.
2. You can choose among different subjects taught in different cities.
3. Your school coordinates the correspondence and paperwork for your application.
4. You'll receive academic credit while enjoying a foreign living experience.
5. It's easier and faster to live in your country of choice as a student than hope that an employer will send you overseas. Such job postings may not be immediate nor in your preferred region or city but when and where the company wants to send you.
6. Your foreign school may organize group activities and local excursions, saving you time, money, uncertainty, and stress compared to exploring an unknown culture alone. Being part of a guided group will be safer, cheaper than booking an independent tour, more educational (because you'll have interpreters), convenient, and fun.
7. It's easier to make friends with your classmates because your subject of study is one of the few things you'll have in common when meeting them for the first time. Classmates will be eager to exchange stories and get to know each other.
8. Your classmates or friends may have informal group outings on weekends; it's fun to travel in a new land with friends. Friends can help you experience the local culture, flavors, and shops while steering you away from price-gouging tourist traps. They can also advise you on significant local events, which neighborhoods to avoid, and what behaviors are taboo.
9. You can expand your circle of friends to an international scale.
10. The experiences broaden and deepen your perspective beyond that of the average person.
11. You gain a mature, international perspective on life by seeing with your own eyes how America differs from the other parts of the world.

Study whatever and wherever you please among your school's subject and program offerings. If foreign language is your fancy, what better way to learn it than among those who speak it every day? Through conversations with locals, you gain insights very different from those here. I learned more Mandarin in Singapore in one year than some students learned in three years at an American university.

If you don't have an opportunity to study abroad through your school, you can research organizations that coordinate these services. Listings of these organizations can be found on the Internet or in reference books available at the library or retail bookstores. You could contact a foreign university directly via mail, phone, fax, or the Internet to ascertain its admission criteria. However, tuition may be much more expensive if you apply directly. Besides completing an application form, you will need to send payment in local currency, your official transcripts, letters of recommendation, and possibly a medical report completed and signed by your physician. You'll also need to apply for a student visa.

When visiting your host country, view it with an open mind. You'll enjoy the experience and learn more. Looking for things to be critical about defeats the whole purpose and will only make you miserable for the time you're there. You'll discover how America's international image differs from its domestic one. You'll realize how life in America shapes a person differently from people abroad.

In traveling to a fair number of places, I did see some ethnocentric American travelers insulting or criticizing citizens in another country—not a good thing for a guest to do. Criticizing people in their own home is not only extremely rude but may also create conflict for you and your associates due to violating local codes of etiquette. American culture has its virtues, but it cannot be applied across the board the world over. Different peoples conduct themselves according to their own customs, norms, and mores. As a temporary resident, local impressions of you will be different than if you were just a tourist. Being cross-culturally sensitive is only proper and a part of your life education. (Cross-cultural sensitivity can also prevent financial losses when doing international business.)

With your degree, internship, extracurricular activities, international experience, and foreign language skills, your résumé will be impressive. Combined with an educated mind, maturity, and self-confidence, your presentation at a job interview will set you apart from others. (Don't forget to apply your interview skills and the finer points about grooming and dress attire.) Interviewers meet lots of people, and they notice everything about a person.

Give yourself the chance to study abroad, have a good time, spread your wings, branch out in life, and return home safely.

17

One More Word

Keep Organized Files

Knowledge is of two kinds. We know a subject ourselves,
or we know where we can find information upon it.
—Samuel Johnson, 1709–1784[78]

Save your college notes; don't discard them. Unless you enroll in graduate school, you won't be taking such copious notes in so many different subjects anytime soon. If you could recall and apply everything your professors and teachers imparted to you, you'd be one hot commodity. You may not be able to retain everything they've taught you, but you have their thoughts recorded in your notes, which are a gold mine of information. Considering the time, work, and expense you put into your notes, it would be wasteful to discard them.

Multi-subject, spiral-bound notebooks are convenient because all your semester's notes are ordered chronologically. Each four- to five-subject notebook represents a semester, can be labeled so, and is easily pulled and reshelved.

Use a separate file folder for storing other papers from each semester, organized by course. For each course, assemble papers in order of syllabus, handouts, tests, quizzes, graded papers and assignments, and speeches. Rubber band or binder-clip each stack of course papers together so they will be easier to sort and recover in the future, and also be less prone to spilling if the file is accidentally dropped.

Standardization and matching are key to file organization. File labeling should be consistent. I labeled each file by semester. To access a specific course's information, excluding lecture notes, I first looked on my transcript to find the right semester. (You could tape or staple a copy of your transcript on the inside left cover of each semester file to serve as a "table of contents.") Then I'd locate the appropriate semester file.

A separate, consolidated file should contain your report cards, final course rankings, transcripts, and administrative paperwork (e.g., your application, admission notice, medical clearance reports, cashier's receipts, approvals, drop forms and confirmations, documents required for graduation, scholarship forms, and correspondence with your college or academic advisor). You can organize contents in this file by date in descending order (an exception was my personal preference to group my report cards together at the front of the file). These files give you an organized paper trail should you encounter administrative complications, apply to graduate school (file information might be used for your statement of purpose), or need to use them for research, your diary, a personal memoir, an example for friends, associates, or children, a reminder of your discipline and college experiences, or even material for writing your own book.

Accept Formal Recognition Offered to You

Any form of recognition is acceptable.
—former NATO officer and U.S. Army Major General

Do not turn back when you are just at the goal.
—Publilius Syrus, fl. first century B.C.E.[79]

Many people feel that their talents and hard work go unrecognized, yet some students decline invitations to join academic honor societies. During my commencement, I was surprised by students asking, "What's Phi Beta Kappa?" when noticing my key pin. One classmate, in his final semester, nearly passed by an invitation from a national honor society because he had never heard of it and thought its $60 lifetime membership fee was excessive. His college of major had already conferred honors upon him. He took my advice to accept the invitation, for which I'm glad.

Saying you're "too busy" to bother, or thinking it's no big deal to decline, is imprudent. Giving yourself every honest advantage doesn't end with your last assignment or exam. If you're offered membership to academic honor societies, whether they are national, regional, school-based, major-specific, or departmental, accept them all; these are rare opportunities for a privileged few. First, lifetime membership fees, if any, are typically less than a dinner at an upscale restaurant. Second, each formal recognition strengthens your résumé for work and graduate school. When seeking that first job after college, employers look closely at your educational qualifications, so every distinction gives you an edge. I don't agree with one person's remark that Phi Beta Kappa won't get you a job. As one recruiter put it, "Sure it will: your résumé goes to the top of the stack for consideration." You can't buy yourself an academic distinction for $50 or $60—it can only be earned by hard intellectual work. An employer who sees academic honors on your résumé knows that you're a cut above the average student. Even stating that you made the Dean's List reflects above-average discipline and performance. No employer will be impressed by your stating that you declined invitations from honor societies. Third, honors are tangible proof of your achievements. You deserve this recognition! Fourth, honor societies offer you networking contacts and extracurricular activities. Fifth, honor societies provide opportunities to hold office positions—another boon to career development and résumé-building. Sixth, honor societies can provide volunteer work for those seeking to contribute to their community.

You can always omit honors from your résumé and conversations whenever you please. But if you decline the invitation in the first place, you may not be able to acquire membership in the society in the future. Waiving formal recognition is analogous to giving up just before the payoff. You've labored for years; why turn it down?

Keep an American Tradition Alive

American culture is built on change. Some of its traditions are disappearing with each generation. But there is one American tradition that I hope you will keep alive. It is a gem that has been with us since the 1940s but that is seldom practiced these days. The tradition is treating others with kindness without expecting anything in return.

Besides asking you to strive for your best in college, there is one request that I ask of the reader: try to make the world a better place within your own capacity. Such action accords with what's in your heart and need not be elaborate or expensive. Being a friend when a friend is needed, telling a loved one how much he or she means to you, being courteous, volunteering for a cause, or doing a job properly instead of emulating popular indifference—all these fit the bill. You don't need a reason to do something nice for another person if your motivation stems from the heart. The acts should not feel forced but are best pegged to whatever feels comfortable to you. And, of course, it's fine to use discretion before acting. The tradition, though originating from simpler times requiring fewer calculated decisions, can still be practiced as long as you don't act naively or blindly. Try doing something good for someone else without expecting something in return. I'm sure you'll notice a change in how you feel about yourself and how others view you. Meanwhile, you'll be making our world a better place in your own way.

Ready to Rock

With regard to excellence, it is not enough to know, but we must try to have and use it.
—Aristotle, 384–322 B.C.E.[80]

Nothing ever becomes real till it is experienced—
Even a proverb is no proverb to you till your Life has illustrated it.
—John Keats, 1795–1821[81]

First ponder, then dare.
—Helmuth Von Moltke, 1800–1891[82]

Everything in this book gives you the strategy that carried me from three Fs to Phi Beta Kappa and five other academic honors. My journey proves that you can succeed if you try. I have given you my formulas. The application, discipline, and perseverance are up to you. First define your parameters, set your goals, and formulate your strategies; then put them into practice, fine-tuning as you go along. Your own perspectives, philosophies, and strategies will evolve as you gain more experience. As you progress, monitor what helps you move forward with honesty and kindness, and what does not. You'll learn a lot about yourself in the process.

When I was a struggling student, I was not uncertain about whether I *could* succeed in school but about *how* to do so. I knew I had it in me to succeed, as should you. By applying and adapting the same methods that helped me, you will reach your potential, too. Search, discover, and understand. Be able to answer for yourself the question, "What have you learned in college?" Give yourself a smile when you succeed. And always believe in yourself.

Appendix

Checklists for Complete Strategy

Keep working one day and one term at a time until the day your school tells you: "Congratulations, you have fulfilled all criteria for graduation!"

Course criteria

____ Determine course criteria within first two class meetings. Read syllabi in class and again at home

____ Assignments

    ____ attendance

    ____ chapter readings

    ____ class participation

    ____ homework papers

    ____ quizzes

    ____ midterms

    ____ term paper

    ____ group project

    ____ final exam

    ____ extra credits

    ____ assignments' percentage breakdowns

    ____ technical criteria for assignments

____ Assess point scale used for assigning grades

____ Assess assignments' point worth

____ Final exam date (know these dates for all courses at the beginning of the semester)

_____ Final exam type
_____ Grading method (curve vs. absolute scale)
_____ Calculate semester grade using percentage weights disclosed by the teacher
_____ Target final exam score (to allocate final exam review efforts effectively over all courses per term)
_____ Penalties for missed assignments or absence
_____ Your image with instructor if your grade is borderline

3-Day Method of exam preparation (see Chapter 11)
_____ Apply core principles for test preparations
_____ Day 1: review portion 1
_____ Day 2: review portions 1 & 2
_____ Day 3: review portions 1, 2, 3
_____ Day 3 or 4: exam, depending on schedule
_____ Option to spread review portions over 4 to 5 days

Graduation criteria
_____ Master checklist of all requirements for graduation (see Chapter 2)

Organize files
_____ Folder for records (consolidated)
    _____ administrative paperwork (see Chapter 17)
    _____ report cards
    _____ final course rankings
    _____ transcript(s)
_____ Separate folder for each term
    _____ contents organized by course (rubber banded or binder clipped together)
    _____ syllabus
    _____ handouts
    _____ tests and quizzes
    _____ graded papers
    _____ graded assignments
    _____ speeches

Approach

____ Seek teachers from whom you can learn well

____ Work hard, honestly, and efficiently (see Chapter 3)

____ Analyze course criteria carefully to tailor approach (see the following and Chapter 5)

____ Apply core study principles (see Chapter 4)

____ Plan your strategy to be organized, streamlined, and thorough

____ Calendar deadlines for *all* courses for the entire semester or quarter

____ Aim for the highest scores and grades commensurate with your ability

____ Plan your time to produce your best work

____ Work in stages to achieve your goals

____ Choose maximum study pace where performance peaks but not ebbs

____ Accept the results of your best efforts

____ Take the time in college to explore, define, and develop yourself

____ Be true to your values when choosing a major

____ Get the most out of your liberal arts courses even if they're not your major

____ Know when to have fun and when to study

____ Know when to stop and smell the roses

____ Give yourself time to reflect on what's happening to you

____ Know when to give yourself a break

____ Engage in "connect and relate" learning

____ Realize the value of today

____ See the big picture

____ Eat properly to fuel yourself for top performance

____ Ensure regular sleep

____ Stay in good health

Notes

1. "Periclum ex aliis facito tibi quod ex usu siet. (A saying.), Loeb Classical Library edition, with occasional changes in the translation." Bartlett, John. (1968). *Bartlett's Familiar Quotations* (14th ed.). Boston: Little, Brown and Company, p. 108b.
2. *Maxim 571.* "Commonly called Publius, but spelled Publilius by PLINY in his *Natural History, 35, sec. 199.* Translated mainly by DARIUS LYMAN. The numbers are those of the translator." Bartlett, op. cit., p. 126b.
3. *Letter 53*, Translated by W. H. FREMANTLE, Bartlett, op. cit., p. 145b.
4. *Inscribed beneath his bust in the Hall of Fame.* This quote was chosen for its philosophical value and not as a political statement about the Confederacy. Robert Edward Lee, 1807–1870, Bartlett, op. cit., p. 620a.
5. *The Bending of the Bough* [*1900*], *act IV.* Bartlett, op. cit., p. 827a.
6. *Maxim 786.* "Commonly called Publius, but spelled Publilius by PLINY in his *Natural History, 35, sec. 199.* Translated mainly by DARIUS LYMAN. The numbers are those of the translator." Bartlett, op. cit., p. 127a.
7. *Origins of Psychoanalysis. Letter to Fliess* [*October 15, 1897*]. Bartlett, op. cit., p. 833b.
8. *Don Quixote, pt. II, bk. IV, ch. 38, p. 724.* Bartlett, op. cit., p. 197a.
9. Leroy S. Rouner, "Resolved: That Phi Beta Kappa Is Gloriously Useless," *The Key Reporter*, Autumn 2000, vol. 66, no. 1, p. 5. "Leroy S. Rouner is professor of philosophy, religion, and philosophical theology & director of the Institute for Philosophy and Religion at Boston University."
10. *Literature and Dogma* [*1873*], *ch. 1.* Bartlett, op. cit., p. 716a.
11. *Ars Amatoria II, 345.* Bartlett, op. cit., p. 128b.
12. *Thyestes 380*, Loeb Classical Library, Bartlett, op. cit., p. 131b.
13. The Quotations Page. http://www.quotationspage.com/quotes.php3?author=Judy+Garland.
14. Rouner, op. cit., p. 4.
15. Ibid., p. 5.
16. *The Just-So Stories* [*1902*]. *The Elephant's Child.* Bartlett, op. cit., p. 876a.
17. *Afoot in England* [*1909*], *ch. 6.* Bartlett, op. cit., p. 789a.
18. Arnold Schwarzenegger (1985). *Encyclopedia of Modern Bodybuilding.* New York: Simon & Schuster, p. 158.
19. *Speech* [*June 24, 1872*]. Bartlett, op. cit., p. 612b.

20. *Life [1932], ch. 24.* Bartlett, op. cit., p. 811b.

21. *Maxim 388.* "Commonly called Publius, but spelled Publilius by PLINY in his *Natural History, 35, sec. 199.* Translated mainly by DARIUS LYMAN. The numbers are those of the translator." Bartlett, op. cit., p. 126a, and *Maxim 780,* ibid., p. 127a.

22. *Maxim 557,* ibid., p. 126b.

23. *From* DIOGENES LAERTIUS, *bk. I, sec. 79.* "Sayings throughout antiquity were variously attributed to the figures known as the 'seven sages.' The list is commonly given as Thales, Solon, Periander, Cleobulus, Chilon, Bias, Pittacus." Bartlett, op. cit., p. 68b.

24. The Quotations Page. http://www.quotationspage.com/quotes.php3?author=Johann+Wolfgang+von+Goethe. Source of date, Bartlett, op. cit., p. 477a.

25. *Discourses, bk. III, ch. 23,* Loeb Classical Library, Bartlett, op. cit., p. 138b.

26. Deng Ming Dao (1999). *Pure Champion.* Unpublished manuscript.

27. Ibid.

28. Sports—Summer Olympic Champions, 1896–2000, *The World Almanac and Book of Facts 2001.* World Almanac Education Group, Inc., p. 902.

29. Robert Kreitner (1995). *Management* (6th ed.). Boston: Houghton Mifflin Company, p. 111.

30. Ibid.

31. *Politics, bk. V, ch. 4,* Chiefly from *The Basic Works of Aristotle,* edited by RICHARD McKEON. Bartlett, op. cit., p. 98b. "Aristotle is quoting a proverb: 'The beginning is the most important part of the work,' *The Republic, bk. I, 377-B,* Plato, ca. 428–348 B.C.E, translated by BENJAMIN JOWETT." Bartlett, op. cit., p. 94a.

32. *Maxim 596.* "Commonly called Publius, but spelled Publilius by PLINY in his *Natural History, 35, sec. 199.* Translated mainly by DARIUS LYMAN. The numbers are those of the translator." Bartlett, op. cit., p. 126b.

33. *Animal Automatism [1874].* Bartlett, op. cit., p. 725a.

34. Source of quote: J. A. DeVito (1999). *Essentials of Human Communication* (3rd ed). New York: Longman, p. 367. Source of date, Bartlett, op cit., p. 87b.

35. *Title of book [1915].* Bartlett, op. cit., p. 951a.

36. *Tatler [1709-1711], no. 147.* Bartlett, op. cit., p. 395b.

37. Source of quote: DeVito, op. cit., p. 224. Source of date, Bartlett, op. cit., p. 206a.

38. *The Divine Comedy. Inferno, canto XV, 99.* Bartlett, op. cit., p. 160b.

39. *This Is My Story [1937].* Following Anna Eleanor Roosevelt's name was the footnote: "I have lost more than a friend, I have lost an inspiration. She would rather light candles than curse the darkness and her glow has warmed the world. —ADLAI E. STEVENSON [November 7, 1962]." Bartlett, op. cit., p. 981b.

40. *But We Were Born Free [1954], ch. 1.* Bartlett, op. cit., p. 1015b.

41. *Fathers and Sons [1862], ch. 16.* Translated by HARRY STEVENS. Bartlett, op. cit., p. 688a.

42. DeVito, op. cit., p. 378.

43. *The Tall Office Building Artistically Considered, Lippincott's Magazine [March 1896].* Bartlett, op. cit., p. 838a.

44. *From* CAIUS JULIUS VICTOR, *Ars Rhetorica I [4ᵗʰ century C.E.]*. "Rem tene; verba sequentur." Bartlett, op. cit., p. 107a.

45. Jaffe, Eugene D. and Hilbert, Stephen (2001). *How to Prepare for the Graduate Management Admission Test, Barron's GMAT,* 12ᵗʰ ed. Barron's Educational Series, Inc. p. 111.

46. From Strunk, William Jr. & White, E. B. Elements of Style 4/e (c) 2000 Published by Allyn and Bacon, Boston, MA. Copyright (c) 2000 by Pearson Education. Reprinted by permission of the publisher.

47. Ibid., p. 20.

48. Jade Snow Wong (1950). *Fifth Chinese Daughter.* New York: Harper; University of Washington Press paperback edition first published in 1989.

49. Interview with Jade Snow Wong, January 10, 2001.

50. Jaffe and Hilbert, op. cit., pp. 118–119.

51. Strunk and White, op. cit., p. 72.

52. Source of quote: DeVito, op. cit., p. 370. Source of date, Bartlett, op. cit., p. 601.

53. *Don Quixote, pt. II, bk. III, ch. 10, p. 502.* Bartlett, op. cit., p. 196a.

54. *Military Review [October 1948].* Bartlett, op. cit., p. 959b.

55. *Discourses, bk. I, ch. 27.* Loeb Classical Library. Bartlett, op. cit., p. 138a.

56. "Franklin D. Roosevelt, quoted, Kansas City Star, June 5, 1977." The Quotations Page. http://www.quotationspage.com/quotes.php3?author=Franklin+D.+Roosevelt. Source of date, Bartlett, op. cit., p. 970b.

57. *Definition of "guts" in The New Yorker [November 30, 1929].* Bartlett, op. cit., p. 1044b.

58. "Aequam memento rebus in arduis Servare mentem." *Odes, bk. II [23 B.C.], ode iii, l. 1.* Bartlett, op. cit., p. 121b.

59. *The Education of Henry Adams,* ch. 20. Bartlett, op. cit., p. 777a.

60. *Le Discours de la Methode, I.* Bartlett, op. cit., p. 327b.

61. DeVito, op. cit., p. 146.

62. *Address, Faneuil Hall, Boston [April 18, 1859].* Bartlett, op. cit., p. 733a.

63. Deng Ming Dao, op. cit., interview with the athlete by the author.

64. See note 26.

65. Ibid.

66. "In der Kunst ist das Beste gut genug." *Italian Journey [March 3, 1787].* Bartlett, op. cit., p. 477b.

67. See note 26.

68. Godwin C. Chu, Chikio Hayashi, and Hiroshi Akuto (1995). *Comparative Analysis of Chinese and Japanese Cultural Values,* East-West Center Reprints, Cultural Studies Series No. 7 (reprinted from *Behaviormetrika,* vol. 22, no.1, 1995). According to this study, some fundamental Confucian concepts are being rejected in mainland China today, due to the Cultural Revolution of 1966–1976. My perspective is that, meanwhile, halfway across the globe, first- and second-generation Chinese Americans continued their Confucian practices and passed the tradition on to their children or students. (I define first-generation Chinese as those born overseas and immigrating to America.) First-generation Chinese immigrants retain the most

of their mother culture and pass their tradition on to the next generation. The degree to which the mother culture is retained gradually diminishes with each subsequent generation born in the West.

69. Ibid., p. 18.

70. Ibid.

71. Ibid.

72. Kreitner, op. cit., p. 402.

73. *Genealogy of Morals [1887], essay 3, aphorism 16.* Bartlett, op. cit., p. 805b.

74. *The Life of Reason [1905-1906], vol. I.* Bartlett, op. cit., p. 867a.

75. *Monostikoi [Single Lines].* Loeb Classical Library translation. Bartlett, op. cit., p. 102b.

76. *Seed for Thought [1949].* Bartlett, op. cit., p. 940b.

77. *Letter to Cadet George S. Patton IV [June 6, 1944].* "Old Blood and Guts." Bartlett, op. cit., p. 987b.

78. *From BOSWELL, Life of Johnson [April 18, 1775].* Bartlett, op. cit., p. 431b.

79. *Maxim 580.* "Commonly called Publius, but spelled Publilius by PLINY in his *Natural History, 35, sec. 199.* Translated mainly by DARIUS LYMAN. The numbers are those of the translator." Bartlett, op. cit., p. 126b.

80. *Nicomachean Ethics, bk. X, ch. 9.* Chiefly from *The Basic Works of Aristotle,* edited by RICHARD McKEON. Bartlett, op. cit., p. 98a.

81. *Letter to George and Georgiana Keats [February 14–May 3, 1819].* Bartlett, op. cit., p. 585b.

82. Attributed aphorism. "Erst wägen, dann wagen." Bartlett, op. cit., p. 597a.

Selected Bibliography

Bartlett, John. *Bartlett's Familiar Quotations*. 14th ed. Boston: Little, Brown and Company, 1968.

Chu, Godwin C., Chikio Hayashi, and Hiroshi Akuto. *Comparative Analysis of Chinese and Japanese Cultural Values*, East-West Center Reprints Cultural Studies Series No. 7, Honolulu: East-West Center, 1995.

Dao, Deng Ming. *Pure Champion*. Unpublished manuscript, 1999.

DeVito, J. A. *Essentials of Human Communication*. 3rd ed. New York: Longman, 1999.

Jaffe, Eugene D., and Stephen Hilbert. *How to Prepare for the Graduate Management Admission Test, Barron's GMAT*. 12th ed. Hauppauge: Barron's Educational Series, Inc., 2001.

Kreitner, Robert. *Management*. 6th ed. Boston: Houghton Mifflin Company, 1995.

Rouner, Leroy S. "Resolved: That Phi Beta Kappa Is Gloriously Useless," *The Key Reporter*, Autumn 2000, vol. 66, no. 1.

Schwarzenegger, Arnold. *Encyclopedia of Modern Bodybuilding*. New York: Simon & Schuster, 1985.

Strunk, William, Jr., and E. B. White. *The Elements of Style*. 4th ed. Boston: Allyn and Bacon, 2000.

The World Almanac and Book of Facts 2001. New York: World Almanac Education Group, Inc., 2000.

Index

To Order

From F to Phi Beta Kappa: Supercharge Your Study Skills

Give the gift of study skills to your friends by ordering additional copies from your bookseller or Chromisphere Press:

Chromisphere Press
P.O. Box 470743
San Francisco, CA 94147
chromisphere@earthlink.net
www.chromisphere.com

Price: $16.95 + $4.00 shipping. California residents, please add 8.5% sales tax.